Sustainable Buildings in Practice

Sustainable Buildings in Practice

What the users think

George Baird

Routledge
Taylor & Francis Group

First published 2010
by Routledge
2 Park Square, Milton Park, Abingdon, Oxon OX14 4RN

Simultaneously published in the USA and Canada
by Routledge
270 Madison Avenue, New York, NY 10016, USA

Routledge is an imprint of the Taylor & Francis Group, an informa business

Designed and typeset by Alex Lazarou
Printed and bound in India by the Replika Press Pvt. Ltd., Sonepat, Haryana

British Library Cataloguing in Publication Data
A catalogue record for this book is available from the British Library

Library of Congress Cataloging in Publication Data
Baird, George, 1938–
Sustainable buildings in practice : what the users think / George Baird.
— 1st ed.
   p. cm.
   1. Sustainable buildings--Evaluation. 2. Buildings--Performance. I. Title.
TH880.B35 2010
720'.47—dc22
                                                    2009020432

ISBN10: 0-415-39932-7 (pbk)
ISBN10: 0-203-86545-6 (ebk)

ISBN13: 978-0-415-39932-6 (pbk)
ISBN13: 978-0-203-86545-3 (ebk)

Contents

CONTENTS

Preface and acknowledgements

No work of this nature happens by accident or without the support and cooperation of a multitude of people – in this case, well over 3000 people contributed, if one counts the number who reported their perceptions, as well as all the building designers whom I interviewed, the building managers who showed me around the buildings, and all my co-authors in whatever capacity they collaborated.

This book is the latest in a 'series' which started with two works of joint authorship with my colleagues here at the Victoria University of Wellington School of Architecture, the first dealing specifically with the energy performance of buildings, the second an overview of building evaluation techniques (Baird *et al.*, 1984; Baird *et al.*, 1996). This was followed by a solo work in which I attempted to demonstrate, via a number of case studies, how environmental control systems, whether active or passive, were being expressed architecturally (Baird, 2001).

One of the rewarding aspects of that latter project was to see the increasing trend towards the use of passive systems – sustainable buildings in current parlance – and the virtually universal adoption of integrated design processes in their development; one of the frustrating aspects was my inability to gather much more than anecdotal evidence of the performance in practice of these buildings from the point of view of their users. Thus the concept emerged of investigating the users' perceptions of some of the current buildings that were pioneering the application of sustainability principles.

An appropriate tool was available in the shape of the standard questionnaire developed by Building Use Studies for use in the well-documented PROBE Studies (Lorch, 2001, 2002). Not only that, I very quickly discovered a network of academics and practitioners who were using this tool in some of the buildings that I wished to investigate. Hence the current project became a collaborative one.

While a short biography of each of my key collaborators is given later and their contribution is noted in the relevant chapters, I should like to mention them all here too.

Drs Maisarah Ali and Shireen Jahnkasim of the International Islamic University in Kuala Lumpur assisted me in the distribution and collection of the questionnaires at the Ministry of Energy, Water and Communications building in Putrajaya. The latter had also undertaken a survey of Menara UMNO for her PhD, the results of which she made available to me.

Jodie Dixon used the questionnaire to assess the performance of five buildings at the University of Newcastle, NSW, Australia as part of her Masters thesis. Two of these, the Student Services Centre and the General Purpose Building, are included here.

Junko Endo of Nikken Sekkei and Professor Toshiharu Ikaga of Keio University were my collaborators for the Tokyo Gas building in Yokohama and the Nikken Sekkei headquarters building in Tokyo.

Leena Thomas of the University of Technology Sydney carried out the survey work at the Torrent Research Centre in Ahmedabad and we worked together on the Institute of Languages Building at the University of New South Wales. Leena and Monica Vandenberg were responsible for the study of the building at 40 Albert Road in South Melbourne.

Sue Turpin-Brooks, at that time Senior Lecturer at Plymouth University, undertook the survey of the Eden Foundation building in England.

Last but by no means least, I am indebted to Barry Austin and Alex Wilson of Arup R&D who had already carried out a survey of the Arup Campus building, but who gave me full access to the data so that I could carry out further analyses.

One of the pleasures of working on this project was to collaborate with so many like-minded people, who not only recognised the importance of building users, but who had also applied this particular methodology.

I must also thank the owners and managers of all the buildings for permission to undertake this project. While it may have been given with a little trepidation in some cases, I trust the result will confirm my assurances that I was not engaged in some kind of fault-finding exercise that would embarrass them or their organisation. As it happens, many were only too eager to add this kind of evaluation to the studies and demonstrations they were already undertaking. By the same token, I must also thank all the architects and engineers who gave so freely of their time to describe the overall design processes involved and to explain some of the finer detail of each of the buildings to me during formal (recorded and transcribed) interviews. All are noted and acknowledged in the relevant case study chapter.

Of course, the unsung heroes and heroines of such an exercise are the 3000 or so building users who responded so agreeably to the questionnaire without too much friendly persuasion on my part or on the part of my collaborators.

While I am grateful to my collaborators around the world, I owe a special debt to a number of outstanding Research Assistants who helped me back at the School of Architecture in Wellington at various stages in the project. From researching and selecting the 'target' buildings, through data entry from the questionnaires and transcription of the taped interviews, to the redrawing of sample plans and sections and analysis of the complete data set, I was assisted by Lauren Christie, Jessie Ferris, Charlotte Goguel, Sephorah Lechat, and Hedda Oosterhoff; outstanding young women, now all graduated with high honours, and with bright futures in architectural practice and research. I must also thank all my colleagues at the School of Architecture for their support – in particular, Dr Michael Donn who covered my teaching duties while I was on research and study leave and Paul Hillier for his photographic advice and support.

I am also grateful to Victoria University of Wellington for funding assistance. In particular a series of grants from the University's Research Fund, a six-month period or Research and Study Leave, together with some strategically timed Overseas Conference Leaves, have enabled me to personally visit all of the buildings, some of them more than once, photograph their key features, undertake the surveys (other than those conducted by my collaborators), and interview the relevant designers.

It is a pleasure to thank Commissioning Editor Caroline Mallinder and the project editor Katherine Morton, of Taylor and Francis for their enthusiasm for the project, together with Production Editor Faith McDonald and her colleagues involved in the production processes.

I have reserved my last and most special thanks for Adrian Leaman of Building Use Studies, to whom I have dedicated this book. Without his enthusiasm for the application of the building evaluation technique that he has developed and refined over many years (he was a contributor to *Building Evaluation Techniques* – Baird *et al.*, 1996) and his willingness to share his expertise, not just with me but also with all of my collaborators, over many many years, this project would not have got off the ground. The key tool for a project such as this is a stable, highly refined, and focused questionnaire, with totally transparent and reliable analytical procedures and a

well-established set of benchmarks. That is what Adrian was able to provide – and he is fun to work with too (see www.usablebuildings. co.uk). And if all that sounds like an endorsement, well, I guess it is – but it is offered sincerely and without qualification.

As to the processes involved in carrying out a project of this kind, I have already alluded to several of the steps involved. Possibly the most important of these, and arguably the most time-consuming, was negotiating permission to carry out user surveys from the owners or occupying organisations of my targeted sustainable buildings. Inevitably some were unable to assist, others turned out to be unsuitable for one reason or another, but several landed in my lap as my network of contacts developed; a small number were buildings that I had studied for my previous book.

Having visited, surveyed, and photographed the building; interviewed members of the design team; entered the data and sent it off to Building Use Studies for analysis (thanks again, Adrian) and interpreted the results, the next step was to develop a coherent and consistent structure for the case study chapters – for the immediate use of myself and my collaborators, and hopefully the ultimate benefit of the reader. The final step was to attempt an overview of the data from all of the buildings.

So how did the users of this set of sustainable buildings perceive them? To find out, please read on.

REFERENCES

Baird, G. (2001) *The Architectural Expression of Environmental Control Systems*, London: Spon Press.

Baird, G., Donn, M. R., Pool, F., Brander, W. D. S. and Chan, S. A. (1984) *Energy Performance of Buildings*, Boca Raton, FL: CRC Press.

Baird, G., Gray, J., Isaacs, N., Kernohan, D. and McIndoe, G. (1996) *Building Evaluation Techniques*, New York: McGraw-Hill.

Lorch, R. (ed.) (2001, 2002) 'Post-occupancy Evaluation', Special Issue of *Building Research and Information*, 29(2): 79–174; and subsequent Forums in 29(6): 456–476 and 30(1): 47–72.

Contributors

Maisarah Ali is the Director of the Center for Built Environment, Kulliyyah of Architecture and Environmental Design, International Islamic University Malaysia. Her research interests are sustainable building, environmental indicators, renewable energy, energy efficiency, asset maintenance management, and repair and rehabilitation of concrete structures.

Barry Austin has 30 years experience in building services engineering. He now leads a team of engineers in Arup's Building Performance and Systems Group which provides specialist consultancy on issues related to the design the performance of buildings. He has specialised in all aspects of energy efficiency in buildings and particularly in the energy-efficient operation of refrigeration plant, heat recovery chillers, and heat pumps.

Jodie Dixon is an architect in Newcastle, NSW, Australia, with experience in post-occupancy building evaluation. She has a Bachelor and Masters degree in Architecture from Newcastle University, NSW. Her design for an award-winning low-energy restaurant and her past role in the research and facilities management of energy-efficient campus buildings have helped refine her knowledge of best practice environmental design. Her architectural practice has a strong focus on delivering acceptable, adaptive levels of occupant comfort in low-energy buildings.

Junko Endo is currently a senior consultant with Nikken Sekkei Research in Tokyo. During her time with Nikken Sekkei she has been involved in the environmental planning of the Institute for Global Environmental Strategies, and in establishing several environmental assessment methods for buildings, including CASBEE.

Toshiharu Ikaga is a professor of Keio University. He worked for Nikken Sekkei Ltd for 21 years and was an associate professor of Tokyo University for two years. He designed and assessed many advanced sustainable buildings, and developed sustainable design guidelines and life cycle assessment tools for national and local governments.

Shireen Jahnkasim is Head of Building Technology at the Faculty of Architecture, International Islamic University Malaysia (IIUM) and has published more than 30 papers locally and internationally. As the co-ordinator of the Environmental and Virtual Reality Research Unit, IIUM, and a LEED AP, she is currently involved in research and development on visualisation and virtual reality tools in strategic decision-making in sustainable design in tropical climates.

Leena Thomas is Senior Lecturer at the University of Technology, Sydney, where she heads the environmental studies strand in the School of Architecture. She specialises in sustainable architecture, integrated design process and post-occupancy evaluation of user experience and environmental performance for buildings in Australia and India.

Sue Turpin-Brooks joined RTP Surveyors in Falmouth in May 2008 as their Practice Manager. A Chartered Building Surveyor since 1989, she pursued private practice work in London until the end of 1993, when she commenced an academic career in Salford, Leeds, and then Plymouth. Particular interests include health and safety aspects of construction and facilities management.

Monica Vandenberg is principal of Encompass Sustainability which specialises in assisting organisations to incorporate sustainability into their business planning process, through strategic planning, culture change, innovation, and learning. She is Executive Director of the Australian Sustainable Built Environment Council and her recent post-graduate studies focused on foresight in the Built Environment.

Alexandra Wilson is a physicist who was part of the Building Performance and Systems Team at Arup where she managed the team's activities in the monitoring of building thermal response and energy use. She has also played a leading role in Arup's project work related to building performance and occupant satisfaction surveys.

Gable end of an Arup Campus pavilion with daylighting/ventilation pod above (see Chapter 9)

This book is dedicated to
Adrian Leaman
of Building Use Studies

North façade of one of the Academic Towers of the MSCS Building
– solar noon on a midsummer day (see Chapter 14)

Introduction

We are all well aware that 'If buildings work well, they enhance our lives, our communities, and our culture' (Baird *et al.*, 1996) or, as Winston Churchill (1943) so eloquently put it, 'We shape our buildings and afterwards our buildings shape us.'

The main aim of this book is to advance the practice of environmentally sustainable building design. It will do this by outlining the design of (or how we have shaped) 30 mixed-mode, passive, and environmentally sustainable commercial and institutional buildings, reporting in detail on the users' evaluations of (or how we have been shaped by) these buildings, and noting some of the lessons that may be learned from their performance.

It is now over a decade since my colleagues and I, in the Introduction to *Building Evaluation Techniques* wrote:

Building evaluation is well established as a concept. Most of the techniques described in this book have reached their current level of sophistication through a process of development and refinement over the last two decades. The main opportunity for further innovation lies in their application. Through evaluation, people get commercial, organisational, operational, and design intelligence and make confident, successful decisions about buildings and operations within buildings. Few, if any, other tools offer such potential for radical improvement in the way we manage, design, and use individual buildings.

(Baird *et al.*, 1996: xxi)

We were firmly of the belief that acquiring and sharing knowledge about building performance was of fundamental importance. In many respects, this book is my personal response to the exhortation that 'the main opportunity for further innovation lies in their [building evaluation techniques'] application'.

BACKGROUND

I make no excuse for applying a technique that focuses on the building users. The '1:10:100 rule' beloved of life-cycle analysts, approximating the ratio of operating costs (1) to combined capital and rental costs (10) to total salary costs of the occupants (100) over the life of a building makes it abundantly clear where attention should be centred.

To quote again from *Building Evaluation Techniques*:

Salary is the single major cost associated with commercial buildings. Over the life of a building, salaries outweigh rent or purchase cost and far outweigh energy and maintenance costs. There is growing evidence of a significant connection between job performance and various physical attributes of the workplace. The costs to organisations are considerable if employees are performing below their full potential because their workplace does not fully meet their needs.

(ibid.: xxiii)

Writing more recently, Yudelson makes it even more explicit:

Here's a mantra and a memory aid: 300–30–3. It costs $300 (or more) per square foot for the average [North American] employee's salary and benefits; $30 per square foot (or less) for rent; and $3 per square foot for energy. To maximise corporate gain, we should focus on improving the output from the $300 person, not hampering that output to save a fraction of $30 on space or a much smaller fraction of $3 on energy.

(Yudelson, 2008: 151)

That message remains unchanged.

However, driven by a growing awareness of the major impact that buildings have on the environment, there has been increasing interest in the development of more sustainable building designs in the past two decades or so. This became abundantly clear to me during the 1990s as I researched the case studies for another book, *The Architectural Expression of Environmental Control Systems* (Baird, 2001). Originally conceived as a celebration of the architectural expression of heating, ventilating, and air conditioning systems, it soon became evident that environmental control of many recent buildings, and most of those with ambitions towards sustainability, was via integrated passive and mixed-mode systems – and equally well worth celebrating.

However, writing of these developments in 2003, Cole sounded a note of caution. His concern was for the apparent emphasis being put on technical systems and their potential for 'reduction in resource use and resultant ecological loadings', however laudable and well intentioned on the part of designers (Cole, 2003: 57). This emphasis is particularly evident in the world-wide development of building sustainability rating tools which up till now have been concerned mainly with the technical features of new designs. Cole's concern was that buildings 'designed with excellent "green" performance standards can be severely compromised because the specification and technical performance fail adequately to account for the inhabitants' needs, expectations and behaviour'.

AIMS AND OBJECTIVES

My overall mission in all of this is to provide an independent and unbiased evaluation of how the users perceive some of our recent sustainable building developments. I am still surprised that building designers (with rare exceptions) do not systematically evaluate their projects for the benefit of their own practices. I do understand that their fees may not cover such activities directly and that they would be reluctant to expose what could be construed as design faults in these risk-averse times. However, one might have expected enlightened self-interest in improving one's practice to have provided some motivation – after all, learning from our mistakes is often said to be one of the best lessons. Academics involved in this field have tended to be more focused on technical aspects of building performance such as energy consumption or life-cycle costs or the performance of particular elements or materials. However, there are encouraging indications that increasing numbers (including the several who collaborated with me for this book) are examining building performance from the users' point of view.

Given that my overarching aim was to advance the practice of environmentally sustainable building design, I sought out and evaluated a world-wide set of commercial and institutional buildings, all of which had well-recognised sustainability credentials or features. I wanted to find out the organisational and climatic context for these projects, how and why they were designed in a particular way and,

most importantly, the users' perceptions of the performance of these buildings in practice.

In the longer term, I intend to assess the potential for including ratings based on users' perceptions in future building sustainability rating tools (BSRTs). All of the tools used to give my set of buildings their sustainability credentials focus on the design and as-built stages of the building process. However, with moves afoot to develop BSRTs for buildings in operation, I anticipate opportunities to incorporate user assessments – particular important when, as noted earlier, salary costs are usually many times the building costs.

OVERALL APPROACH AND METHODOLOGY

During the past five years (though mainly in 2005–2007), I have investigated the performance in practice of a range of commercial and institutional buildings worldwide. Around 30 buildings in 11 countries have been studied – in all cases, either recipients of national awards for sustainable design or highly rated in terms of their country's building sustainability rating tool(s). In several instances, I was able to collaborate with other academics active in this field.

Generally speaking, these investigations involved me in undertaking one or more visits to each of the buildings. During these visits a structured, recorded interview was conducted (later transcribed) with a key architect and environmental engineer from the design team, and a detailed tour undertaken of each building and its facilities, photographing key features, and collecting relevant documentation.

These investigations also included the personal distribution and collection of a questionnaire survey seeking the users' perceptions of a range of factors. The questionnaire has evolved over several decades, from a 16-page format used for the investigation of sick building syndrome in the UK in the 1980s, to a more succinct two-page version. Developed by Building Use Studies (BUS, 2004) for use in the Probe investigations (BRI, 2001/2), it is available under licence to other investigators. The 60 or so questions cover a range of issues. Fifteen of these elicit background information on matters such as the age and sex of the respondent, how long they normally spend in the building, and whether or not they see personal control of their environmental conditions as important.

However, the vast majority ask the respondent to score some aspect of the building on a 7-point scale, typically from 'unsatisfactory' to 'satisfactory' or 'uncomfortable' to 'comfortable', where a '7' would be the best score (note, however, that in several instances a '4' would be the best score, while in others a '1' would be best).

The following aspects are covered:

- *operational* – space needs, furniture, cleaning, meeting room availability, storage arrangements, facilities, and image;
- *environmental* – temperature and air quality in different climatic seasons, lighting, noise, and comfort overall;
- *personal control* – of heating, cooling, ventilation, lighting, and noise;
- *satisfaction* – design, needs, productivity, and health.

Analysis of the responses yielded a mean value (on a 7-point scale) for each variable. In addition to calculating these mean values, the analysis also enables the computation of a number of ratings and indices in an attempt to provide indicators of particular aspects of the performance of the building or of its 'overall' performance.

THE BUILDINGS SURVEYED

The buildings surveyed were as follows, by country:

- Australia: 60 Leicester Street, Melbourne; 40 Albert Road, South Melbourne; the Red Centre Building, UNSW, Sydney; Institute of Languages, UNSW, Sydney; Student Services Centre, Newcastle University, NSW; General Purpose Building, Newcastle University, NSW; Scottsdale Forest Ecocentre, Tasmania
- Canada: Computer Science and Engineering Building, York University, Ontario; Liu Institute, University of British Columbia, Vancouver; Military Families Resource Centre, Toronto; National Works Yards, Vancouver
- Germany: Sciencepark, Gelsenkirchen
- India: Torrent Research Centre, Ahmedabad (both conventionally and evaporatively air-conditioned buildings)
- Ireland: St Mary's Credit Union, Navan
- Japan: Tokyo Gas, Yokohama; Nikken Sekkei Building, Tokyo

- Malaysia: Menara UMNO, Penang; Ministry of Energy, Water and Communications Building, Putrajaya
- New Zealand: the Campus Reception and Administration Building, Auckland University of Technology; the Landcare Research Laboratory, Auckland; the Mathematics and Statistics and Computer Science Building, Christchurch
- Singapore: Institute of Technical Education, Bishan
- United Kingdom: Arup Campus, Solihull; City Hall, London; Foundation Building, Eden Project, St Austell; Gifford Studios, Southampton; Renewable Energy Systems Building, Kings Langley; ZICER Building, University of East Anglia, Norwich
- USA: Natural Resources Defense Council, Santa Monica, California; NRG Systems, Hinesburg, Vermont.

These were selected on the basis of their sustainability 'credentials'. Virtually all of them were recipients of national awards for sustainable or low energy design, or were highly rated in terms of their respective country's building sustainability rating tool or in some way pioneered green architecture. I had studied six of them (the Red Centre, Sciencepark, Torrent Research Centre, Tokyo Gas, Menara UMNO, and the Institute of Technical Education) for my previous book (Baird, 2001) on the expression of environmental control and was keen to see how they performed from the users' point of view. Of course, willingness on the part of the building owner and tenants to be surveyed was also an essential prerequisite, and not all building owners felt in a position to accept my overtures, and a small number proved unsuitable for one reason or another.

Of the 30 buildings selected, 13 accommodated office activities predominantly, ten were tertiary level academic teaching buildings, four housed laboratories or research organisations, and two contained a combination of industrial and administrative functions.

While most of the buildings were in temperate climates of one kind or another (see later), a significant number were located in hot–humid climates. Their systems of ventilation ranged from full air conditioning, through mixed-mode (concurrent, changeover, and zoned) to natural ventilation (both conventional and advanced) and in one case Passive Downdraft Evaporative Cooling (PDEC).

STRUCTURE OF THE BOOK

Immediately following this introductory chapter I shall present an overview of the findings from the entire set of buildings. This will serve not only to summarise the characteristics and users' perceptions of this particular set, but also to explain the nature of the scoring systems used and the computation of the various indices employed. Readers anticipating some kind of league table of the 30 cases will be sorely disappointed. While I have not been averse to comparing their overall performance to that of a set of more conventional buildings (Baird and Oosterhoff, 2008), that was not my aim. Rather, it was to assess their performance in context, analyse the scores and comments, and highlight common issues. Following the introduction to each Part, each case study is presented in detail. They have been grouped broadly by climatic zone, roughly in order of increasing wintertime outside design temperature, as follows:

Part 1: Cold–Temperate Zone (six case studies)
NRG Systems Facility, Hinesburg, Vermont, USA
Computer Science and Engineering Building, York University, Ontario, Canada
Military Families Resource Centre, Toronto, Ontario, Canada
Sciencepark, Gelsenkirchen, Germany
National Works Yards, Vancouver, British Columbia, Canada
Liu Institute, University of British Columbia, Vancouver, Canada

Part 2: Medium–Temperate Zone (11 case studies)
Gifford Studios, Southampton, England
Arup Campus, Solihull, England
ZICER Building, University of East Anglia, Norwich, England
Renewable Energy Systems Building, Kings Langley, England
City Hall, London, England
The Foundation Building, Eden Project, St Austell, Cornwall, England
The Mathematics and Statistics and Computer Science Building, Canterbury University, Christchurch, New Zealand
St Mary's Credit Union, Navan, Ireland
Scottsdale Forest Ecocentre, Tasmania, Australia
Tokyo Gas, Kohoku New Town, Yokohama, Japan
Nikken Sekkei Building, Tokyo, Japan

Part 3: Warm–Temperate Zone (nine case studies)
The Landcare Research Laboratory, Auckland, New Zealand
The Campus Reception and Administration Building, Auckland University of Technology, New Zealand.
60 Leicester Street, Melbourne, Victoria, Australia
40 Albert Road, South Melbourne, Victoria, Australia
The Red Centre Building, University of New South Wales, Sydney, NSW, Australia
Institute of Languages, University of New South Wales, Sydney, NSW, Australia
General Purpose Building, University of Newcastle, NSW, Australia
Student Services Centre, University of Newcastle, NSW, Australia
Natural Resources Defense Council, Santa Monica, California, USA

Part 4: Hot–Humid Zone (four case studies)
Institute of Technical Education, Bishan, Singapore
Ministry of Energy, Water and Communications Building, Putrajaya, Malaysia
Menara UMNO, Penang, Malaysia
Torrent Research Centre, Ahmedabad, Gujarat, India

The rationale for this grouping was that climate is a major driver of the environmental control options available to design teams and it would be of interest to juxtapose the solutions adopted and the users' responses to them.

Following the briefest of introductions to each group of buildings, the following structure has been adopted for the individual case study chapters to enable easy reference and cross-comparison: the context; the design process; the design outcome; and users' perceptions of the building – covering overall response, significant factors, user comments, and overall performance indices. In some cases, it has been possible to include other reported aspects of performance.

REFERENCES

Baird, G. (2001) *The Architectural Expression of Environmental Control Systems*, London: Spon Press.

Baird, G., Gray, J., Isaacs, N., Kernohan, D. and McIndoe, G. (1996) *Building Evaluation Techniques*, New York: McGraw-Hill.

Baird, G. and Oosterhoff, H. (2008) 'Users' Perceptions of Health in Sustainable Buildings', in E. Finch (ed.) *Proceedings of CIB W70 International Conference on Facilities Management, Edinburgh, June 2008*, London: International Council for Research and Innovation in Building and Construction.

BRI (2001/2) 'Special Issue – Post-occupancy Evaluation', *Building Research and Information*, 29(2): 79–174; and subsequent 'Forums' in 29(6): 456–76 and 30(1): 47–72.

BUS (2004) Website: available at: www.usablebuildings.co.uk (accessed 12 December 2007).

Churchill, W. (1943) *House of Commons, Hansard*, 28 October, London: HMSO.

Cole, R. J. (2003) 'Green Buildings – Reconciling Technological Change and Occupant Expectations', in R. J. Cole and R. Lorch (eds) *Buildings, Culture and Environment*, Oxford: Blackwell.

Yudelsen, J. (2008) *The Green Building Revolution*, Washington, DC: Island Press.

Looking up into a ventilation chimney at the CS&E Building

1

Overview of the buildings and their performance

As previously intimated, I shall present an overview of the findings from the entire set of buildings in this chapter. This will serve not only to summarise the characteristics and users' perceptions of this particular set, but also to explain the nature of the scoring systems used and the computation of the various indices employed.

Following a description of the nature of the buildings and their users, an outline will be given of the working arrangements of the latter and the extent of their involvement with the building. Next, the users' perception scores for individual performance factors will be presented, together with a number of indices and rating scales, designed to give an indication of performance over a range of factors. The derivation of these indices and rating scales will be explained at this point. It is recommended that readers make themselves thoroughly familiar with the characteristics of these indices and rating scales in order to appreciate their application and presentation in the individual case study chapters that follow.

As well as asking the users to rate the individual factors on a 7-point scale, the questionnaire also invited brief comment on several of these. While the individual case study chapters will scrutinise the comments in more detail, a section of this chapter will be devoted to outlining their general tenor. A limited amount of statistical analysis was also undertaken to gauge the extent of correlations between the various individual factors and indices of performance and some of the key findings will be presented. Finally, an attempt will be made to summarise some of the main overall issues that emerged from the study of this set of sustainable buildings.

However, no overview can possibly do justice to the detailed information, analyses, and insights contained in the individual case study chapters. Having 'digested' this overview, I trust readers will be encouraged to dip into the case studies, perhaps starting with buildings of a type and in a climatic zone with which they are particularly concerned.

THE BUILDINGS

The 30 buildings were spread over 11 countries and a number of continents: six from North America (four from Canada and two from the USA); eight from Europe (six from the UK and one each from Germany and Ireland); ten from Australasia (seven from Australia and three from New Zealand); and six from Asia (two from Malaysia, two from Japan, and one each from Singapore and India).

As noted earlier, virtually all were recipients of national awards for sustainable or low energy design, or were highly rated in terms of their respective country's building sustainability rating tool (BREEAM in the UK, CASBEE in Japan, LEED in the USA, Green Globes in Canada, etc.) or in some way pioneered sustainable architecture.

The buildings were also located in a range of climatic zones. For the purpose of this exercise, these have been broken down into four categories which I have labelled Cold–Temperate (with wintertime design temperatures of -5°C or less), Medium–Temperate (with wintertime design temperatures between -4°C and zero), Warm–Temperate (with wintertime design temperatures ranging from +3°C to +7°C), and Hot–Humid (with temperatures ranging up to +40°C or more). The six cold–temperate zone buildings were located in Canada, the USA (Vermont), and Germany; the 11 medium–temperate in the UK, Ireland, Tasmania, and the South Island of New Zealand; the nine warm–temperate in mainland Australia, the North Island of New Zealand, and the USA (Santa Monica, California); and the hot–humid in Malaysia, Singapore, and India.

The 30 buildings were all commercial or institutional in nature, housing anything from 15 to around 350 staff with a mean of approximately 66 per building. Thirteen of the buildings accommodated office activities predominantly, ten were tertiary-level academic teaching buildings, four housed laboratories or research organisations, and two contained a combination of light industrial and administrative functions.

In terms of the ventilation systems employed in these buildings, 15 had what have been termed *advanced natural ventilation* systems, broadly defined as natural ventilation where some of the ventilation openings are automated or some specially designed natural ventilation elements have been incorporated into the design. Most of the remainder (some 13 buildings) utilised a *mixed-mode* system of ventilation – these were predominately *changeover* systems where the mechanical systems were designed to operate during cold or hot conditions, and the natural ventilation systems during mild conditions. Two buildings had *zoned* systems where large parts of the building were either air conditioned or naturally ventilated. Only three of the buildings were fully air conditioned with predominantly sealed facades. Astute readers will have realised that amounts to 31 cases, rather than 30 – the reason for this is that one of the case studies (the Torrent Research Centre in Ahmedabad) had both air conditioned and advanced naturally ventilated buildings, and these were surveyed separately. Fuller details of the systems of environmental control are given in the individual case study chapters.

Most had been built or refurbished in the course of the past decade, and all of them had been occupied for a year or more before the survey work was carried out, giving most occupants sufficient time to experience their new surroundings over at least a full annual cycle.

THE OCCUPANTS

Overall, there were some 2035 respondents to the questionnaires. While not everyone scored every question (the questionnaire simply asked them to fill in as many as they could), the vast majority did so. The staff numbers responding ranged from a low of 13 (the small staff group at the Toronto Military Families Resource Centre) to a high of 334 (London City Hall), with a mean of approximately 66 persons per building. In a number of the academic buildings, responses were also sought from the students. A shorter questionnaire was use for this – the data are not included here but are presented in the relevant case study chapters.

For 98 per cent of the respondents (43.3 per cent female, 56.7 per cent male), the building was their normal place of business – the rest tended to be contractors of one kind or another. They worked 4.73 days per week on average and 8.01 hours per day, of which around 6.48 were spent at their desk or work space and 5.47 at a computer screen. The ratio of under-30s to over-30s was 32.6 to 67.4 per cent and most (75.1 per cent) had worked in the building for more than a year, but only 38.5 per cent at the same desk or work area. In broad terms, around 30 per cent of respondents either had a single office or shared with more than eight others, with around 13.3 per cent each sharing with either one, two to four, or five to eight colleagues. On average, slightly over half the occupants (51.5 per cent) had a window seat.

SCORING OF THE INDIVIDUAL FACTORS

Table 1.1 lists the means and standard deviations of the users' perception scores for each of the 45 factors that respondents were asked to score. Each factor corresponds to a specific question – these are necessarily abbreviated to fit the table, but reflect the nature of the full question posed to the building users.

The factors have been grouped into the following categories:

- Operational (eight factors)
- Environmental, with the following four sub-categories:
  - temperature and air in winter (eight factors) – not applicable in the case of the hot–humid climatic zone buildings
  - temperature and air in summer (eight factors)
  - lighting (five factors)
  - noise (six factors)
- Personal control (five factors)
- Satisfaction (five factors).

For some 22 of the factors, a score of 7 would be considered the ideal; in 15 cases, a score of 4 would be deemed best; and in seven instances a score of 1 would be the ultimate target. The relevant factors are noted in Table 1.1. The only exception to these guidelines is the Productivity factor which is expressed as the percentage by which the respondents thought their productivity had increased or decreased.

Of the 22 factors for which a score of '7' would be the ideal, no less than 17 had an average score greater than 4.00, the mid-point of the scale. Seven of these were greater than 5.00, indicating that for this set of buildings, the occupants perceived the following factors as reasonably satisfactory, on average:

- image (to visitors)
- furniture (in the occupant's work area)
- cleaning (standard of)
- availability of meeting rooms
- meets work requirements
- lighting overall
- needs (building as a whole).

TABLE 1.1

Means and Standard Deviations of the users' perception scores for each factor they were asked to rate on a 7-point scale

Factor	Mean	SD	Factor	Mean	SD
OPERATIONAL					
Image to visitors	5.62	0.959	Cleaning	5.27	1.010
Space in building	4.81	0.840	Availability of meeting rooms	5.15	0.853
Space at desk – too little/much[4]	4.32	0.533	Suitability of storage arrangements	4.20	0.740
Furniture	5.18	0.529	Facilities meet work requirements	5.32	0.638
ENVIRONMENTAL					
Temp and Air in Winter			Temp and Air in Summer		
Temp Overall	4.42	0.682	Temp Overall	4.32	0.966
Temp – too hot/too cold[4]	4.65	0.564	Temp – too hot/too cold[4]	3.43	0.705
Temp – stable/variable[4]	4.23	0.625	Temp – stable/variable[4]	4.23	0.485
Air – still/draughty[4]	3.55	0.660	Air – still/draughty[4]	3.26	0.540
Air – dry/humid[4]	3.39	0.341	Air – dry/humid[4]	3.82	0.506
Air – fresh/stuffy[1]	3.71	0.724	Air – fresh/stuffy[1]	3.85	0.798
Air – odourless/smelly[1]	3.03	0.654	Air – odourless/smelly[1]	3.17	0.634
Air overall	4.44	0.611	Air overall	4.33	0.858
Lighting			Noise		
Lighting Overall	5.15	0.733	Noise Overall	4.42	0.836
Natural light – too little/much[4]	3.94	0.485	From colleagues – too little/much[4]	4.31	0.446
Sun & Sky Glare – none/too much[1]	3.73	0.616	From other people–too little/much[4]	4.35	0.583
Artificial light – too little/much[4]	4.14	0.325	From inside – too little/much[4]	4.09	0.620
Art'l light glare – none/too much[1]	3.37	0.523	From outside – too little/much[4]	3.87	0.749
			Interruptions – none/frequent[1]	3.94	0.707
PERSONAL CONTROL			**SATISFACTION**		
Heating [30.97 & 16.768]	2.82	1.134	Design	4.99	1.079
Cooling [31.97 & 14.853]	2.81	1.003	Needs	5.16	0.775
Ventilation [28.48 & 17.541]	3.42	1.091	Comfort Overall	4.91	0.835
Lighting [26.41 & 14.710]	3.85	1.210	Productivity	+4.07%	10.02%
Noise [27.14 & 15.355]	2.48	0.756	Health	4.25	0.712

NOTES: (a) the means listed in this table are the averages of the mean scores for each building (as opposed to the mean of the individual respondent scores which could have a slightly different value); (b) unless otherwise noted, a score of 7 is 'best'; superscript 4 implies a score of 4 is best, superscript 1 implies a score of 1 is best; (c) the numbers in square brackets are the percentages of respondents (mean and SD) who thought personal control of that aspect was important.

That is not to say that every building scored well on these factors. As indicated by the standard deviation (SD) figures, there was quite a spread of scores (but more on that later). The five factors below the mid-point of the scale were all in the Personal Control category (more on these later too).

In the case of the 15 factors where a score of 4.00 would be deemed best, the averages for no less than 11 of them were clustered between 3.50 and 4.50. The four exceptions all related to temperature and air in winter and summer, where it was perceived to be too cold and dry in winter, and too hot and still in summer, on average.

For the seven factors where a score of 1 would represent the ultimate, all of the average scores were less than 4.00, the mid-point of the scale. It is good to see, given the effort that has been put into the design of the ventilation systems for these buildings, that the air was perceived to be well on the odourless side of the odourless/smelly scale in both winter and summer.

Finally, in this overview of the individual factors, it was particularly encouraging to see that the users considered their productivity to have increased by 4.07 per cent on average as a result of the environmental conditions in the building.

Turning now to the mean scores within each of the categories, it can be seen that of the eight operational factors, five were greater than 5.00. However, the mean score for Storage was only 4.20, indicating that a perceived lack of storage could be an issue in many cases. Interestingly, with an average score of 4.32 (on a scale where 4.00 represents the ideal) there is a hint that some occupants consider they have too much space at their desk or work area.

In the case of the four Environmental sub-categories, there were mixed results. Temperature Overall and Air Overall averaged out at around 4.43 and 4.32 in winter and summer respectively, just over the mid-point and on the satisfactory side of their respective scales. As mentioned earlier, the air was perceived to be well on the odourless side of the odourless/smelly scale, but only just on the fresh side of the fresh/stuffy scale in both winter and summer. In general, conditions were perceived to be on the cold, still, and dry side in winter and on the hot and still side in summer.

Of the Environmental factors, Lighting Overall, with a mean score of 5.15 was the highest by far, with mean values close to the ideal for the amount of both natural and artificial light. While the scores for glare were less than the scale mid-point (the ideal was 1.00 in this instance), the SD values hint at some variability in users' perceptions.

The mean score for Noise Overall, at a modest 4.42, was similar to that for Temperature and Air Overall. Noise from colleagues and other people seemed to be the main 'culprit' in this instance, with interruptions scoring 3.94 on a scale where 1 would be the ideal.

As noted earlier, all five of the Personal Control factors rated well below the mid-point of their scales (where 7 would be the ideal). Lighting, at 3.85 had the highest figure, while Noise, at 2.48 had the lowest. On average, around 29 per cent of the occupants rated personal control as important.

As far as the Satisfaction factors were concerned, Design, Needs, and Comfort Overall all averaged out close to a score of 5 (on a scale where 7 is the ideal) while Health, at 4.25 was above the scale mid-point, implying that the occupants perceived themselves to be healthier in these buildings, on average. Interestingly, an earlier analysis had indicated that the occupants of these buildings perceived themselves to be healthier than the occupants of a more conventional set of buildings (Baird and Oosterhoff, 2008). The fifth factor, Productivity, also scored well on the positive side, though with an SD value of around 10 per cent, there is clearly some variation between the building averages.

To illustrate typical score distributions, histograms of six factors (Image, Needs, Design, Health, Comfort, and Productivity) are presented in Figures 1.1 (a)–(f) respectively. All, apart from Productivity, are factors for which a score of 7 would be the ideal. The means and medians for this set of buildings are greater than the scale mid-point of 4 but the spread of the individual building means is evident.

OVERALL INDICES AND RATING SCALES

Having considered the individual factors for this set of buildings and clarified the characteristics of the scoring system, this section will overview the performance of the buildings in terms of a number of indices and rating scales. While it is useful, indeed essential, to be able to look in detail at the individual factor scores, it can also be instructive, as well as convenient to consider groups of related factors together.

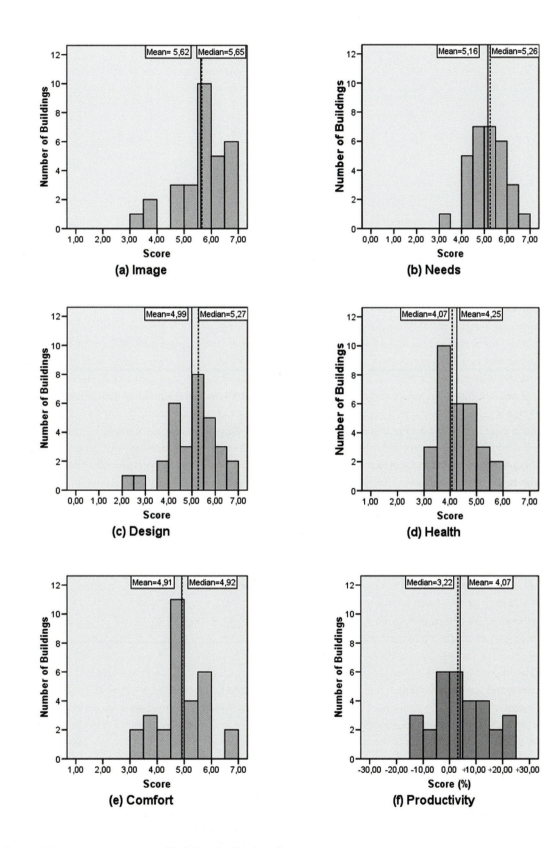

1.1 Distribution of the average scores, across all buildings, for six selected factors: (a) Image; (b) Needs; (c) Design; (d) Health; (e) Comfort Overall; (f) Productivity

To some extent, this kind of consideration is already integrated into the questionnaire in terms of the environmental factors, where respondents are asked to score Lighting Overall, Noise Overall, Temperature Overall, and Air Overall (the latter in both in winter and summer) as well as a range of factors within each of these categories; they are also asked to score their Comfort Overall. In addition to these 'integrating' scores, the Building Use Studies (BUS) analysis package calculates a number of indices and rating scales. These will now be described and the results for this set of buildings outlined, noting that I will borrow heavily from Sections 3 and 4 of a paper to the 2008 World Sustainable Building Conference (Baird *et al.*, 2008).

First, it should be made clear that each of the factors has been assigned a benchmark (copyright BUS) on its 7-point scale. At any given time, these benchmarks are simply the mean of the scores for each individual factor, averaged over the last 50 buildings entered into the BUS database. As such, each benchmark score may be expected to change over time as newly surveyed buildings are added and older ones withdrawn. Nevertheless none of them was observed to have changed significantly during the five years or so over which these buildings were surveyed.

In the case of our set of buildings, some 41.5 per cent of the nearly 1400 scores (31 buildings by 45 factors) were 'better' than the corresponding benchmark at the time of analysis, 35.9 per cent were close to the benchmark figure, and some 22.6 per cent turned out 'worse'.

The Comfort, Satisfaction, and Summary Indices, and the Forgiveness Factor

The Comfort Index attempts to encapsulate, in a single figure, an overview of users' perceptions of that aspect of the building's performance. This index is formulated from the Z-scores for Comfort Overall, together with the main environmental factors of Lighting Overall, Noise Overall, Temperature Overall in both winter and summer, and Air Overall in both winter and summer. The Z-scores are derived from (actual score – benchmark) / (benchmark standard deviation). They are standardised scores with mean = 0 and standard deviation = 1, and are used here to give equal weights to the seven constituent values of the index.

The formula for calculating the Comfort Index is simply the average of the Z-scores for these seven factors, i.e.

$$\frac{(Z_{comfort} + Z_{light} + Z_{noise} + Z_{tempwinter} + Z_{tempsummer} + Z_{airwinter} + Z_{airsummer})}{7}$$

The Comfort Index is based on a scale of -3 to +3, where +3 is considered 'best' (the mid-point lies on zero). Figure 1.2(a) illustrates how this set of buildings performs when measured by the Comfort Index. The majority of the buildings (24 of the 29 cases considered – complete data were not available in two cases) were above the mid-point of the scale in terms of comfort. Ten of these were greater than +1.00 and all the climatic zones and ventilation types were well represented. Some five cases were less than the mid-point but none of these fell below -1.00.

In the same way as the Comfort Index, the Satisfaction Index attempts to encapsulate, in a single figure, the users' overall satisfaction with the building. It is formulated from the Z-scores of the overall ratings for Design, Needs, Health, and Productivity. The formula for calculating this index is simply the average of the Z-scores for these factors, i.e.

$$SI = \frac{(Z_{design} + Z_{needs} + Z_{health} + Z_{productivity})}{4}$$

As before, the Satisfaction Index is based on a scale of -3 to +3 where +3 is considered 'best' (the mid-point lies on zero). As shown in Figure 1.2(b), 25 of the 29 cases were above the scale mid-point and 13 of these were greater than +1.00. Only four cases were less than the mid-point and, again, none of these dropped below -1.00. Overall, these buildings were found to perform higher in terms of 'satisfaction' (mean = 1.05) than they did for 'comfort' (mean = 0.79).

The Summary Index is simply the arithmetical average of the Comfort and Satisfaction Indices. Figure 1.2(c) illustrates the distribution of this index which, as might be expected, lies somewhere between the comfort and satisfaction distribution with a mean value of 0.92. As can be seen, 25 cases (or 86 per cent) are above the mid-point

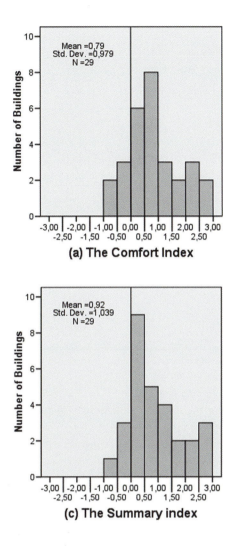

1.2 Distribution of overall performance indices across all buildings: (a) the Comfort Index; (b) the Satisfaction Index; (c) the Summary Index; (d) the Forgiveness Factor

of the scale and only four (or 14 per cent) are below. Nine of the buildings had indices greater than 1.00 for both satisfaction and comfort, though not necessarily at the same level.

In addition to these indices, a so-called Forgiveness Factor is also calculated. This is simply the ratio of the score for Comfort Overall to the average of the scores for the six environmental factors Lighting Overall, Noise Overall, Temperature Overall in both winter and summer, and Air Overall in both winter and summer. It represents an attempt to quantify the users' tolerance of the environmental conditions in the building. 'Values greater than 1 are taken to indicate that occupants may be more tolerant, or "forgiving", of the conditions' (Leaman and Bordass, 2007). While the typical values would range from 0.80 to 1.20, for this set of buildings the mean

value of the Forgiveness Factor was 1.08. As indicated in Figure 1.2(d), 22 of the 29 cases considered had values greater than 1.00, around half were greater than 1.10, and two buildings attained values greater than 1.20.

Rating scales

Two rating scales, one made up of 'Ten Factors' and one using 'All Factors' (around 45 in total), are used to provide an overall performance assessment of the buildings from the users' point of view. Each factor in the rating scale is scored on a scale from 1 to 5, depending on whether it is perceived as being significantly worse, slightly worse, the same as, slightly better, or significantly better than the BUS benchmarks and the scale mid-point. These scores

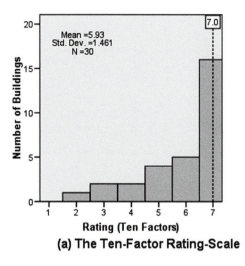

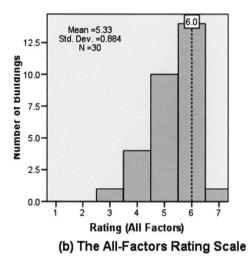

1.3 Distribution of the Rating Scales across all buildings: (a) the Ten-Factor Rating Scale; (b) the All-Factors Rating Scale

are then summed and the percentage is then transformed to the following 7-point scale where:

1. (0–14.3 per cent) is 'Very Poor';
2. (14.428.6 per cent) is 'Poor';
3. (28.7–42.9 per cent) is 'Below Average';
4. (43–57.2 per cent) is 'Average';
5. (57.3–71.4 per cent) is 'Above Average';
6. (71.5–85.7 per cent) is 'Good Practice';
7. (85.8–100 per cent) is 'Exceptional'.

The variables included in the Ten-Factor Rating Scale are – Comfort Overall, Design, Health, Image, Lighting Overall, Needs, Noise Overall, Productivity, Temperature Overall in Summer, and Temperature Overall in Winter. While it could be argued that there is a certain amount of arbitrariness in the selection of the above variables and the terminology employed for the Rating Scale, and that the scoring process requires careful judgement, I believe they have the inestimable merits of simplicity and transparency, and can be readily interpreted in the context of the particular building.

Looking first at the 7-point rating scale incorporating ten factors, no less than 16 buildings made it into the 'Exceptional' category with a further five close behind in the 'Good Practice' category. Ten of the 11 countries were represented in these 21 buildings. While most of these were in temperate climatic zones, three were in hot–humid climates (two of them air conditioned). Of the 21, ten had advanced natural ventilation, eight were mixed-mode, and three were air conditioned. Figure 1.3(a) demonstrates that, of the

30 buildings in this sample, more than half were in the 'Exceptional' category with a score of 7. Only three buildings were considered to be 'Below Average' or less.

This high percentage of excellent buildings continues even when 'All Factors' were input into the rating scale as can be seen in Figure 1.3(b). Although only one building was still rated as 'Exceptional' (7 on the scale), 24 out of the remaining 29 were considered to be 'Good Practice' or 'Above Average'.

It is evident that taking all 45 or so factors into account proved to be a tougher test on the 7-point rating scale for most of the buildings. The median for the group had slipped from 7 to 6 and while only one building had retained its 'Exceptional' status, at the other end of the spectrum the lowest rated building had moved up from 'Poor' to 'Below Average'. Overall, only four buildings were unchanged and 22 had gone down; four buildings had improved their rating – presumably factors other than those included in the ten-factor scale were scoring better.

The highest ranking was achieved by a building with advanced natural ventilation in a temperate climate, while the lowest had zoned mixed-mode ventilation in a hot–humid climate. Both had been designed with the intent of exploiting natural ventilation for owner–occupier clients who, while not overtly cognisant of sustainability issues, were nevertheless interested in the long-term performance of their buildings.

TABLE 1.2

Overall numbers of respondents offering positive, balanced, and
negative comments on 12 aspects of performance (35% average comment rate)

Aspect	Number of respondents				
	Positive	Balanced	Negative	Total	Ratio (-ve/+ve)
Overall Design	314	151	413	878	1.32
Needs Overall	101	76	417	593	4.13
Meeting Rooms	96	54	410	560	4.27
Storage	47	73	407	527	8.66
Desk/Work Area	134	86	341	561	2.54
Comfort Overall	126	57	208	391	1.65
Noise Overall	37	92	494	623	13.35
Lighting Overall	140	90	304	534	2.17
Productivity	114	150	209	473	1.83
Health	114	111	255	480	2.24
Work Well	715	–	–	715	1.27
Hinder	–	–	905	905	
TOTALS	1938	939	4363	7240	2.25
PER CENT	26.8	13.0	60.2	100	–

OVERVIEW OF THE USERS' COMMENTS

In addition to scoring the various factors listed on the questionnaire, the building users were invited to comment on ten aspects of the building. These corresponded directly to the following factors: Design; Needs; Meeting Rooms; Storage; Desk/Work Area; Comfort Overall; Noise Overall; Lighting Overall; Productivity; and Health. In addition, respondents were invited to give examples of 'things which usually work well' and 'things which can hinder effective working'.

By no means all the occupants took up these invitations, but a significant number did so and it is of interest to overview the nature of their responses (these will be analysed in more detail in the individual case study chapters). As far as the average comment rate is concerned (the number of respondents who made a comment on individual factors, compared to the total number of respondents), this amounted to approximately 35 per cent overall, ranging from just under 20 to just over 60 per cent.

In terms of the nature of their responses, the comments were placed into three categories: *positive* (extolling the virtues of the building); *negative* (noting problems attributed to the building); and *balanced* (where the respondent was neutral about the effect of the building on their work, or made a combination of positive and negative comments). Table 1.2 lists the overall numbers of respondents offering comments on these various aspects of the building and calculates the ratio of negative to positive comments.

The overall nature of the comments certainly supported the view that building users are more likely to complain rather than praise. Overall, only around 26.8 per cent of comments were positive, while 13.0 per cent were balanced and 60.2 per cent negative – the overall ratio of negative to positive comments was 2.25:1. Nevertheless, five of the factors had ratios better than or similar to that overall ratio of 2.25 – in ascending order, these were Design (1.32), Comfort (1.65), Productivity (1.83), Lighting (2.17), and Health (2.24), while

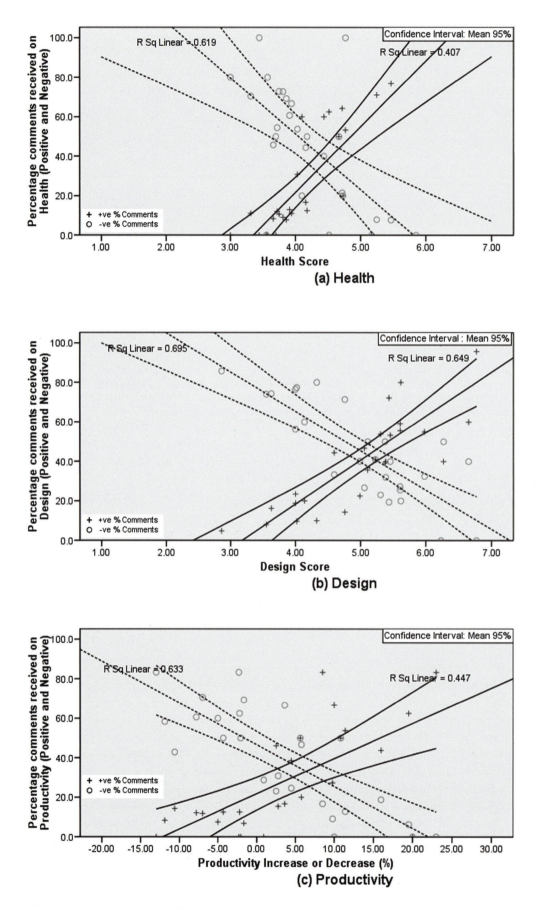

1.4 Plots of the correlations between scores and both positive and negative comments for three factors: (a) Health; (b) Design; (c) Productivity

the ratio of Hindrances to things that Work Well was 1.27. At the opposite extreme, Noise and Storage had ratios of 13.35:1 and 8.66:1 respectively – portents of a common issue.

In terms of numbers of comments received, Design attracted by far the most with 878 – over 12 per cent of the total received – and also had the lowest ratio of negative to positive comments. Next in order was Noise with 623 comments (around 8.6 per cent of the total), but with far and away the highest ratio of negative to positive comments. Clearly, both figures are useful in making an assessment of any particular aspect of performance

CORRELATIONS BETWEEN COMMENTS AND SCORES

Given that not all respondents ventured a comment, it was of interest to see if there was any inherent bias or correlation between the nature of the comments and the scores. For this analysis, the positive, negative, and balanced comments for each building (expressed as a percentage of the total number of comments received for that building) were correlated against the scores for the corresponding factors.

Of the ten factors tested, seven exhibited a reasonable degree of correlation between both the percentage positive and negative comments, and the corresponding factor scores. It was reassuring to note that in all ten cases the trends of the positive and negative comments were as one would have anticipated (the greater the percentage of positive comments, the higher the score; the greater the percentage of negative comments, the lower the score) while correlation between the balanced comments and scores was relatively very weak. Figure 1.4 plots these relationships for the three factors with the best correlations – Health, Design, and Productivity – noting that the R Sq Linear figures indicate the percentage of variation explained by the corresponding regression line.

In the case of Health, for example (Figure 1.4(a)), as the percentage of positive comments increased, so too did the score; similarly, the higher the number of negative comments, the lower the score. In both instances, despite total comment rates around the 25 per cent mark, a reasonable percentage of the variation was explained by their respective regression lines (40.7 per cent in the case of the positive comments, 61.9 per cent in the case of the negative).

All three graphs in Figure 1.4 further illustrate the apparent propensity of building users to offer negative rather than positive comments. If one takes the mid-point score of 4.00 as a 'break-even' point between unsatisfactory and satisfactory, it can be seen that it only requires around 25 per cent of the comments to be of a positive nature to reach that figure. On the other hand, it appears to require around 50–60 per cent of the comments to be negative before the score dips below the mid-point.

While one would need to undertake further case studies and extend the analysis to the other factors to ascertain the generality of this finding, it is certainly an intriguing one – and one that has the potential to lead to the development of a new tool for the analysis of building performance.

Whatever the outcome of that investigation, it was auspicious to see a good correlation between the scores and both the number and nature of the comments in these instances.

CORRELATIONS BETWEEN RATING SCALES, INDICES, AND FACTORS

Previous studies of this kind (BRI, 2001, 2002) had shown that strong correlations existed between several of the factors analysed in this type of survey work. Hence it was felt appropriate to see whether that was the case for this particular set of sustainable buildings and to check on the strength of correlation of the factors incorporated into the various rating scales and indices.

Rating scales

Table 1.3 ranks the Pearson correlation coefficients for 20 individual factors in relation to the 7-point and percentage alternatives of the Ten-Factor Rating Scale (the ten actually incorporated in the rating scale are indicated by *). As noted in Table 1.3, several of these 20 factors were also involved in one or other of the two main indices (Satisfaction and Comfort) and in one or other of two of the groups of factors (Satisfaction and Operational) used to describe the users' responses (see also Table 1.1).

Using the rule of thumb that correlation coefficients in the ranges 0.8–1.0, 0.6–0.8, and 0.4–0.6 indicate very strong, strong, and moderate relationships respectively (Salkind, 2005: 88), it can be seen that the

TABLE 1.3

Ranked Pearson correlation coefficients for the 20 factors involved in the
Ten-factor Rating Scale (indicated by an asterisk *), in the Satisfaction and Comfort Indices,
and in the Operational and Satisfaction groupings

Factor	Pearson correlation Ten-factor Rating Scale		Satisfaction or Comfort Index	Satisfaction or Operational Group
	7-Point Scale	Percentage Scale		
*Comfort	0.858	0.896	Comfort	Satisfaction
*Design	0.857	0.895	Satisfaction	Satisfaction
*Needs	0.816	0.841	Satisfaction	Satisfaction
*Productivity	0.790	0.844	Satisfaction	Satisfaction
*Noise	0.749	0.787	Comfort	
Space in Bldg	0.749	0.782		Operational
*Health	0. 682	0.729	Satisfaction	Satisfaction
Air-summer	0.673	0.731	Comfort	
Facilities	0.669	0.718		Operational
*Image	0.636	0.648		Operational
Storage	0.635	0.654		Operational
*Temp-summer	0.624	0.680	Comfort	
*Temp-winter	0.589	0.627	Comfort	
Meeting Rooms	0.566	0.578		Operational
Air-winter	0.483	0.526	Comfort	
Furniture	0.466	0.476		Operational
*Lighting	0.345	0.417	Comfort	
Space at Desk	0.225	0.219		Operational
Cleaning	0.166	0.166		Operational
Average Control	0.158	0.209		

top four of the 20 – Comfort, Design, Needs, and Productivity – are in the very strong category, the next nine are strong, and four are moderate – virtually all with correlations that were significant at the 0.01 level (two-tailed). The remaining three have only a very weak or non-existent relationship with this rating scale.

It will be noted that the correlation coefficients for the percentage scale are generally higher than those for the 7-point scale. However, as the trends were substantially the same and the correlation coefficient between the two was 0.984, it was felt there was ample justification for using either, as appropriate to the circumstances. While histograms using only the 7-point scale were used earlier in this chapter to illustrate the overall performance of the entire set of buildings, the results from using both rating scales will be presented in the individual case study chapters.

As far as the Ten-Factor Rating Scale was concerned, the correlation coefficients for Comfort, Design, Needs, and Productivity were all greater than 0.8, while those for Noise, Health, Image, Temperature in Summer, and Temperature in Winter were all greater than 0.6, with correlations significant at the 0.01 level (two-tailed). Only Lighting fell below that threshold, but even it was significant at the 0.05 level (two-tailed).

It is worth noting too that several other factors came into the strong relationship category, namely Space in the Building, Air in Summer, Facilities, and Storage, while Meeting Rooms, Air in Winter, and Furniture were moderately related.

In the case of the All-Factors rating scale, the correlation coefficients for Comfort and Productivity were again found to be greater than 0.8, while Air in Summer, Noise, Design, Needs, Facilities, Temperature in Summer, Space in Building, Health, Air in Winter, and Lighting were all greater than 0.6. Temperature in Winter, Storage, Meeting Rooms, and Image had moderate relationships significant at the 0.05 level (two-tailed) only, while the remaining four – Furniture, Space at Desk, Cleaning, and Average Control – had only very weak or non-existent relationships.

There was a strong correlation (0.884) between the 7-point and the percentage scales in the case of the All-Factors Rating Scale too; and between the All-Factors and Ten-Factor Rating Scales (0.878 for the percentage scale, 0.789 for the 7-point scale).

Returning to Table 1.3, it can be seen that all of the factors included in the Satisfaction Index had correlation coefficients in the strong to very strong category – this is also reflected in the very strong correlations found between the Satisfaction Index and the Percentage Rating Scales (0.820 and 0.824 for the Ten-Factors and All-Factors, respectively). In the case of the Comfort Index, the corresponding correlation coefficients were slightly lower at 0.776 and 0.763, respectively, and the individual factor correlations ranged from very strong to moderate, with Comfort, reassuringly, being the strongest of all. In a similar way, most of the five factors included in the Satisfaction Group had very strong correlations with the rating scales, while six of the eight factors in the Operational Group were in the strong to moderate category (with Space at Desk and Cleaning the exceptions).

Indices

The Comfort Index was specified as dependent on the scores for the following seven factors: Comfort Overall, Lighting Overall, Noise Overall, Temperature Overall in both winter and summer, and Air Overall in both winter and summer. Their ranking order, in terms of the correlation coefficients between them and the Comfort Index, was found to be Comfort Overall (0.875), Air in Summer (0.822), Temperature in Winter (0.806), Air in Winter (0.796), Noise Overall (0.783), Temperature in Summer (0.748), and Lighting (0.562). All of which was reasonably reassuring of the utility of this index, as specified.

In the case of the Satisfaction Index, the ranking order of the four factors in terms of their correlation coefficients was Productivity (0.954), Design (0.913), Health (0.912), and Needs (0.888), all in the very strong category.

Given that the Summary Index is simply the average of the Comfort and Summary Indices, it was to be expected that they would be highly correlated, with coefficients of 0.973 and 0.981 respectively.

Individual factors

A limited investigation was carried out of the correlations between seven of the 45 or so factors. Even this limitation resulted in some 21 coefficients (involving all 45 factors would have produced 990!). Those selected were Comfort, Design, Needs, Productivity, Health, Facilities, and Image.

To a substantial extent, this order also represents their ranking in terms of their correlations with one another. Comfort, Design, and Needs, for example, were all very strongly correlated with five of the other factors and strongly correlated with the remaining one. Productivity and Health were very strongly correlated with four of the other factors, and strongly correlated with the remaining two. Facilities was strongly correlated with three factors and moderately with the other three, while Image was only moderately correlated with all six.

The strongest individual correlation coefficient was found to be between Design and Needs (0.938), while the lowest for this set was between Image and Facilities (0.578), though even this was significant at the 0.01 level (two-tailed).

Overall, these findings gave one confidence that the factors being assessed, the indices, and the rating scales were all relevant to the users' perceptions of the performance of these buildings.

OVERALL ISSUES AND OBSERVATIONS

While the focus of the book and the survey questionnaire on which many of its findings are based are on the users' perceptions of this particular set of sustainable buildings, it is by no means the whole story. Informed readers will be well aware that the priorities of the client, the experience of the architectural and engineering team, their commitment to integrated design, and the time available for the whole process can all have a profound influence on the building and its eventual performance.

It will probably come as no surprise to learn that in the vast majority of cases, the clients for these buildings had a strong commitment to the principles and practice of sustainability. Indeed, several had environmental policies in place within their organisations well prior to the design and construction of these buildings, and those that had not were open to giving serious consideration to this kind of approach.

The clients for the academic buildings, for example, tended to have a long-term view of their building projects, at the very least in terms of future energy costs, but usually in terms of their broader environmental impact and of course their educational influence. In several instances, the clients were actively involved in some aspect of 'environmental business' and were clearly motivated by the desire to demonstrate their commitment to the principles of sustainability. While some embraced the idea that the building could also act as a demonstration of a number of leading edge practices, most required a rigorous economic case be made before approving their incorporation in the design. While many of the buildings were owner–occupied and the client could be expected to take a long-term view, this was by no means universal – several were leased (in one case a specific environmental lease had been drawn up) while others were designed with possible future leasing in mind.

All of these issues were also reflected in the clients' choices of the design teams for their projects. Most of them were local practitioners, familiar with the culture and climate of the locality, and with established track records and in some cases a philosophical commitment to the application of environmentally sustainable design principles. As well as that commitment, most of these practitioners were experienced in employing integrated design processes to achieve their sustainability aims – architects and engineers working together from the outset, fully cognisant of the downstream impact of early design concept decisions.

In terms of the operation of these buildings, a large number were under the care of the facilities management department of their organisation, be it a university campus or a municipality. Where the buildings housed a technically sophisticated organisation, operation and maintenance were carried out by staff in-house. In a few instances a manager had been appointed specifically to oversee the running of the building. Despite the frequent assertion that a user manual had been prepared for the building occupants, I was able to sight a copy only rarely.

Many particular issues are noted in the case study chapters. In the remaining few paragraphs of this overview I should like to pick up on a few of the more common items from that miscellany, starting with what one could term design issues.

As evidenced by the nature of the comments and to some extent the scores for these factors, Noise and Storage issues were by far the commonest source of complaint. In the case of the former, juxtaposing offices with other activities such as auditoria, meeting rooms, showrooms, visitor areas, even corridors with hard surfaces and wooden floors is probably a planning issue. Noise and disturbance within the open plan offices themselves could probably be alleviated by the establishment of appropriate etiquette and some education of the staff on the implications of moving from cellular to open-plan offices, as well as appropriate layout and acoustical design. In the case of storage, despite an average score of 4.20, the high ratio of negative to positive comments indicates that this is an issue for many people – it would appear that the paperless office is still some way off.

Among the other issues that seemed to arise reasonably frequently was the incidence of direct glare from the sun. This was noted in buildings in every climatic zone and is somewhat surprising, given the predictability of sun angles – perhaps more care needs to be taken with internal layouts and the positioning of workstations in relation to the sun.

Temperature issues of one kind or another were relatively pervasive too, with summer overheating being noted in several of the naturally ventilated or mixed-mode temperate zone buildings. By contrast, several of the fully air conditioned buildings were deemed to be on the cold side in summer – a hint that their set points could possibly be raised. Of particular interest was the finding that many of the buildings in the warm–temperate zone were felt to be on the cold side in winter – an indication that more attention should be given to this aspect of design.

The importance of commissioning was stressed by several of the clients and designers and there was ample evidence of this being undertaken. In some cases this was still ongoing, particularly in those instances where the project incorporated novel or 'demonstration' features. Allied to this, post-occupancy evaluations of one kind or another had already been carried out in several of the buildings prior to my visits.

Despite the temperature issues noted above, as far as the occupants were concerned, there were indications of a growing acceptance of a wider temperature band and tolerance for internal thermal conditions to change gradually in accordance with the seasons. The occupants also appreciated being able to see or feel the effect of their operating any of the control systems to which they had access – natural ventilation openings were mentioned in this respect.

Several other trends and innovations were also noted. Among these were a growing number of buildings with full fresh-air ventilation systems and a large variety of ventilation chimneys and other devices designed to enhance the flow of natural ventilation. A variety of heating and cooling systems were also in evidence, ranging from biomass boilers, solar hot water, and seasonal heat storage to ground and water source heat pumps, aquifers, and passive downdraft evaporative cooling.

Space does not permit the inclusion of further statistical analyses of the users' scores and ratings of these buildings as a whole or interpretation of the factors influencing their perceptions. However, it is anticipated that a companion website will be set up for that purpose. This would include papers describing more detailed analyses of specific factors, and further case studies undertaken since the book was written.

Following this overview chapter, each case study is now presented in detail, grouped broadly into the following climatic categories: Part 1 Cold–Temperate (six case studies); Part 2 Medium–Temperate (11 case studies); Part 3 Warm–Temperate (nine case studies); and Part 4 Hot–Humid (four case studies).

REFERENCES

Baird, G., Christie, L., Ferris, J., Goguel, C. and Oosterhoff, H. (2008) 'User Perceptions and Feedback from the "Best" Sustainable Buildings in the World', in *Proceedings of SB08 – the World Sustainable Building Conference, Melbourne*, September.

Baird, G. and Oosterhoff, H. (2008) 'Users' Perceptions of Health in Sustainable Buildings – Worldwide', in E. Finch (ed.) *Proceedings of CIB-W70 International Conference in Facilities Management*, Edinburgh, June, London: International Council for Research and Innovation in Building and Construction.

BRI (2001, 2002) 'Post-occupancy Evaluation', Special Issue of *Building Research and Information*, 29(2): 79–174, and subsequent 'Forums', 29(6): 456–76 and 30(1): 47–72.

Leaman, A. and Bordass, B. (2007) 'Are Users More Tolerant of "Green" Buildings?' *Building Research and Information*, 35(6): 662–73.

Salkind, N. J. (2005) *Statistics for People who (Think They) Hate Statistics*, Thousand Oaks, CA: Sage.

Part 1

Buildings in Cold–Temperate Climates

Chapters 2–7

The following six case studies are all located in what could be classed broadly as cold–temperate climates, with wintertime outside design temperatures ranging from -21°C to -5°C. As can be seen, they are predominantly Canadian locations, together with one from the north-east of the USA and the other in the Ruhr Valley of Germany. They will be described in the following order:

The buildings located in Germany and Vancouver have advanced natural ventilation, while those in the more severe climates of the north-east of North America are changeover mixed-mode.

Freestanding tracker photo-voltaic panels framing the NRG Systems Facility

2
NRG Systems Facility
Hinesburg, Vermont, USA

THE CONTEXT

NRG Systems moved into its new 4320m² facility in August 2004. As a well-established and rapidly expanding manufacturer of wind measuring equipment, the company was strongly committed to renewable energy. Its owners (Jan and David Blittersdorf) *were* determined that their new facility would reflect these values, describing their previous building which they had outgrown as a tin box, neither energy efficient nor a good work environment (Nelson, 2005). 'The Blittersdorfs were very clear that they wanted it to be one of the best environmentally performing buildings and a great place for the people who were working in it, and they stayed focused on these two goals' (Maclay, 2005).

The building is located on the edge of the rural town of Hinesburg, some 20km south of Burlington, the main city in the north of the State of Vermont (latitude 44.5°N) where the winter and summer design temperatures are -21.2°C and +29.1°C respectively (ASHRAE, 2001: 27.20–1). The site is at the foot of the south-facing slope of a small hill (Figure 2.1) – ideal for catching the sun, providing shelter from north-west winds in winter and exposure to south-west winds in summer, making use of natural drainage, and even providing a suitable location for a wind turbine on the ridge-line.

Soon after the building's completion the architects won the 2004 Honor Award for Excellence in Architecture from the Vermont

2.1 The building in its rural setting at the foot of the hill – note the wind turbine at the top. This view is of the main south façade – note the fixed photo-voltaic panels covering the sloping roof, and the tracker panels out front. The uppermost strip of windows provides daylight to the warehouse area behind

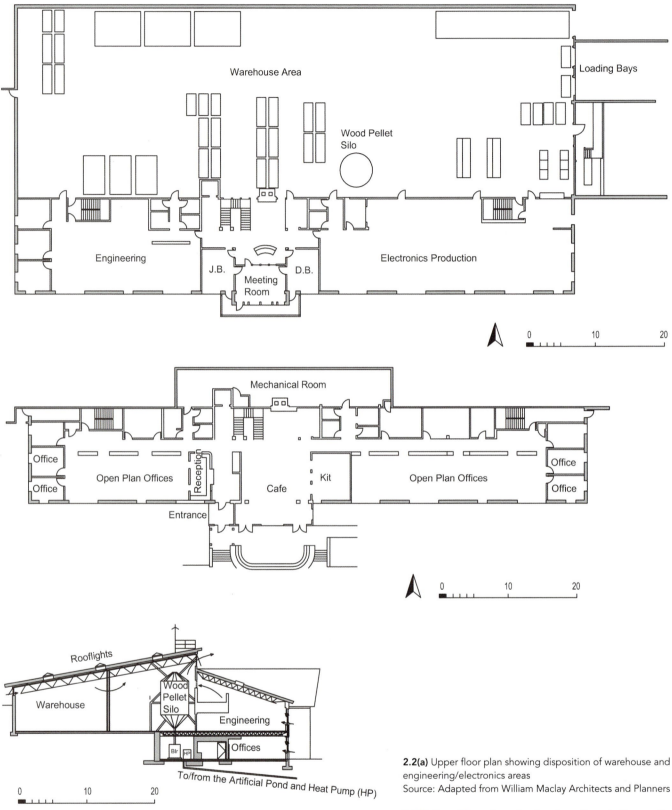

Warehouse Area

Loading Bays

Wood Pellet Silo

Engineering

J.B.

Meeting Room

D.B.

Electronics Production

0   10   20

Mechanical Room

Office

Office

Open Plan Offices

Reception

Cafe

Kit

Open Plan Offices

Office

Office

Entrance

0   10   20

Rooflights

Warehouse

Wood Pellet Silo

Engineering

Blr   HP

Offices

To/from the Artificial Pond and Heat Pump (HP)

0   10   20

2.2(a) Upper floor plan showing disposition of warehouse and engineering/electronics areas
Source: Adapted from William Maclay Architects and Planners

2.2(b) Plan of lower floor showing disposition of offices, café area, and mechanical room
Source: Adapted from William Maclay Architects and Planners

2.3 Cross-section – note the disposition of fixed and openable windows for daylighting and natural ventilation, and how the building is bermed into the site
Source: Adapted from William Maclay Architects and Planners

2.4 Central portion and eastern end of the south façade. The central portion houses a café area on the lower level, and a main meeting room on the upper. Note the continuous horizontal band of glazing at high level on each of the two floors and the warehouse, the former with horizontal louvres inside and view windows below. The western end of this façade has a similar layout. Note too the strip of photo-voltaic panels between the floors

2.5 Internal view showing the window arrangement. The upper daylighting windows are fitted with sets of horizontal louvres designed to reflect sunlight onto the ceiling and avoid glare in the working area – they are adjusted manually by means of the long vertical rod. The opening of these windows is motorised, and may be actuated centrally by the building management system or locally using the switch in the centre of this shot. The lower sections of the view windows may be opened manually

Chapter of the American Institute of Architects for the project, and subsequently won Efficiency Vermont's 2005 Better Building by Design Award. Also in 2005, the building achieved Gold in Version 2 of the US Green Building Council's LEED Certification process for New Construction (LEED, 2006).

The design process and architectural outcome have been described elsewhere in some detail (LEED, 2006; NRG Systems, 2004; Nelson, 2005; Simmon, 2005). What follows is the briefest of outlines.

THE DESIGN PROCESS
Selected from a short-list of four firms, William Maclay Architects and Planners took on the design leadership for the project. Arguably the leading environmentally focused firm in the State of Vermont, its principal, Bill Maclay, had been practising in this mode for several

2.6 Lower floor open plan office area – daylighting and view windows to the right, and open street to the left of the wooden partitioning

2.7 Upper floor engineering area – daylight and view windows to the left, sloping roof with skylights above, mezzanine level on upper right, and fully exposed mechanical and electrical services distribution

2.8 General view of the warehouse area. Note the strips of daylighting windows at high level to the left and right of shot, and the regular layout of the square-shaped skylights in the roof. The large silo for the storage of a year's worth of wood pellets is on the left, partly obscured by some open shelving

decades from his small office in nearby Waitsfield (Maclay, 2005). Also joining the design team right from the start was energy consultant Andy Shapiro from nearby Montpelier, with whom Maclay had worked for more than 15 years on a range of projects where energy efficiency was a major design criterion (Shapiro, 2005). Clearly, this was an experienced team with an environmental focus and an intimate knowledge of the local environment.

The design process was a relatively long one, taking around two years all together and involving not only the detailed assessment of NRG Systems' existing operations, but the investigation of a range of sites. When refurbishment of their existing building turned out not to be viable, and sites near the existing facility proved to be unsuitable, it took a zoning change to secure the selected site.

The overall design process was a fully integrated one that not only included all the other members of the design team and the company managers, but also the entire staff from the various departments (Maclay, 2005); and while the prospect of possible LEED accreditation was not a major driver of the design, there was little doubt the building was going to be a prime candidate.

For the majority of his projects, Maclay's preference is to keep the design outcome as simple as possible, but in this case his technically sophisticated clients encouraged the use of mixed-mode systems of environmental management with integrated and relatively complex controls for the active and passive systems.

THE DESIGN OUTCOME

Building layout, construction, and passive environmental control systems

Rectangular in plan (80m by 40m approximately) and with its long axis orientated east–west (Figures 2.2a and 2.2b), the building is bermed into the lower slopes of a hillside (Figure 2.3). The envelope underwent a series of tests to ensure it was made as airtight as possible to minimise air infiltration. The building fabric was designed with high levels of insulation (ranging from around 100mm in the walls and floors to 150mm in the roof) and minimum thermal breaks, while all the windows were triple-glazed.

2.9 NRG Systems, Hinesburg – Mechanical Room – the two wood-pellet boilers on the left and the back-up propane boiler on the right – all domestic scale. The pellet storage silo is located in the warehouse area immediately above – see Figures 2.3 and 2.8

2.10 NRG Systems, Hinesburg – Mechanical Room – showing the layout of the five heat pumps; domestic hot water storage cylinders at the rear

2.11 NRG Systems, Hinesburg – Some of the 12 freestanding tracker photo-voltaic panels, and the pond used to collect and control storm-water runoff and act as a heat sink when the building requires cooling

The front section of the southern façade (Figure 2.4) is two storeys high, the lower level (Figure 2.2b) containing the reception area and groups of offices either side of a central café area; the upper level (Figure 2.2a) housing engineering and electronics areas on either side of the Blittersdorfs' offices and main meeting room.

For daylighting purposes, both levels have a continuous approx 600mm high strip window at high level (Figure 2.4). These windows are fitted with horizontally slatted adjustable blinds which, on sunny days, are designed to reflect light onto the ceiling while avoiding direct sun penetration and glare, and admit diffuse light at other times (Figure 2.5). Both levels have south-facing view windows located at intervals under the continuous strip. The roof of the upper level, which slopes up over a mezzanine walkway towards the warehouse area behind (Figure 2.3), incorporates skylights that are carefully located to avoid direct sun penetration onto the working area. The large warehouse area itself has a continuous strip of glazing at high level along both its north and south façades (Figures 2.3 and 2.4), together with a grid of skylights (total area approximately 3 per cent of the floor area) on its roof (Figure 2.3) – designed to provide adequate light on sunny days. The artificial lighting systems for all of these areas are designed to enable a logical system of dimming in step with the prevailing natural lighting conditions.

The offices (Figure 2.6) and engineering–electronics areas (Figure 2.7) have a mixed-mode system of ventilation (more of which later) with both automated and manually operated windows on all façades. Apart from a couple of extract fans, the warehouse area (Figure 2.8) is entirely naturally ventilated via motorised windows at high level, and with openings between the production and warehouse areas designed to enable air transfer from the former to the latter, before exhausting to the outside.

Active environmental control systems

When use of the passive systems is inappropriate, a number of active systems are used to heat, cool, and ventilate the building. The central plant for these is housed in a very accessible Mechanical Room (Figure 2.2b) on the lower level, immediately behind the office area and below the warehouse.

Heating is provided by two 140,000 Btu/hr (41kW) wood-pellet-fired boilers (Figure 2.9) gravity-fed from a 30-ton silo in the warehouse

TABLE 2.1

Average scores for each factor and whether they were significantly better, similar to, or worse than the BUS benchmarks

OPERATIONAL FACTORS

Factor	Score	Worse	Similar	Better		Factor	Score	Worse	Similar	Better
Image to visitors	6.98			●		Cleaning	5.93			●
Space in building	6.25			●		Availability of meeting rooms	6.71			●
Space at desk – too little/much^4	4.56		●			Suitability of storage arrangements	6.05			●
Furniture	6.29			●		Facilities meet work requirements	6.55			●

ENVIRONMENTAL FACTORS

Temp and Air in Winter	Score	Worse	Similar	Better		Temp and Air in Summer	Score	Worse	Similar	Better
Temp Overall	6.11			●		Temp Overall	5.00			●
Temp – too hot/too cold^4	4.11			●		Temp – too hot/too cold^4	3.32		●	
Temp – stable/variable^4	2.67		●			Temp – stable/variable^4	3.82		●	
Air – still/draughty^4	2.33	●				Air – still/draughty^4	2.34	●		
Air – dry/humid^4	2.95	●				Air – dry/humid^4	4.97	●		
Air – fresh/stuffy^1	2.72			●		Air – fresh/stuffy^1	2.74			●
Air – odourless/smelly^1	2.03			●		Air – odourless/smelly^1	2.08			●
Air Overall	6.32			●		Air Overall	5.65			●

Lighting	Score	Worse	Similar	Better		Noise	Score	Worse	Similar	Better
Lighting Overall	5.86			●		Noise Overall	4.67			●
Natural light – too little/much^4	4.35		●			From colleagues – too little/much^4	4.26		●	
Sun & Sky Glare – none/too much^1	3.58			●		From other people – too little/much^4	4.00			●
Artificial light – too little/much^4	3.79		●			From inside – too little/much^4	4.19		●	
Art'l light glare – none/too much^1	2.42			●		From outside – too little/much^4	2.03		●	
						Interruptions – none/frequent^1	3.50			●

CONTROL FACTORS [b]

Factor	%	Score	Worse	Similar	Better		SATISFACTION FACTORS	Score	Worse	Similar	Better
Heating	14%	2.37		●			Design	6.77			●
Cooling	23%	2.37		●			Needs	6.68			●
Ventilation	25%	3.40		●			Comfort Overall	6.56			●
Lighting	20%	3.45		●			Productivity %	19.51			●
Noise	34%	2.76	●				Health	5.47			●

NOTES: (a) unless otherwise noted, a score of 7 is 'best'; superscript ^{4} implies a score of 4 is best, superscript ^{1} implies a score of 1 is best; (b) the per cent values listed here are the percentages of respondents who thought personal control of that aspect was important.

TABLE 2.2

Numbers of respondents offering positive, balanced, and negative comments on 12 performance factors.

Aspect	Number of respondents			
	Positive	Balanced	Negative	Total
Design	23	1	–	24
Needs	5	2	4	11
Meeting Rooms	9	2	1	12
Storage	3	3	5	11
Desk/Work Area	8	10	–	18
Comfort Overall	11	2	1	14
Noise Overall	3	5	11	19
Lighting Overall	7	3	7	17
Productivity	10	5	1	16
Health	10	2	1	13
Work Well	32	–	–	32
Hinder	–	–	27	27
TOTALS	121	35	58	214
PER CENT	56.5	16.4	27.1	100

immediately above – with a small propane-fired boiler for back-up. Cooling is provided by a set of five heat pumps (Figure 2.10) which reject their heat to the 1.3 million gallon (approx 5 megalitres) artificial pond in front of the building which also serves to control stormwater runoff and as a recreational facility. The air handling units for the office and the engineering/electronics areas are also housed here – these are full fresh-air systems with intakes at high level on the south façade and equipped with heat recovery wheels.

Pipes embedded in the floor-slab enable underfloor heating and cooling of the entire building. The offices and engineering/electronics areas have carbon dioxide-controlled mixed-mode ventilation via the air handling units and opening windows with red and green indicators letting the occupants know when opening or closing the windows is preferable (but not mandatory). The warehouse area's natural ventilation may be supplemented by a couple of extract fans at either end of the space.

Several photo-voltaic systems, with a total capacity of 67kW, have been incorporated in the building design. Some 35kW have been incorporated onto the south sloping roof, a further 7kW form an elongated awning on the south façade (Figure 2.4), while 12 freestanding tracker panels of 2.2kW are each mounted around the pond (Figure 2.11).

USERS' PERCEPTIONS OF THE BUILDING

Overall response

The building was surveyed during November 2005. Of the 44 respondents (virtually all the employees in the building during the time of the survey), some 37 were based in the office or manufacturing areas, the remaining seven in the warehouse area. For almost all of them (30 per cent female, 70 per cent male), the building was their normal place of business, working on average 5.0 days per week and 8.8 hours per day, of which around 6.9 were spent at their desk or work space 4.1 at a computer. In the latter case there was a wide variation, depending on the nature of their job – while more than one-third of respondents used their computer from six to nine hours per day, more than one-third used it for less than two hours. The ratio of under-30s to over-30s was 18:82 per cent and most (80 per cent) had worked in the building for more than a year at the same desk or work area. More than half shared with five or more others, while the rest were equally divided between those with single offices and those sharing with one to four others.

Significant factors

The average score for each of the survey questions is listed in Table 2.1. Table 2.1 also indicates those factors that the staff perceived as being significantly better, similar to, or worse than the benchmark and/or scale mid-point. In this case, some 27 aspects were significantly better, only four significantly worse, while the remaining 14 aspects had much the same score as the benchmark. In terms of the eight operational factors, this building scores better than the benchmark in seven instances. The only exception was the score for desk space.

While the overall scores for temperature and air in both summer and winter were all considerably higher than their corresponding benchmarks, there was some variability in the individual aspects. The air itself was fresh and odourless in both seasons of the year, but was perceived to be on the dry and still side, and too hot in summer.

Lighting overall scored better than the benchmark and scale mid-point, and both 'glare' scores were better than their respective benchmarks and scale mid-points. However, there was a suggestion of too much natural light and too little artificial light in the average scores. Noise overall scored highly too, but there was a perception of too little noise from outside and possibly a little too much from colleagues and other internal sources.

Relatively small percentages of staff (14–25 per cent) rated personal control of heating, cooling, ventilation, and lighting as important and scored these factors the same or better than their benchmarks, but lower than the mid-point. Control of noise, on the other hand, was perceived as important by 34 per cent of staff. Perceptions of the satisfaction factors (design, needs, comfort overall, productivity, and health) were all significantly better than their respective benchmarks, including and very much higher than the scale mid-point in every case.

Users' comments

Overall, some 214 responses were received from staff under the 12 headings where they were able to add written comments – some 37.8 per cent of the 528 potential (44 respondents by 12 headings). Table 2.2 indicates the numbers of positive, balanced, and negative comments – in this case, around 56.5 per cent were positive, 16.4 per cent balanced, and 27.1 per cent negative.

The design of the building attracted one of the highest response rates, with virtually all of the comments positive. Comments on comfort overall, while less numerous, were overwhelmingly positive too. The same went for health, though respondents did concede that it was probably healthier outside in this rural environment.

Despite the scores indicating there was too much work space, more than half of the negative comments were concerned with a lack of space. The issue of space was mentioned relatively frequently in the Work Well and Hinder categories too, this time favouring the former approximately 2:1.

Noise issues related to the open-plan and connected nature of the warehouse and office–manufacturing areas were noted frequently under both the noise overall and hinder categories. Comments on light overall were evenly divided between positive and negative.

Overall performance indices

The Comfort Index, based on the overall scores for comfort, noise, lighting, temperature, and air in winter and summer, works out at +2.50, while the Satisfaction Index, based on the design, needs, health, and productivity scores, is +3.35, noting that the scale mid-point in these instances is zero on a nominal -3 to +3 scale.

The Summary Index, being the average of the Comfort and Satisfaction Indices, works out at +2.93, while the Forgiveness Factor, calculated to be 1.17 in this instance, indicates that staff are likely to be relatively more tolerant of minor shortcomings in individual aspects such as winter and summer temperatures, air quality, lighting, and noise (a factor of 1 being the mid-point on a scale that normally ranges from 0.8 to 1.2).

In terms of the Ten-Factor Rating Scale, the building was 'Exceptional' on the 7-point scale, thanks to a calculated percentage value of 100 per cent. When All-Factors were taken into account, the percentage value worked out at 76 per cent, comfortably within the 'Good Practice' band.

ACKNOWLEDGEMENTS

I must express my gratitude to Jan and David Blittersdorf for granting permission for me to undertake this survey. Particular thanks go to their Personal Assistant Kathy Magnus for introducing me to staff around the building and to Bill Maclay and Andy Shapiro for assisting my understanding of the building and its design.

REFERENCES

ASHRAE (2001) *ASHRAE Handbook: Fundamentals, SI Edition*, Atlanta, GA: American Society of Heating Refrigerating and Air-Conditioning Engineers.

LEED (2006) 'Overview (et seq.)', available at: http://leedcasestudies.usgbc.org/overview.cfm?ProjectID=420 (accessed 23 September 2007).

Maclay, B. (2005) Transcript of interview held on 23 November 2005, Waitsfield, Vermont, USA.

Nelson, S. (2005) 'NRG Systems: An Architectural Tour de Force', *Builder/Architect, Vermont Edition*, 12(3): 4–8.

NRG Systems (2004) 'Tour Our New Green Building (et seq.)', available at: www.nrgsystems.com/about/green_building.php (accessed 7 January 2005).

Shapiro, A. (2005) Transcript of interview held on 22 November 2005, Montpelier, Vermont, USA.

Simmon, V. L. (2005) 'Zealous by Design', *Business People Vermont*, 22(5): 3–6.

Rooftop ventilation chimney at the CS&E Building

3
Computer Science and Engineering (CS&E) Building
York University, Ontario, Canada

THE CONTEXT

Completed in 2001, the approximately 10,700m² (115,000ft²) Computer Science and Engineering (CS&E) Building fronts onto Campus Walk in the heart of the Keele Campus of York University, Ontario (Figure 3.1).

York University had sustainability policies and guidelines in place prior even to the commencement of planning for this building in 1997 (Czarnecki, 2003; McMinn, 2002) and 'From the outset of project planning, the University's goal was that this construction would be the first green institutional project in Ontario' (Macaulay and McLennan, 2006: 151).

As the name implies, the building accommodates the Department of Computer Science and Engineering, with lecture theatres, computing and research laboratories, and staff offices on an 'infill' site between existing campus buildings.

Located just north of the city of Toronto at approximately 44°N latitude, the 1 per cent design temperatures are around -17.2°C and +28.7°C respectively (ASHRAE, 2001: 27.24–5).

In 2001, the building was joint winner (with the Druk White Lotus School in India) of the Arup World Architectural Award in the best green building category (*Architecture Week*, 2002). In 2002, it also received the Consulting Engineers of Canada Award of Excellence and the Governor General's Medal for Architecture.

3.1 Wintertime view from the south-west. The south façade fronts onto Campus Walk, with the rear of the main lecture theatre behind the glass façade on the upper right – as well as the fixed external horizontal shading, large rotating vertical shading panels are positioned immediately behind the glass. The lights in the main entrance foyer are visible at ground level immediately below. The undergraduate computing laboratories are also located on the ground floor behind the west façade, with staff offices in the two floors immediately above behind the copper external cladding

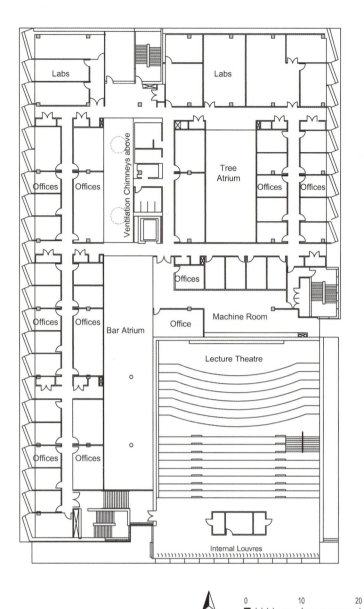

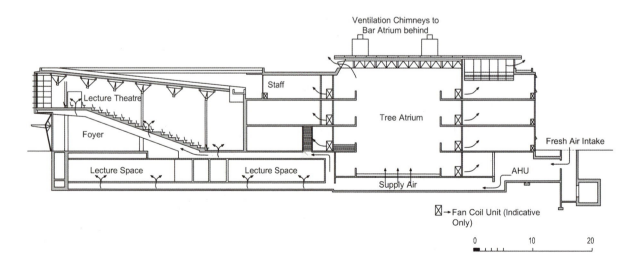

3.2 Second floor plan, with the main lecture theatre, and the two smaller lecture halls immediately below, taking up the south-east quadrant. Note the location of the tree and bar atria, with offices and laboratories grouped around them; and the orientation of the glazing of the office windows on the east and west façades
Source: Adapted from Busby and Associates

3.3 North–south cross-section indicating overall layout of lecture halls and office/laboratory spaces, together with the main air distribution routes
Source: Adapted from Busby and Associates

3.4 View of the east façade. The sloping part on the left of shot indicates the main lecture theatre is immediately behind. To the right of shot, the glazing of the offices on Levels 2 and 3 is orientated to catch the morning sun. The upper part of the tree atrium is just visible above roof level

3.5 View of the tree atrium. Note the offices to the right and left, and circulation spaces in front (and to the rear) of the shot. Fresh air enters at low level (see also Figure 3.7) and acts as the supply to the adjacent spaces via local fan coil units (see Figure 3.11). The air exits via the automated windows at high level

THE DESIGN PROCESS

Following a short-listing process, the design team for the project was a joint venture of Busby and Associates of Vancouver and Architects Alliance of Toronto. They, together with mechanical engineers Keen Engineering and other consultants, took a fully integrated approach to the design process. Busby and Keen had already worked together on sustainable projects in the Vancouver area – several of their principals were involved in the Canadian and US Green Building Councils, while they and many of their staff were LEED accredited (Bonda, 2003).

Given the client's goal for a sustainable building, planning with this in mind was a high priority from the outset. Again, according to Macaulay and McLennan (2006), 'The project kicked off with an all-day design charette at York, led by Bob Berkebile of BNIM [Berkebile Nelson Immenschuh McDowell] Architects in Kansas, Missouri.' Berkebile had been founding chair of the AIA's Committee on the Environment and had led charettes for earlier projects of this

3.6 A busy research laboratory on the Basement Level – note the limited glazing area

3.7 Typical staff office showing the window arrangement. This office is on the west façade with the glazing oriented north-north-west to avoid afternoon summer solar heat gain – the remainder of the west façade is copper clad externally (see also Figure 3.10). Offices on the east façade have a similar arrangement, but with the glazing oriented south-south-east to capture the morning sun

3.8 Typical local fan coil unit in an equipment cupboard adjacent to a circulation corridor. Air (that has been supplied via the tree atrium) is drawn in from the corridor via the grille above the door, filtered, conditioned as necessary, and supplied to the nearby offices and research laboratories

nature. This time, the aim was 'to define sustainability goals and identify features that would lead to good indoor air quality and user satisfaction while not exceeding the capital budget'.

Decisions about key issues required a consensus of the design team members and the client, in the knowledge that achieving some degree of sustainability in a climate as extreme as Southern Ontario might involve rather more risk than in the relatively mild conditions of Vancouver. Nevertheless, the use of passive natural ventilation and a more tolerant view of the thermal conditions acceptable in transient spaces, for example, were accepted as central to the concept.

THE DESIGN OUTCOME

The design background and outcome have been described elsewhere in some detail (see Macaulay and McLennan, 2006: 38–9,116–17 and 149–60 in particular; Czarnecki, 2003; McMinn, 2002). What follows is the briefest of outlines.

Building layout, construction, and passive environmental control systems

The CS&E Building is rectangular in plan (Figure 3.2), approximately 67m by 30m, oriented on the major axes of the grid (long axis north–south), and located between existing campus buildings immediately to the east and west. It has four floors – a recessed basement, ground floor, and two upper levels (Figure 3.3).

A raked 950-seat lecture theatre occupies the ground and upper levels. It is located in the south-east section of the building (Figures 3.2 and 3.4) together with two 200-seat lecture halls in the basement level underneath (Figure 3.3). The building has two full-height atria – one a circulation space running north–south and connecting entrance areas at each end of the building (Figure 3.2); the other in the centre of the north-east section of the building where it is surrounded by offices (Figures 3.2 and 3.5). These atria (termed the 'bar atrium' and 'tree atrium' respectively) play an integral part in both the ventilation and the lighting of the building.

3.9 Roofscape looking towards the third floor Staffroom. Note the sloping grassed roof over the main lecture theatre (foreground right); the opening windows of the tree atrium projecting above the grassed roof of the third floor (centre rear of shot); and the two ventilation chimneys over the north end of the bar atrium (upper left)

3.10 View of the building from the north-west. Note the orientation of the glazing of the offices on the second and third floors (see also Figure 3.7)

3.11 Looking up into one of the two ventilation chimneys (see also Figure 3.9), designed to enable air to exhaust from the north end of the bar atrium area

Large computing laboratories are located along the west façade on the ground floor, while the remainder of that floor and the basement, and most of the two upper floors contain offices, research laboratories, and associated service spaces (Figures 3.6, 3.7, and 3.8).

Walls and roof have high R-values, the latter with a layer of soil under grass and wild flowers, the main function of which is to assist in the management of stormwater (Figure 3.9). The double-glazed windows have thermally broken frames, while the internally exposed concrete structure provides a significant amount of thermal mass. As succinctly expressed by McMinn (2002):

> The material palette of the building exterior combines pre-cast concrete, copper sheathing and large areas of glazing, with an interior of exposed structural concrete, drywall, maple millwork and extensive use of glass partitions separating offices and labs from circulation areas.

Fixed horizontal canopies and the upper floor overhang shade the south façade glazing (Figure 3.1), while a manually operated set of wide vertical internal louvres provide further control options for the space at the rear of the large lecture theatre. The buildings immediately to the east and west are neither close enough nor high enough to provide solar shading to the upper floors of the building – there, a 'sawtooth' design has been adopted for the fenestration (Figure 3.2), with the glazing angled to capture wintertime solar gain on the east (Figure 3.4), and to prevent summertime solar gain on the west (Figure 3.10).

Active environmental control systems

Heat exchangers in the basement of the building are connected to the Keele Campus district (steam) heating and (chilled water) cooling systems. These in turn supply hot and chilled water to a distributed system of fan coil units in the laboratory and office spaces (Figure 3.8) as well as the air handling units (AHUs) serving the lecture theatres and the atria.

The main air supply is tempered via a 'subterranean air plenum' (McMinn, 2002) buried under the building (Figure 3.3), and while the lecture theatres are necessarily mechanically ventilated when in use, a mixed-mode approach has been taken to the thermal environmental control of the rest of the building.

TABLE 3.1

Average scores for each factor and whether they were significantly better, similar to, or worse than the BUS benchmarks

	Score	Worse	Similar	Better		Score	Worse	Similar	Better
OPERATIONAL FACTORS									
Image (5.74)	5.83			●	Cleaning	5.97			●
Space in building	4.65			●	Availability of meeting rooms	5.09			●
Space at desk – too little/much^4	4.51		●		Suitability of storage arrangements	4.17		●	
Furniture	5.42			●	Facilities meet work requirements	5.50			●
ENVIRONMENTAL FACTORS									
Temp and Air in Winter					Temp and Air in Summer				
Temp Overall	4.47			●	Temp Overall	4.41			●
Temp – too hot/too cold^4	4.14		●		Temp – too hot/too cold^4	4.75		●	
Temp – stable/variable^4	3.40		●		Temp – stable/variable^4	3.74		●	
Air – still/draughty^4	3.83		●		Air – still/draughty^4	3.78		●	
Air – dry/humid^4	3.27		●		Air – dry/humid^4	3.82		●	
Air – fresh/stuffy^1	4.16		●		Air – fresh/stuffy^1	3.87			●
Air – odourless/smelly^1	3.29		●		Air – odourless/smelly^1	3.13			●
Air Overall	4.38			●	Air Overall	4.33			●
Lighting					**Noise**				
Lighting Overall (5.24)	5.49			●	Noise Overall (4.81)	4.28		●	
Natural light – too little/much^4	2.99	●			From colleagues – too little/much^4	4.24		●	
Sun & Sky Glare – none/too much^1	2.61			●	From other people – too little/much^4	4.66	●		
Artificial light – too little/much^4	4.65	●			From inside – too little/much^4	4.50	●		
Art'l light glare – none/too much^1	3.25			●	From outside – too little/much^4	3.59	●		
					Interruptions – none/frequent^1	4.01		●	

	%	Score	Worse	Similar	Better		Score	Worse	Similar	Better
CONTROL FACTORS [b]						**SATISFACTION FACTORS**				
Heating	32%	1.59	●			Design (5.62)	5.11			●
Cooling	31%	1.59	●			Needs (5.32)	5.34			●
Ventilation	28%	2.18	●			Comfort Overall (5.27)	4.91			●
Lighting	42%	4.23		●		Productivity % (+13.55)	+2.54			●
Noise	46%	2.23		●		Health (4.45)	3.86		●	

NOTES: (a) unless otherwise noted, a score of 7 is 'best'; superscript ^{4} implies a score of 4 is best, superscript ^{1} implies a score of 1 is best; (b) the per cent values listed here are the percentages of respondents who thought personal control of that aspect was important ; (c) student scores are in brackets – the temperature and air scores cover all seasons.

TABLE 3.2

Numbers of staff (students in brackets) offering positive, balanced, and negative comments on 12 performance factors

Aspect	Number of respondents			
	Positive	Balanced	Negative	Total
Overall Design	10	4	14	28
Needs Overall	4	4	11	19
Meeting Rooms	3	0	12	15
Storage	2	6	12	20
Desk/Work Area	7	2	10	19
Comfort	3 (2)	2 (2)	7 (17)	12 (21)
Noise Sources	0 (1)	6 (2)	19(28)	25 (31)
Lighting Conditions	6	2	13	21
Productivity	6	4	3	13
Health	1 (0)	3 (1)	9 (11)	13 (12)
Work Well	27	–	–	27
Hinder	–	–	40	40
TOTALS (Staff only)	69	33	150	252
PER CENT (Staff only)	27	13.1	59.5	100

During summer and winter conditions, for example, an AHU supplies fresh tempered air to the atria, where it in turn acts as an air supply to the fan coil units serving the adjacent offices and research laboratories in the surrounding spaces. In spring and autumn, the perimeter windows may be opened for fresh air ventilation, with air transfer to the atria via the corridors and eventual exhaust via automatic windows at the top of the tree atrium (Figure 3.5) or two large ventilation chimneys at the north end of the bar atrium (Figure 3.11).

USERS' PERCEPTIONS OF THE BUILDING

Overall response

In this case, responses were sought from both staff (academic, research, and administrative) and undergraduate students, the former using the standard questionnaire, the latter a shorter version. The survey was conducted during November 2005.

For all of the 70 or so staff respondents (36 per cent female, 64 per cent male), the building was their normal place of work, most (78 per cent) working five days per week or more, and averaging 7.1 hours per day. There were equal proportions of those aged over 30 and under 30 and most (81 per cent) had worked in the building for more than a year, some 69 per cent at the same desk or work area. Around 33 per cent worked alone while the rest shared with one or more colleagues (some 60 per cent with up to eight others). Hours per day spent at desk and computer averaged 6.1 and 5.9 respectively. The respondents were split 40:10:25:25 per cent between the Basement, First (Ground), Second, and Third floors respectively.

Of the 94 students who responded to the shorter questionnaire, most (70 per cent) had used the building (the ground floor computing laboratories mainly) for more than a year, averaging 4.2 days per week and 4.0 hours per day, most of which (3.4 hours) was spent at a computer screen.

Significant factors

The average scores of the staff and students for each of the relevant survey questions are listed in Table 3.1. This table also indicates those aspects of the building that the staff perceived as being significantly better, similar to, or worse than the benchmark and/or scale mid-point. Overall, some 19 aspects were significantly better, 8 significantly worse, while the remaining 18 aspects had much the same score as the benchmark.

In terms of the eight operational aspects, staff scored this building above the benchmark in six instances, and about the same as the benchmark or scale mid-point in two cases. Of these latter, storage, at 4.17, was well above the corresponding benchmark, while space at desk, at 4.51, scored slightly on the 'too much' side of the scale mid-point. Cleaning (5.97) and image (5.83) scored highest in this set.

In terms of the environmental factors, the air in the building was perceived to be particularly fresh and odourless in summer, though less so in winter. The air was also perceived to be slightly on the still and dry side with stable temperatures that were perceived to be too cold in both winter and (perhaps surprisingly) summer. Despite these apparent shortcomings, temperature and air overall scored well (higher than the corresponding benchmarks and the scale mid-point) in both seasons. Lighting overall scored highly (5.49) and glare from both daylight and artificial light did not appear to be a major issue. However, there was a perception, on average, of too much artificial light and too little natural light (remembering that 40 per cent of respondents were located in the basement floor). Noise overall, at 4.28, was close to the benchmark and higher than the scale mid-point – the main issues appeared to be a perception of too much noise from other people and sources inside the building, and too little from outside.

The staff did not perceive themselves as having very much control over heating, cooling, or ventilation (the scores were all less than what is a relatively low set of benchmarks), but less than one-third of respondents rated this as important. Rather more saw control of lighting and noise as important, but only in the former case was a reasonable score attained.

Of the Satisfaction variables (design, needs, comfort overall, productivity, and health), all were better than their respective benchmarks. Similarly, all but health were higher than the scale mid-point, and even it, at 3.86, was significantly higher than its benchmark value.

As indicated in Table 3.1, the undergraduate student perceptions (responses to only ten overall variables were sought in the shorter questionnaire) were all significantly higher than both the BUS Benchmark figures and the scale mid-point. Most were greater than 5 and Productivity averaged +13.55 per cent. While the students scored lighting, needs, and image slightly lower than the staff, the other seven aspects ranged from around 0.4 to 1.0 higher.

Users' comments

Overall, some 252 responses were received from staff under the 12 headings where they were able to add written comments – some 30.0 per cent of the 840 potential (70 respondents by 12 headings). The number of comments was approximately in proportion to the number of respondents on each floor of the building. Table 3.2 indicates the numbers of positive, balanced, and negative comments overall – in this case, around 27.4 per cent were positive, 13.1 per cent balanced, and 59.5 per cent negative.

Generally speaking, the individual comments ranged over a wide spectrum of factors, with only a few issues or trends apparent. Arguably chief among those, and reflecting the relatively low scores for some of its aspects, was noise – comments here were predominantly negative. Noise was also the dominant issue reported under the heading of things that hinder. Sources included construction noise, students entering/leaving the lecture theatres, machine room noise, and sounds from adjacent offices.

Design received most comments – no single issue dominated and there were just as many positive and balanced comments as there were negative. Aspects working well included the lighting (on all floors) and the use of space in the building, while storage and meeting room availability came in for some negative comments.

The 64 comments from students (representing only 5.7 per cent of the potential) on comfort, health, and noise were predominantly negative. Noise issues, mostly due to the proximity and activities of other students, dominated.

Overall performance indices

The Comfort Index for the staff, based on the scores for comfort overall, noise, lighting, temperature, and air in winter and summer, works out at +0.80, while the Satisfaction Index, based on the design, needs, health, and perceived productivity scores, is +0.82, both higher than the scale mid-point (noting these indices are scaled from -3 to +3).

The Summary Index, being the average of these, works out at +0.81, while the Forgiveness Factor, calculated to be 1.08 in this instance, indicates that the staff as a whole are likely to be relatively tolerant as far as minor shortcomings in individual aspects such as winter and summer temperatures, air quality, lighting, and noise are concerned (a factor of 1 being the mid-point on a scale that normally ranges from 0.8 to 1.2).

In terms of the Ten-Factor Rating Scale, the building was comfortably within the 'Exceptional' band of the 7-point scale, thanks to a calculated percentage value of 94 per cent. When All-Factors were taken into account, the percentage value worked out at 72 per cent, right on the 'Above Average'/'Good Practice' borderline.

Applying the same system to the ten factors assessed by the undergraduate students, a percentage value of 100 per cent was obtained, at the top end of the 'Exceptional' band.

ACKNOWLEDGEMENTS

I must thank Peter Cribb, Chair of the Department of Computer Science, and Tahir A. Mohammed, Director of Facilities Development, for their ready permission for me to survey the building and its occupants; thanks also to Kathy Wardle and Peter Busby of Busby Perkins and Will, and Kevin R. Hydes of Stantec Consulting (formerly of Keen Engineering) for helping my understanding of the design of the building.

REFERENCES

Architecture Week (2002) 'World Architecture Arup Awards', *Architecture Week*, 21 August 2002, available at: www.architectureweek.com/2002/0821/news_1–1.html (accessed 10 January 2008).

ASHRAE (2001) *ASHRAE Handbook: Fundamentals, SI Edition*, Atlanta, GA: American Society of Heating Refrigerating and Air-Conditioning Engineers.

Bonda, P. S. (2003) 'Architecture as Philosophy – Peter Busby's Deeply Green Vision of Design', *Interiors and Sources*, October, available at: www.isdesignet.com/articles/detail.aspx?contentID=3967 (accessed 10 January 2008).

Czarnecki, J. E. (2003) 'Without Architectural Fanfare, Busby + Associates and Architects Alliance Demonstrate Sustainability in a Northern Climate with York University's Computer Science Building', *Architectural Record*, 191(2): 138.

Macaulay, D. R. and McLennan, J. F. (2006) *The Ecological Engineer*, vol. 1: *Keen Engineering*. Kansas City, MO: Ecotone Publishing.

McMinn, J. (2002) 'Code Green: A Benchmark is Set for Green Design at a Suburban Toronto Campus', *Canadian Architect*, January, available at: www.cdnarchitect.com/issues/ISarticle.asp?id=70722&story_id=CA133273&issue=01012002&PC (accessed 10 January 2008).

Entrance foyer of the Toronto MFRC

4
Military Families Resource Centre (MFRC)
Toronto, Ontario, Canada

THE CONTEXT

The 1840m² Toronto Military Families Resource Centre (TMFRC) (Figure 4.1) was officially opened in June 2003. It was built for the Department of National Defence Canada to serve the needs of personnel in the Greater Toronto area.

Established in 1992, the TMFRC caters to the needs of the spouses and children of military personnel through a variety of programmes. Principal among these is the Children's Playgarden Child Care Centre inspired by the Reggio Emilia approach to child care in which, *inter alia*, 'the environment is an important component' (TMFRC, 2007). Other functions include a youth centre, distress counselling services, physical and educational programmes, and a library.

Housed initially in a former military administration building, when the Centre was forced to move, the opportunity was taken to redefine its needs and space requirements. A major partnering workshop held in May 2001 asserted their mission 'To design the best facility to deliver TMFRC programs in a functional, efficient, safe and welcoming environment to meet the needs of our community' (Agree Inc, 2001).

With a staff of around 25, the building can accommodate 49 full-time day-care children, 24 nursery school children, and approximately

4.1 Northerly façade with a single-storey row of offices in the centre foreground and the two-storey circular plan entrance area to the left of shot. The sloping roof over the multi-function activity space dominates the upper level. Note too the air intake grilles and exhaust cowls of the mechanical ventilation system, as well as the glazing, much of it openable to enable natural ventilation

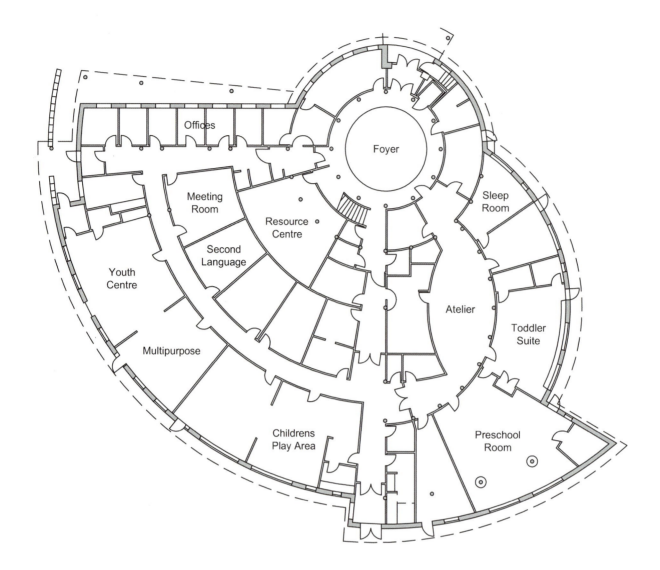

4.2 Ground floor plan – note the circular plan foyer area, the child-care areas 'curving' around the perimeter, and the 'straight' row of offices on the north façade
Source: Adapted from Public Works Government Services Canada

4.3 Long section with main entrance on the right, children's play area on the ground floor to the left, and large multi-function activity space on the upper level
Source: Adapted from Public Works Government Services Canada

0 — 10

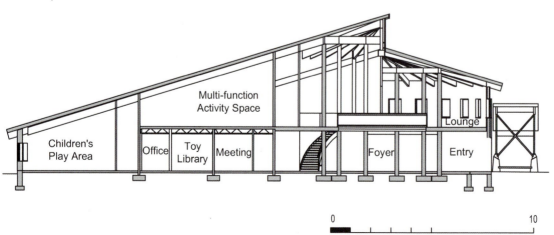

0 — 10

4.4 Inside the two-storey entrance foyer area. Resource Centre straight ahead on the ground floor; high level internal glazing of the large multi-function activity space visible on the upper floor

4.5 Atelier and kitchen/dining area in the ground floor children's area

20 in the youth programme. In addition, there is a multi-purpose room that seats 50 and two classrooms that seat ten each (Doucette, 2005; Tom, 2005).

The building is located in the Downsview district of the City of Toronto. The site is fairly open and reportedly 'at the highest elevation in Toronto with extreme exposure to wind'. The latitude of Toronto is around 44°N and its 1 per cent design temperatures are approximately -17.2 and +28.7°C (ASHRAE, 2001: 27.24–5).

The building won the Canadian Wood Council's 2003 Green by Design Award in the institutional category (PWGSC, 2004), and achieved four Globes out of five in the Canadian version of the Green Globes building sustainability rating tool (GBI, 2005).

With the Department of National Defence having a programme in place for sustainable design, and the underlying concerns of the occupants for the environment, these issues were always going to be high on the agenda – though with no specific budget allowance, a well-integrated design approach was essential.

What follows is the briefest of outlines of the design process and architectural outcome.

THE DESIGN PROCESS

The process started in early 2000, with the TMFRC defining its minimum requirements. The following year saw these requirements developed, via a partnering process involving all the key stakeholders (see, for example, the May 2001 Agree Workshop referred to earlier) into a range of built options – several compact, angular and longitudinal forms were considered and rated before the final layout was selected. According to the TMFRC (2003):

> The design of the building was inspired by: (1) our centre values; (2) our understanding of the principles of the Reggio Emilia approach and the importance of environment; and (3) our desire to ensure a healthy workplace for staff, a play space for children and a programming space for adults.

4.6 View of the Toddler Suite – kitchen area visible through the glazed partition wall. Note the exposed services at high level (sprinkler pipes and air supply/extract ducts)

4.7 Typical one-person office. Note openable section at lower section of the window

4.8 Large multi-function activity space on the upper level of the building. Note the high-level internal glazing on upper left 'borrowing' daylight from the foyer area, and the exposed air supply ducts and sprinkler pipes

The design team comprised an in-house team of architects and mechanical services engineers from the Toronto office of Public Works and Government Services Canada (PWGSC) together with Ontario-based structural and electrical engineers Totten Sims Hubicki (TSH) Associates, under the overall leadership of architect Richard Doucette who had recently joined PWGSC from private practice.

Given the environmental agendas of the Department of National Defence and the TMFRC, together with Doucette's interest in sustainable design and his predilection for involving both the end users and all of the design team right from the start of a project, it will come as no surprise that the Green Globes assessment notes under Project Management – Integrated Design Process are fairly positive (GBI, 2005). 'A team approach [was] used throughout the design process involving collaboration between architect, engineers, consultants, and occupants. Evidence of environmental goals established [in] the early stages of the design process.'

Doucette himself (2005) recalls it as an intensely integrated process, with around 100 meetings over the two-and-a-half year design and construction period, covering everything from the form of the building to the selection of the furniture.

THE DESIGN OUTCOME

Building layout, construction, and passive environmental control systems

The form that emerged from this relatively lengthy process was for a compact two-floor circular plan with sloping roof structures, with roughly 1340m² on the ground level and 500m² at the upper level (Figures 4.2 and 4.3).

On the ground level, the main child-care accommodations arc around the perimeter of the building, nautilus-like in plan (Figure 4.2), from a circular two-storey high entry foyer area (Figure 4.4). These accommodations (Figures 4.5 and 4.6) are linked by an internal corridor, on the inner side of which are situated the service areas and other classrooms. A row of offices also radiates from the foyer area, making up the north façade of the building (Figures 4.1 and 4.7). The upper level contains a large multi-function activity space (Figure 4.8), a couple of offices, and some mechanical plant rooms,

4.9 Looking down into the pre-school child care areas from the upper floor 'balcony' space. Note the extensive use of glazed partitions

4.10 View of the exterior from the north-east. Note the openable windows at high, mid, and low levels

4.11 Looking up towards the high-level glazing above the foyer area, some of which is openable. Note too the exposure of some of the mechanical and electrical services

as well as 'balcony' spaces open to and overlooking the foyer and pre-school areas on the east side of the ground floor (Figure 4.9).

Roof, walls, and floor slab are well insulated and clear double-glazing is used throughout. The perimeter and roof-level glazing (Figures 4.10 and 4.11) is designed to enable daylight penetration to the majority of the spaces that are in frequent use, such as the child-care areas and the offices; interior glazed partitions are also used to good effect (Figures 4.4, 4.6, and 4.8). All of the windows at both high and low level have openable sections to enable natural ventilation to take place when climatic conditions allow – typically from spring to autumn (Figures 4.1, 4.10, and 4.11).

Active environmental control systems

An underfloor heating system, served by a gas boiler located on the upper level, is the primary heating source for the building, while a small air handling unit distributes fresh air, heated or cooled as appropriate, to all of the occupied spaces. The ducts for the latter have been left exposed (Figures 4.6, 4.8, and 4.11) – as with many other aspects of the building, this is to enable the children to gain an understanding of how it works.

USERS' PERCEPTIONS OF THE BUILDING

Overall response

The building was surveyed during November 2005. For virtually all of the 13 respondents (92 per cent female, 8 per cent male), representing almost all of the occupants at the time of the survey, the building was their normal place of business. They worked 4.8 days per week on average and 7.6 hours per day, of which around 6.6 were spent at their desk or in a child-care space and 3.0 at a computer. The ratio of under-30s to over-30s was 75:25 per cent and most (77 per cent) had worked in the building for more than a year at the same desk or work area. The proportions were equally divided between those with a single office and those who shared with one or more colleagues.

TABLE 4.1

Average scores for each factor and whether they were significantly better, similar to, or worse than the BUS benchmarks

	Score	Worse	Similar	Better		Score	Worse	Similar	Better
OPERATIONAL FACTORS									
Image to visitors	6.62			●	Cleaning	6.00			●
Space in building	6.42			●	Availability of meeting rooms	6.40			●
Space at desk – too little/much⁴	5.42		●		Suitability of storage arrangements	5.27			●
Furniture	6.08			●	Facilities meet work requirements	6.31			●
ENVIRONMENTAL FACTORS									
Temp and Air in Winter					*Temp and Air in Summer*				
Temp Overall	5.27			●	Temp Overall	5.92			●
Temp – too hot/too cold⁴	3.20	●			Temp – too hot/too cold⁴	4.50		●	
Temp – stable/variable⁴	4.33		●		Temp – stable/variable⁴	3.70		●	
Air – still/draughty⁴	3.33	●			Air – still/draughty⁴	3.60		●	
Air – dry/humid⁴	3.50		●		Air – dry/humid⁴	3.78		●	
Air – fresh/stuffy¹	3.89		●		Air – fresh/stuffy¹	3.09			●
Air – odourless/smelly¹	3.40		●		Air – odourless/smelly¹	3.62		●	
Air Overall	5.00			●	Air Overall	4.90			●
Lighting					**Noise**				
Lighting Overall	5.69			●	Noise Overall	5.67			●
Natural light – too little/much⁴	4.50	●			From colleagues – too little/much⁴	3.91		●	
Sun & Sky Glare – none/too much¹	4.09		●		From other people – too little/much⁴	4.73	●		
Artificial light – too little/much⁴	4.18		●		From inside – too little/much⁴	4.67	●		
Art'l light glare – none/too much¹	4.83	●			From outside – too little/much⁴	3.55	●		
					Interruptions – none/frequent¹	2.90			●
CONTROL FACTORS [b]					**SATISFACTION FACTORS**				
Heating	23%	2.17 ●			Design	6.23			●
Cooling	31%	2.17 ●			Needs	6.38			●
Ventilation	0%	2.91	●		Comfort Overall	5.92			●
Lighting	8%	5.25		●	Productivity %	+20.00			●
Noise	8%	3.33 ●			Health	5.17			●

NOTES: (a) unless otherwise noted, a score of 7 is 'best'; superscript ⁴ implies a score of 4 is best, superscript ¹ implies a score of 1 is best; (b) the per cent values listed here are the percentages of respondents who thought personal control of that aspect was important.

TABLE 4.2

Numbers of respondents offering positive, balanced, and negative comments on 12 performance factors

Aspect	Number of respondents			
	Positive	Balanced	Negative	Total
Overall Design	2	–	–	2
Needs Overall	1	1	2	4
Meeting Rooms	1	–	2	3
Storage	1	1	2	4
Desk/Work Area	2	1	1	4
Comfort	1	–	–	1
Noise Sources	–	1	2	3
Lighting Conditions	–	–	1	1
Productivity	–	–	–	–
Health	–	–	–	–
Work Well	4	–	–	4
Hinder	–	–	3	3
TOTALS	12	4	13	29
PER CENT	41.4	13.8	44.8	100

Significant factors

The average scores for each of the survey questions are listed in Table 4.1. Table 4.1 also indicates those factors that the staff perceived as being significantly better, similar to, or worse than the benchmark and/ or scale mid-point. In this case, some 21 aspects were significantly better, 9 were significantly worse, while the remaining 15 aspects had much the same score as the benchmark.

In terms of the eight operational aspects, this building scores better than the benchmark in virtually every case. Only in relation to space at desk is there a suggestion that there is too much!

Overall scores for temperature and air in both winter and summer were well over their respective benchmarks and the scale mid-point. Nevertheless, the more detailed scores reveal that respondents perceived the temperature as too hot and the air as too still in winter (this may have been due to technical/contractual issues that have since been resolved).

While lighting overall scored very well, the occupants indicated there was too much of it, both artificial and daylight. While glare from the artificial lighting was an issue, that from sun and sky was less of a problem.

Noise overall scored very well too, but there appeared to be too much internal noise of one kind or another (possibly not surprising in this kind of facility) and too little from outside. The building wasn't quite an interruption-free zone, but scored very well on this aspect.

Personal control did not rate of particularly high importance in this building.

All of the satisfaction variables came out significantly higher than their corresponding benchmarks and the scale mid-point. At +20.0 per cent, perceived productivity gains were remarkably high.

Users' comments

Overall, some 29 responses were received from staff under the 12 headings where they were able to add written comments – some 18.6 per cent of the 156 potential (13 respondents by 12 headings). Table 4.2 indicates the numbers of positive, balanced, and negative comments – in this case, around 41.4 per cent were positive, 13.8

per cent balanced, and 44.8 per cent negative. With so relatively few respondents and numbers of comments, it was not possible to pick out any common issues or trends.

Overall performance indices

The Comfort Index, based on the comfort overall, noise, lighting, temperature, and air quality scores, works out at +2.08, while the Satisfaction Index, based on the design, needs, health, and perceived productivity scores, is +2.82, noting that the scale mid-point in these instances is zero on a -3 to +3 scale.

The Summary Index, being the average of the Comfort and Satisfaction Indices, works out at +2.45, while the Forgiveness Factor, calculated to be 1.09 in this instance, indicates that staff are likely to be relatively forgiving of minor shortcomings in individual aspects such as winter and summer temperatures, air quality, lighting, and noise (a factor of 1 being the mid-point on a scale that normally ranges from 0.8 to 1.2).

In terms of their average perception scores for the ten overall study variables, the staff rated the building as 'Exceptional', with a score of 100 per cent. When all 45 variables considered here were taken into account, the building 'scored' around 72 per cent – at the borderline of the 'Above Average' and 'Good Practice' bands.

ACKNOWLEDGEMENTS

I must express my gratitude to Susan Tom, Child Care Centre Supervisor, for granting permission for me to undertake this survey. Particular thanks go to architect J. Richard Doucette of Public Works and Government Services Canada, and to Jiri Skopek of ECD Energy and Environment Canada for assisting my understanding of the building and its design.

REFERENCES

Agree Inc (2001) Toronto Military Family Resource Centre – Workshop Record, Toronto, 22 May.

ASHRAE (2001) *ASHRAE Handbook: Fundamentals, SI Edition*, Atlanta, GA: American Society of Heating Refrigerating and Air-Conditioning Engineers.

Doucette, J. R. (2005) Transcript of interview held on 1 December 2005, Toronto, Ontario, 29 pp. plus Appendices.

GBI (2005) 'Green Globes Case Study – Toronto Military Families Resource Centre, Green Building Initiative', available at: www.thegbi.org/assets/ case_study/toronto_mfrc.pdf (accessed 4 December 2007).

PWGSC (2005) 'Outstanding Architectural Achievement', available at: www.pwgsc.gc.ca/db/text/archives/2004/summer2004/002-archtc-e.html (accessed 19 April 2006).

TMFRC (2003) 'Special Building Edition', Toronto: Toronto Military Families Resource Centre.

TMFRC (2007) 'Children's Playgarden', available at: www.tmfrc.com/playg_ whoweare.html (accessed 4 December 2007).

Tom, S. (2005) Transcript of interview held on 29 November 2005, Toronto, Ontario.

5

Sciencepark
Gelsenkirchen, Germany

THE CONTEXT

The Sciencepark (Wissenschaftspark), Gelsenkirchen, is located on the site of a former steel mill. The building is comprised of nine three-storey pavilions, each connected to one side of a continuous three-storey gallery some 300m in length, which together provide some 19,200m^2 of office and laboratory accommodation (Figures 5.1 and 5.2). A full height 10m-wide glazed arcade is located on the other side of the gallery, and parking for around 180 cars is provided in the basement area underneath (Figure 5.3). One of the many projects commissioned by the Emscher Park Internationale Bauausstellung (IBA) as a means of revitalising the industrial base of the Ruhr, this commenced construction in 1992, reaching completion three years later, winning the 1995 German Architecture Prize.

The aim of this particular project was to build a facility that would attract research and development organisations involved in ecological energy technologies. Located at a latitude of around 51°N in the low-lying northern part of Germany, the region has a reasonably temperate climate, with winter and summer 1 per cent design temperatures of around -7°C and +28°C respectively (ASHRAE, 2001: 27.34–5).

THE DESIGN PROCESS

This building resulted from a 1989 competition won by the well-established small practice of Uwe Kiessler and Partner of Munich which had been involved in the design of a range of building types over the previous decades. Herbert Nowak of Ingenieurbüro Trumpp, with whom Kiessler had built up a strong relationship over many years, was the designer of the engineering services on this project. In this instance, the Fraunhofer Institute in Freiberg was also retained to carry out simulations of the thermal environmental conditions in parts of the building.

Having grown up in this part of the country, Uwe Kiessler was familiar with the kinds of buildings used in the traditional industries. His idea was 'to create a new kind of industrial building, with offices and laboratories – not to have little buildings in nice situations, but to have one straight, long building' (Ausbach and Nowak, 1998) with the aim of attracting ecological energy technologies.

Despite the relative vagueness of what was meant by a science park, the IBA's overall theme of 'working in the park' was well established. Hence, the placement of the new building along one side of the site, thus enabling a park to be developed over the remainder (Figure 5.4), was a key decision – in full keeping with the 'working

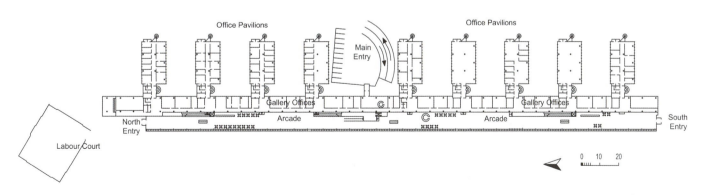

5.1 Ground floor plan showing the nine pavilions linked by their services towers to the elongated, north–south running gallery/arcade. The curved shape at upper-centre indicates the entry to the underground car park
Source: Adapted from Kiessler + Partner

5.2 Cutaway model showing two pavilions linked to a section of gallery/arcade, with indicative floor layouts. Note too the rooftop photo-voltaic arrays oriented due south

5.3 Cross-section through a typical pavilion and gallery/arcade area. Arrows indicate the anticipated natural ventilation airflow directions in the arcade
Source: Adapted from Kiessler + Partner

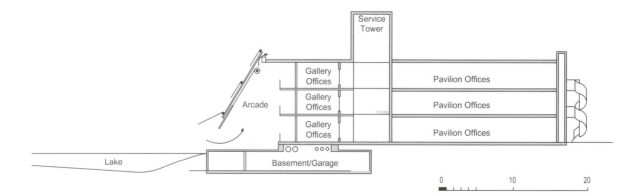

5.4 Looking southwards from the Labour Court building. Sloping west façade of the arcade and north entry to the 'walk in the park' on the left, artificial lake in the centre, and the main expanse of the park to the right. Window-cleaning gantry evident at the north end of the façade

5.5 View along the east side of the building indicating the spaced-out gable ends of a number of pavilions (those shown are to the south of the main entrance). Services areas and fire escape stairs in evidence

in the park' theme, and designed to bring nature back into the city (Fisher, 1998: 5).

In terms of the design process, the members of the team – including Herr Nowak of Ingenieurbüro Trumpp – met regularly on a weekly basis. The design philosophy at Kiessler's office did not allow heating and cooling matters to be dealt with as an engineering afterthought – such considerations were an integral part of the architectural design process from the very start. Using natural ventilation and night cooling for the pavilions and gallery spaces, for example, to avoid the need for mechanical ventilation and refrigeration systems, was fundamental to the concept. The involvement of the Fraunhofer Institute in the simulation of alternative solutions from an energy use point of view was also an indication of Kiessler's serious intent in this regard.

THE DESIGN OUTCOME

Building layout, construction, and passive environmental control systems

The final shape of this 'form looking for a function' (Dawson, 1996) is of an elongated, three-storey gallery on a north–south axis, located on the eastern edge of a park (Figures 5.1 and 5.4). The nine three-storey research pavilions, with their flexible partitioning systems, are spaced out along the eastern edge of the gallery (Figures 5.1 and 5.5), while on the west side, facing the park is a full height, triangular cross-section, glazed arcade (Figures 5.6 and 5.7) . The basement parking and services area extends over the full width of the arcade and gallery (Figure 5.3).

The nine 12.60m-deep three-storey pavilions are well separated from one another and designed to allow for natural cross-ventilation. This is achieved through the use of a 1.44m façade module. Alternate modules contain either a fixed glazed element or an element comprised of a glazed French door alongside what has been termed a ventilation lamella (Figure 5.8). This latter consists of a rainproof, louvred, fly-screened opening, with a timber internal door under the control of

5.6 Looking northwards towards the Labour Court building. South entrance to the 'walk in the park' on the right; lower sections of the sloping façade all in their closed position; roller blinds arrangement evident but none deployed

5.7 Inside the arcade, looking north. Open gallery corridor on the immediate right, view to the park and lake to the left

5.8 Internal view of a typical façade module showing a ventilation lamella (comprised of a rainproof, louvred, flyscreened opening, and a timber internal door under the control of the occupants) with French door alongside and radiators under the short window sill

the occupants; apart from its conventional function of allowing the occupants direct control of the amount of fresh air during the working day, this device enables night-time cooling without compromising the security of the building.

The orientation and spacing of the pavilions allow solar heat gains to the short east and the long south façades. Externally these gains are controlled by motorised canvas roller blinds (Figure 5.9)

56

5.9 View into the space between two pavilions. The roller blinds are fully deployed on the east façade of the gallery offices – note the angle of the shadow on that façade at the time (the sun is to the south-east of the building). Those on the south façade of the adjacent pavilion (to the right of the picture) are not yet deployed, and none is fitted on the south façade (on the left of the picture)

5.10 Exterior view of environmental controls for a typical façade – this one of the upper floors of the south-east corner of a pavilion – showing vertical blinds, lamella, roller blind arrangement, and window details

5.11 On the roof of the gallery looking north towards the Labour Court building in the distance. The exhaust fans and natural ventilation openings from the arcade are on the left and the photo-voltaic panel array on the right. The structures on the far right are the services towers linking the individual pavilions to the gallery

and internally by vertical adjustable blinds (Figure 5.10), the former centrally, the latter directly by the occupants. The thermal mass of the exposed concrete ceilings is also available as a store for heat or coolth as appropriate. In the case of the gallery spaces, their plan depth of 5.44m allows for single-sided natural ventilation, using the same façade module as the pavilions.

Passive and active environmental control systems

Thermal environmental control was achieved in both the pavilion/gallery spaces and in the arcade through a combination of active and passive systems.

Connection to the local district heating system provides hot water at 120°C for the building. Heating mains run in the basement serve 12 heat exchangers, three serving the different zones of the arcade's underfloor heating system and one for each of the pavilions. In the latter cases, vertical distribution is via ducts at either end of the pavilions, one in the stair tower, the other on the eastern façade, and horizontal distribution to the perimeter radiators is in the raised floor.

The controls to the central heating radiators, located conventionally under each module, are programmed to turn them off when the French windows or ventilation lamellae are opened (Figure 5.8). Water pipes in the slab, used for heating the arcade in the winter, in summertime are employed to take heat away from the slab for use in preheating other parts of the building and the process hot water needed in the laboratories and wash-hand basins.

The sloping façade of the 300m-long arcade is completely glazed and faces almost due west and is thus potentially subject to massive heat gains during the latter part of the day (Figures 5.4 and 5.6). Several means of coping with such conditions have been incorporated into the design, most noticeably the 38 glazed openable panels 7m by 4.5m on the lower third of the 38 façade modules. These panels can be completely raised and lowered in their sloping guide rails by a pair of electric motors located within the apex of the arcade to allow fresh air to enter the arcade, making use of the cooling potential of the lake water on its way. Smaller, automatically controlled

TABLE 5.1

2002 Survey – Average scores for each factor and whether they were significantly better, similar to, or worse than the BUS benchmarks

OPERATIONAL FACTORS

	Score	Worse	Similar	Better		Score	Worse	Similar	Better
Image to visitors	5.75			●	Cleaning	4.61		●	
Space in building	3.53	●			Availability of meeting rooms	5.45			●
Space at desk – too little/much^4	4.53		●		Suitability of storage arrangements	4.44			●
Furniture	5.61			●					

ENVIRONMENTAL FACTORS

Temp and Air in Winter / **Temp and Air in Summer**

	Score	Worse	Similar	Better		Score	Worse	Similar	Better
Temp Overall	4.53			●	Temp Overall	2.31	●		
Temp – too hot/too cold^4	4.58	●			Temp – too hot/too cold^4	1.86	●		
Temp – stable/variable^4	4.14			●	Temp – stable/variable^4	4.58		●	
Air – still/draughty^4	3.16	●			Air – still/draughty^4	3.57		●	
Air – dry/humid^4	3.07		●		Air – dry/humid^4	3.27	●		
Air – fresh/stuffy^1	3.80			●	Air – fresh/stuffy^1	4.60		●	
Air – odourless/smelly^1	3.19			●	Air – odourless/smelly^1	3.49		●	
Air Overall	4.62			●	Air Overall	2.50	●		

Lighting / **Noise**

	Score	Worse	Similar	Better		Score	Worse	Similar	Better
Lighting Overall	5.12			●	Noise Overall	4.76			●
Natural light – too little/much^4	4.45		●		From colleagues – too little/much^4	3.28		●	
Sun & Sky Glare – none/too much^1	4.51	●			From other people – too little/much^4	3.51		●	
Artificial light – too little/much^4	4.00			●	From inside – too little/much^4	3.82		●	
Art'l light glare – none/too much^1	3.11			●	From outside – too little/much^4	4.14		●	
					Interruptions – none/frequent^1	3.16			●

CONTROL FACTORS ^{b} / SATISFACTION FACTORS

	%	Score	Worse	Similar	Better		Score	Worse	Similar	Better
Heating	49%	3.47		●		Design	4.96			●
Cooling	47%	2.04	●			Needs	4.78			●
Ventilation	43%	4.12		●		Comfort Overall	4.88			●
Lighting	35%	4.63			●	Productivity %	+1.43			●
Noise	29%	4.78		●		Health	3.69		●	●

NOTES: (a) unless otherwise noted, a score of 7 is 'best'; superscript ^{4} implies a score of 4 is best, superscript ^{1} implies a score of 1 is best; (b) the per cent values listed here are the percentages of respondents who thought personal control of that aspect was important.

TABLE 5.2

2006 Survey – Average scores for each factor and whether they were significantly better, similar to, or worse than the BUS benchmarks

	Score	Worse	Similar	Better		Score	Worse	Similar	Better
OPERATIONAL FACTORS									
Image to visitors	5.63			●	Cleaning	4.27		●	
Space in building	3.56	●			Availability of meeting rooms	5.50			●
Space at desk – too little/much⁴	4.25		●		Suitability of storage arrangements	4.00		●	
Furniture	5.32			●	Facilities meet requirements	5.96			●
ENVIRONMENTAL FACTORS									
Temp and Air in Winter					Temp and Air in Summer				
Temp Overall	4.30		●		Temp Overall	2.63	●		
Temp – too hot/too cold⁴	4.59	●			Temp – too hot/too cold⁴	2.00	●		
Temp – stable/variable⁴	4.45		●		Temp – stable/variable⁴	4.37		●	
Air – still/draughty⁴	3.32	●			Air – still/draughty⁴	3.07		●	
Air – dry/humid⁴	2.96	●			Air – dry/humid⁴	2.86	●		
Air – fresh/stuffy¹	3.44			●	Air – fresh/stuffy¹	4.57		●	
Air – odourless/smelly¹	3.19			●	Air – odourless/smelly¹	3.33			●
Air Overall	4.82			●	Air Overall	3.04	●		
Lighting					**Noise**				
Lighting Overall	5.27			●	Noise Overall	4.37			●
Natural light – too little/much⁴	4.30	●			From colleagues – too little/much⁴	3.86		●	
Sun & Sky Glare – none/too much¹	4.20	●			From other people – too little/much⁴	3.93			●
Artificial light – too little/much⁴	4.07			●	From inside – too little/much⁴	3.90		●	
Art'l light glare – none/too much¹	3.00			●	From outside – too little/much⁴	4.27	●		
					Interruptions – none/frequent¹	3.46			●

		Score	Worse	Similar	Better		Score	Worse	Similar	Better
CONTROL FACTORS[b]						**SATISFACTION FACTORS**				
Heating	39%	3.79		●		Design	4.60		●	
Cooling	32%	1.97	●			Needs	4.53		●	
Ventilation	35%	5.17			●	Comfort Overall	4.93			●
Lighting	29%	5.60			●	Productivity %	-2.27		●	
Noise	19%	2.83		●		Health	3.57		●	

NOTES: (a) unless otherwise noted, a score of 7 is 'best'; superscript ⁴ implies a score of 4 is best, superscript ¹ implies a score of 1 is best; (b) the per cent values listed here are the percentages of respondents who thought personal control of that aspect was important.

air exhaust openings at the apex (and accessible from the roof) run the full length of the arcade – should natural ventilation pressures prove insufficient, then the 18 smoke exhaust fans (total capacity 220,000m³/s) may be pressed into service (Figure 5.11). To assist in the control of solar heat gains and glare, the exterior surface was fitted with roller blinds.

The 210kWp photo-voltaic system installed on the roof of the building (Figures 5.11 and 5.2) feeds straight to the local electricity network. The 190,000kWh or so it produces each year are not used directly in the building, nor is the rooftop array of panels an integral part of its design.

USERS' PERCEPTIONS OF THE BUILDING

Overall response

Two surveys were undertaken at this building, the first in 2002, the second in 2006. The following notes will report the overall findings and indicate any notable differences in the average responses between the two surveys.

For both sets of respondents (51 in 2002; 30 in 2006), the building was their normal place of business, on average, working around 4.5 days per week and 8.3 hours per day, of which 6.8 were spent at their desk and 5.6 at a computer. The majority (some 82 per cent) were over 30 and around 70 per cent had worked in the building for more than a year at the same desk or work area. Around half had single offices, while the rest shared with one or more colleagues. Over 90 per cent were near to a window. The female:male proportions differed between the two surveys, being 40:60 per cent in 2002 and 60:40 per cent in 2006.

Significant factors

The average scores for each of the survey questions are listed in Tables 5.1 and 5.2 for the 2002 and 2006 surveys respectively. The tables also indicate those aspects of the building that the users perceived as being significantly better, similar to, or worse than the benchmark and/or scale mid-point at these times.

Of the 44 aspects surveyed in 2002, some 19 were significantly better, nine significantly worse, while the remaining 16 had much the same score as the benchmark. By 2006, of the 45 aspects surveyed, some 17 were significantly better, 12 were significantly worse, while the remaining 16 had much the same score as the benchmark. Of the 44 aspects surveyed on both occasions, some 32 had remained more or less the same, three had improved, and nine had not scored quite so well, though in most instances the differences in average scores were relatively small.

In terms of operational aspects, the scoring pattern was fairly similar both years, with most aspects rated reasonably well. While the building scored very highly (5.96 in 2006) for 'meets work requirements', there was a suggestion of there being too much desk space and relatively inefficient use of the space in the building generally. The score for storage had fallen from 4.44 to 4.00.

Scores for temperature and air overall in winter and summer (4.62/4.82 and 2.50/3.05 respectively in 2002/2006) indicated a pronounced difference in perception between the two seasons. Winter conditions were characterised as still, dry, and slightly too cold, but fresh and relatively odourless, while in summer, conditions were seen as still, dry, and odourless too, but stuffy and, with scores of 1.86 and 2.00 in 2002 and 2006, far too hot.

Lighting overall scored well in both surveys, as did the artificial lighting and the (lack of) glare from it. However, there appeared to be a perception of too much natural light together with attendant glare issues. Noise overall scored slightly less well than lighting overall both years; the building scored well for lack of interruptions, but there seemed to have been a slight increase in the perception of noise from outside.

Depending on the aspect considered, between 20 and 50 per cent of respondents rated personal control as important – scoring cooling, ventilation, and lighting much higher than the benchmark, heating and noise about the same, with cooling predictably very much worse.

Of the Satisfaction variables (design, needs, comfort overall, productivity, and health), all were significantly better than their respective benchmarks in 2002. By 2006, all but comfort overall had dropped closer to their respective benchmarks.

Of the differences between 2002 and 2006, it can be seen that temperature and air in summer score slightly higher in 2006 (though at 2.63 and 3.04 respectively they are still relatively low), while

TABLE 5.3

Numbers of respondents offering positive, balanced, and negative comments on 12 performance factors in 2002 and 2006

Aspect	Number of respondents			
	Positive	Balanced	Negative	Total
Overall Design	7 (4)	1 (2)	6 (3)	14 (9)
Needs Overall	3 (1)	2 (1)	7 (6)	12 (8)
Meeting Rooms	0 (1)	1 (0)	3 (1)	4 (2)
Storage	0 (2)	1 (0)	4 (2)	5 (4)
Desk/Work Area	4 (0)	0 (0)	3 (0)	7 (0)
Comfort	0 (0)	0 (0)	3 (5)	3 (5)
Noise Sources	0 (0)	0 (0)	6 (8)	6 (8)
Lighting Conditions	3 (2)	1 (1)	8 (6)	12 (9)
Productivity	1 (0)	1 (1)	2 (5)	4 (6)
Health	2 (0)	2 (1)	3 (4)	7 (5)
Work Well	9 (3)	–	–	9 (3)
Hinder	–	–	14 (4)	14 (4)
TOTALS	29(13)	9 (6)	59 (44)	97 (63)
PER CENT	29.9 (20.6)	9.3 (9.5)	60.8 (69.9)	100.0
OVERALL TOTALS	42	15	106	160
OVERALL PER CENT	26.2	9.4	64.4	100

temperature in winter, design, and needs scored slightly lower though still close to their respective benchmarks and above the scale mid-point.

Users' comments

In terms of user comments, similar percentage response rates were elicited in both 2002 and 2006 (15.8 per cent and 17.5 per cent respectively).

Overall, some 160 responses were received from staff under the 12 headings where they were able to add written comments – 97 in 2002, 63 in 2006 (15.8 per cent of the 612 potential in 2002; 17.5 per cent of the 360 potential in 2006). Table 5.3 indicates the numbers of positive, neutral, and negative comments in both years. Overall, around 26.2 per cent were positive, 9.4 per cent neutral, and 64.4 per cent negative, with an apparent slight shift towards the negative over the period.

While response rates were relatively low, design attracted the highest number on both occasions with roughly equal positive and negative comments. While comfort attracted very few comments, it was found that there were a relatively large number of comments (nine in 2002 and 14 in 2006) among several of the other categories (design, needs, space, hinder, productivity, and health) about the occurrence and effects of high summer temperatures, in the arcade in particular.

Noise attracted entirely negative comment in both surveys. Mainly, these referred to internal noise from activities in adjacent spaces and the arcade, as well as impact noise from the wooden floors. This aligned with the generally moderate scores for different aspects of noise described above. Lighting attracted a relatively large number of comments (second only to design). Two-thirds of these were negative and mainly related to the operation of the exterior blinds on the pavilion and gallery façades – sun and sky glare *per se* were hardly mentioned under this heading, but half the comments under hinder in 2002 related to the effect of bright sunlight.

Overall performance indices

The Comfort Indices, based on the comfort overall, noise, lighting, temperature, and air quality scores, work out at +0.53 and +0.20 in 2002 and 2006 respectively, which are significantly better than the scale mid-point in both cases, while the corresponding Satisfaction Indices, based on the design, needs, health, and perceived productivity scores, are +0.54 and +0.07 respectively, which are also significantly higher than the scale mid-point (noting these are both around zero on a -3 to +3 scale).

The Summary Indices, being the average of the Comfort and Satisfaction Indices, work out at +0.53 and +0.13 respectively, while the Forgiveness Factors, calculated to be 1.22 and 1.21 in this instance, indicate that staff as a whole are likely to be relatively more tolerant of minor shortcomings in individual aspects such as winter and summer temperatures, air quality, lighting, and noise (a factor of 1 being the mid-point on a scale that normally ranges from 0.8 to 1.2).

In 2002, in terms of the Ten-Factor Rating Scale, the building was 'Good Practice' on the 7-point scale, thanks to a calculated percentage value of 83 per cent. When All-Factors were taken into account, the percentage value worked out at 72 per cent, just inside the 'Good Practice' band. The corresponding ratings in 2006 were slightly lower – 'Good Practice' with 76 per cent on the Ten-Factor Rating Scale, and 'Above Average' with 65 per cent on the All-Factors.

OTHER REPORTED ASPECTS OF PERFORMANCE

Some years prior to these surveys, Fisher (1998), as part of his Cambridge University MPhil Degree in Environmental Design in Architecture, used a brief questionnaire to assess the response of some 25 building occupants to the environmental conditions they experienced in their offices and in the arcade. His findings are summarised elsewhere (Baird, 2001) but worth repeating here:

His results suggested 'that most people are reasonably satisfied with the thermal performance of the building in winter' (even more so in spring and autumn), but 'are less happy with peak summer temperatures'. It seemed too that the occupants were well pleased with the environmental control features over which they had direct local control, namely the lamellae and the windows [Figure 5.8]. No mention is made of the interior vertical blinds, but the exterior roller blinds, over which the occupants had no control and which obscure the view completely when down, rated poorly. Originally designed to be controlled automatically, their operation during days of rapidly changing external light conditions was deemed to be disturbing. They are now operated manually, but can only be fully open or fully closed on any given floor – hardly ideal [Figure 5.9].

In response to a question whether the arcade (18°C was specified) should be heated to room temperature in winter, most respondents thought that a temperature between that outside and their (pavilion) room would be adequate. Spring daytime temperatures around 25°C were recorded – summertime temperatures exceeding 35°C were reported, though the position of the blinds and openings at the time is not known.

No particular surprises there, but encouraging to note the apparent acceptance of the lamellae, despite their relative novelty.

(Baird, 2001:77)

The summertime overheating issue was investigated by Kasule and Till (2002) who monitored maximum average temperatures in the arcade area ranging from 28°C on the lower levels to around 40°C on the upper floor. This appeared to be the result of wind damage to the external roller blinds on the arcade façade rendering them ineffective, together with insufficient outlet area for the hot air to escape at the top, and no coordination of their control with the air inlet openings. The solution proposed was a combination of 'inside shading devices with proper air circulation between glass and the device' in combination with louvre windows that would allow the available outlet area to be increased, but it is not known if this has ever been implemented.

ACKNOWLEDGEMENTS

My thanks go to Stefanie Ausbach of Kiessler + Partner, Architects, Munich, and to Herbert Nowak of Ingenieurbüro Trumpp, Grafelfing, whom I interviewed in connection with the design of the building; to Geschäftsführer Dr H-P. Schmitz-Borchert and Sabine von der Beck of vdB Public Relations, for their assistance during my visit to Wissenschaftspark. I should also like to thank Peter Fisher for permission to quote from his findings.

REFERENCES

ASHRAE (2001) *ASHRAE Handbook: Fundamentals, SI Edition*, Atlanta, GA: American Society of Heating Refrigerating and Air-Conditioning Engineers.

Ausbach, S. and Nowak, H. (1998) Transcript of interview of 18 September 1998.

Dawson, L. (1996) 'Arcadian Assembly', *The Architectural Review*, 1195: 30–5.

Fisher, P. (1998) 'Rheinelbe SciencePark Gelsenkirchen – an Environmental Case Study', unpublished MPhil essay, St Edmund's College, Cambridge.

Kasule, S. and Till, P. (2002) 'Overheating in Buildings – Investigation and Solutions', in A. A. M. Sayigh (ed.) *Proceedings of World Renewable Energy Conference VII (WREC 2002)*, Oxford: Elsevier Science.

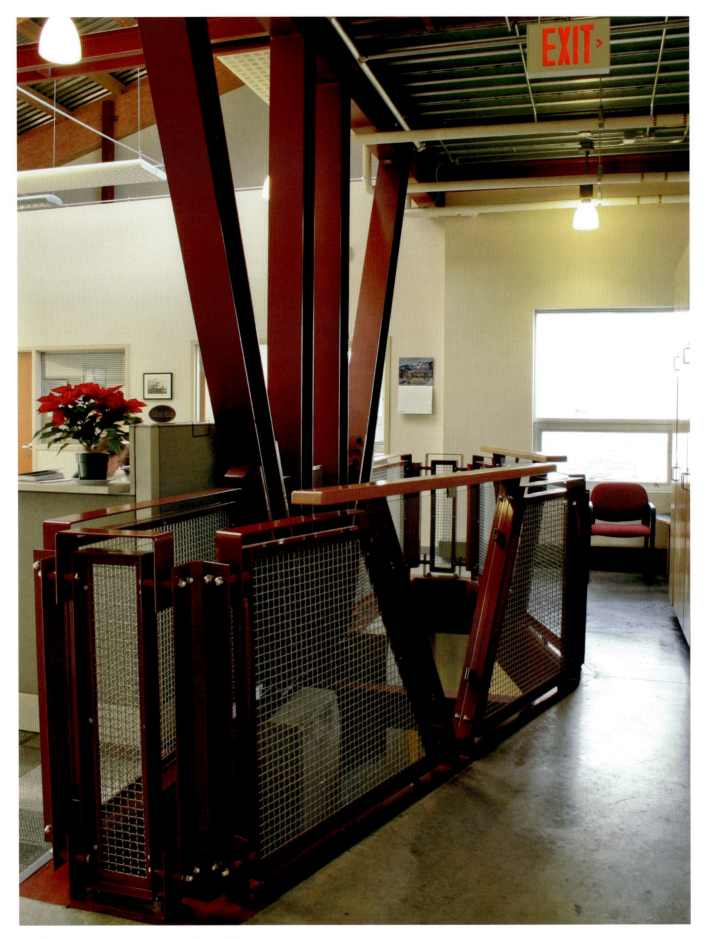

Inter-floor-slab opening and structure at National Works Yards

6

National Works Yards
Vancouver, British Columbia, Canada

THE CONTEXT

Completed in early 2004 and officially opened in June of that year, the National Works Yards occupy a 12-acre (5-hectare) site close to the centre of Vancouver, British Columbia, the city that it serves. The site accommodates a range of facilities associated with the construction, maintenance, and administration of the City's transport infrastructure – the roads and sidewalks, their signage and markings, traffic signals and lighting, parking operations, and the like. It provides a base for around 400 employees.

This new facility replaces an existing one and consolidates a number of the above operations that were previously scattered around the City. Its development was seen as an opportunity to promote and implement the City's sustainability policies, and the project was seen 'as a model to guide future building designs' and a commitment given to reporting 'back on costs and lessons learned' (Bremner, 2004). A plaque at the entrance proclaims the building to be 'Continuing Vancouver's commitment to a sustainable city'.

While several buildings are located on the site, it was the major Administrative Centre and the smaller Parking Operations buildings (Figure 6.1) that were the main focus of this sustainable design effort. While both buildings achieved LEED Gold certification, it is the former that is the subject of this case study.

6.1 View of the two-storey Administration Centre with its mono-pitched roof from the south-west with low-angle winter sunshine on its south façade. The Parking Operations building is the smaller single-storey structure in the distance, on the other side of the main entrance to the Yards

6.2 View of the two-storey Administration Centre with its mono-pitched roof from the south-east. The main entrance control to the Yard and the building is in the foreground. The Parking Operations building is to the right just out of shot

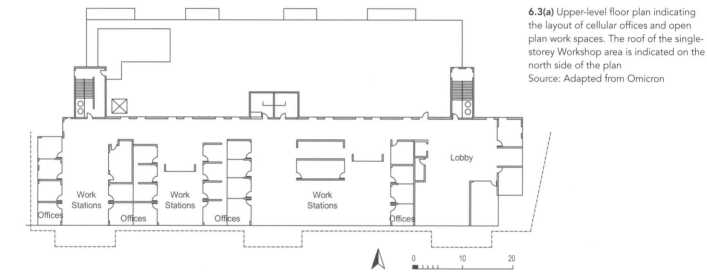

6.3(a) Upper-level floor plan indicating the layout of cellular offices and open plan work spaces. The roof of the single-storey Workshop area is indicated on the north side of the plan
Source: Adapted from Omicron

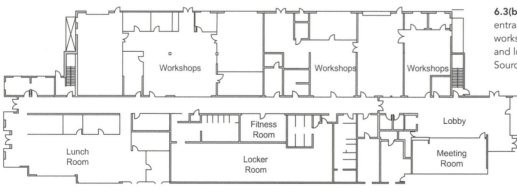

6.3(b) Plan of the ground floor showing entrance lobby and central corridor, with workshops to the north and locker room and lunch room facilities to the south
Source: Adapted from Omicron

6.4 Interior of the upper floor indicating one mix of cellular offices and open-plan workspace. Note the use of structural steel and engineered wood, the high-level glazing on the north façade, and the arrangement of suspended lights and radiant heating panels. Note too the low-level December sun penetration

6.5 Interior of the upper floor indicating another arrangement of cellular offices and open-plan workspace. Note the motorised louvred natural ventilation opening beside the high-level glazing on the north façade as well as the openable windows at low level. Again, the suspended radiant heating panels are quite evident, though none of the circular floor grilles through which fresh air is supplied are visible in this shot. Low-level December sun penetrating the south glazing is producing angled patterns on the right-hand wall; tough roller blinds are provided should this prove to be a glare issue

Located on the western seaboard of Canada, at a latitude of 49°N, the 1 per cent design temperatures are around -4.7°C and +23.2°C (ASHRAE, 2001: 27.22–3). The Administrative Centre, with a score of 44 (out of a possible 69) was the first to receive LEED Gold certification from the Canadian Green Building Council, under LEED BC (British Columbia) criteria. It also received the Canadian Institute of Steel Construction 2004 BC Steel Design Award (Architectural Division) and an Honourable Mention in the inaugural Canadian 'Outside the Box' annual awards (2004).

THE DESIGN PROCESS

Following a fairly lengthy planning phase during which the basic site plan had been established (Hanvey, 2005), the Vancouver-based multi-disciplinary firm Omicron Architecture Engineering Construction Services Ltd was commissioned to design and build the new facility. As a firm that provides architectural, engineering (structural, mechanical, and electrical), and construction services (common in the Far East, but relatively unusual in North America and Europe), Omicron was well placed to undertake an integrated approach to the overall design of the buildings – virtually essential if the client's objective of a sustainable design is to be achieved.

The Architect of Record for the project was Omicron's Scott M. Kemp, with Peter Bremner as the Project Manager on behalf of the client, the City of Vancouver. While the site layout had been predetermined, the configuration of the buildings was completely open, giving the design team for the Administration Centre ample scope to introduce innovative sustainable design and construction practices.

6.6 Main locker room with high-level glazing on the south façade. Air handling units and ducting at high level serve the office floors above

6.7 Lunch room with south-facing glazing on the right and offices at the rear and to the left of shot. Note the deployment of suspended radiant panel heaters and the air supply ductwork serving the lunch room itself and the offices above

6.8 View from the north-east with the main entrance on the left of shot. Note the single-storeyed workshops along the north of the building and the high-level glazing on the upper floor, some with louvred openings. The three vertical stacks on the right are exhausts from the paint booth

THE DESIGN OUTCOME

The design background and outcome (the process took around two-and-a-half years) have been described elsewhere in some detail (Patterson, 2004; DTI, 2005). What follows is the briefest of outlines, together with more detail of the environmental control systems.

Building layout, construction, and passive environmental control systems

The two-storey Administration Centre fronts onto National Avenue on the southern perimeter of the site (Figures 6.1 and 6.2). The upper floor (approximately 95m by 20m with its long axis east–west – Figure 6.3(a)) accommodates a series of single offices and open-plan work stations (Figures 6.4 and 6.5), together with associated meeting rooms. The ground floor immediately below (Figure 6.3(b)) houses an extensive locker room for the large number of employees for whom the building is a base (Figure 6.6), together with a lunch room (Figure 6.7), a few offices, and a large meeting room beside the main entrance. A single-storey series of workshops is also located along the northern side of the ground floor (Figures 6.8, 6.9, and 6.10).

According to Omicron (2008):

> The building is a composition of four major components: mass, frame, skin and cover. The mass construction of the walls and slabs consists of high volume fly ash concrete tilt panels. Structural frames made from local wood and high recycled content steel support the second floor and roof. The skin of the building is a combination of high performance curtain wall and corrugated metal siding. The cover is a large inclined roof, which is highly reflective to reduce heat island effect.

The R-values of the walls, roof, and double-glazed windows are reported (DTI, 2005) to be approximately 2, 2.5, and 0.4m^2.$^\circ$C/W respectively. The building's east–west orientation, in combination with a mono-pitched roof with its high point on the north edge (Figures 6.1 and 6.8) enable glare-free daylighting of the upper floor. Roof overhangs and sunshades on the south edge were designed to minimise direct sun penetration during the summer (Figures 6.1, 6.2, and 6.11).

6.9 General view of the Signals Workshop on the ground floor

6.10 General view of the Signwriting Workshop on the ground floor

6.11 Close-up view of part of the south façade. The mechanical plant room and bicycle storage are located behind this section of tilt-up slab with embossed motif on the ground floor. Note the openable windows on the upper floor offices (indicated by the thicker glazing bars) and the solar shading canopy above

Active environmental control systems

Heating and cooling to the building are via high-level suspended radiant panels mainly (Figures 6.4, 6.5, and 6.7), together with some fan convectors. The hot or chilled water to these is supplied by the combination of a ground source heat pump and a gas-fired boiler located on the ground floor. The heat pump is designed to cover all the cooling load and half the maximum heating demand, with 24 boreholes, some 120m in depth under the adjacent car park, providing the required heat source/sink.

The mixed-mode ventilation system is comprised of a full fresh air displacement system (Figure 6.7) with CO_2 sensor control, together with manually openable windows around the perimeter – control of the latter being at the behest of the occupants. A number of large penetrations between the ground and upper floors (Figures 6.3(a) and 6.3(b)), together with openings at high level on the north façade (Figures 6.5 and 6.7) assist the flow of air through the building.

Occupancy sensor control is used for the artificial lighting systems. The building has been equipped with waterless urinals, and a rainwater harvesting system has been installed and the water collected used in the (dual-flush) WCs. A sedum roof has been laid out over the single-storey workshop area, and some photovoltaic panels installed in some of the rooflights, but these are mainly for demonstration purposes.

USERS' PERCEPTIONS OF THE BUILDING

Overall response

In this case, responses were sought from both the Centre staff and the Roads staff who only used the building as a base, the former using the standard questionnaire, the latter the shorter version. The survey was conducted during December 2005.

For all of the 35 or so Centre staff respondents (26 per cent female, 74 per cent male), the building was their normal place of work, most (89 per cent) working five days per week, and averaging 7.0 hours per day. The majority (some 88 per cent) were over 30 and had worked in the building for more than a year, some 80 per cent at the same desk or work area. Around 46 per cent worked alone while the rest shared with one or more colleagues. Hours

TABLE 6.1

Average scores for each factor and whether they were significantly better, similar to, or worse than the BUS benchmarks

		Score	Worse	Similar	Better			Score	Worse	Similar	Better
OPERATIONAL FACTORS											
Image	(4.82)	5.94			●	Cleaning		2.34	●		
Space in building		5.03			●	Availability of meeting rooms		5.69			●
Space at desk – too little/much⁴		4.97		●		Suitability of storage arrangements		3.66		●	
Furniture		5.43			●	Facilities meet work requirements		4.86		●	
ENVIRONMENTAL FACTORS											
Temp and Air in Winter						*Temp and Air in Summer*					
Temp Overall	(4.87)	3.94		●		Temp Overall		3.28	●		
Temp – too hot/too cold⁴		4.93	●			Temp – too hot/too cold⁴		2.67	●		
Temp – stable/variable⁴		4.75	●			Temp – stable/variable⁴		4.38		●	
Air – still/draughty⁴		4.06			●	Air – still/draughty⁴		3.29		●	
Air – dry/humid⁴		3.48		●		Air – dry/humid⁴		3.39	●		
Air – fresh/stuffy¹		4.13		●		Air – fresh/stuffy¹		4.31		●	
Air – odourless/smelly¹		3.34		●		Air – odourless/smelly¹		3.62		●	
Air Overall	(4.39)	3.84	●			Air Overall		3.58		●	
Lighting						**Noise**					
Lighting Overall	(4.05)	5.52			●	Noise Overall	(4.05)	4.68			●
Natural light – too little/much⁴		4.12			●	From colleagues – too little/much⁴		4.06			●
Sun & Sky Glare – none/too much¹		3.97		●		From other people – too little/much⁴		4.24		●	
Artificial light – too little/much⁴		4.15		●		From inside – too little/much⁴		4.12		●	
Art'l light glare – none/too much¹		3.55			●	From outside – too little/much⁴		4.39	●		
						Interruptions – none/frequent¹		4.03		●	
CONTROL FACTORS ᵇ						**SATISFACTION FACTORS**					
Heating	43%	1.52	●			Design	(4.61)	5.06			●
Cooling	24%	1.70	●			Needs	(3.91)	4.44		●	
Ventilation	14%	2.70		●		Comfort Overall	(4.52)	4.53			●
Lighting	14%	1.73	●			Productivity %	(+0.87)	+0.91		●	
Noise	38%	1.79	●			Health	(3.52)	3.81		●	

NOTES: (a) unless otherwise noted, a score of 7 is 'best'; superscript ⁴ implies a score of 4 is best, superscript ¹ implies a score of 1 is best; (b) the per cent values listed here are the percentages of respondents who thought personal control of that aspect was important ; (c) Roads staff scores are in brackets – the temperature and air scores cover all seasons.

TABLE 6.2

Numbers of centre staff (Road staff in brackets) offering positive, balanced, and negative comments on 12 performance factors

Aspect	Number of respondents			
	Positive	Balanced	Negative	Total
Overall Design	7	4	4	15
Needs Overall	–	–	11	11
Meeting Rooms	2	–	3	5
Storage	–	–	10	10
Desk/Work Area	4	–	5	9
Comfort	3	2	3 (4)	8
Noise Sources	–	2	8 (1)	10
Lighting Conditions	2	2	5	9
Productivity	–	5	2	7
Health	1	2	8 (4)	11
Work Well	19	–	–	19
Hinder	–	–	24	24
TOTALS (centre staff only)	38	17	83	138
PER CENT (centre staff only)	27.5	12.3	60.2	100

per day spent at desk and at a computer averaged 6.0 and 4.8 respectively. The respondents were split evenly between the two floors of the building.

Of the 23 Roads staff who responded to the shorter questionnaire, most (78 per cent) had used the building for more than a year, worked a five-day week, but were in the building for less than two hours per day.

Significant factors

The average scores of the Centre staff and the Roads staff for each of the relevant survey questions are listed in Table 6.1. Table 6.1 also indicates those aspects of the building that the Centre staff perceived as being significantly better, similar to, or worse than the benchmark and/or scale mid-point. Overall, some 12 aspects were significantly better, 12 were significantly worse, while the remaining 21 aspects had much the same score as the benchmark.

In terms of the eight operational aspects, this building scores above the benchmark in four instances, and about the same as the

benchmark or scale mid-point in three cases. Only cleaning, with a score of 2.38, was rated as unsatisfactory.

In terms of the environmental factors, Centre staff's perceptions of lighting overall and noise overall were both better than their respective benchmarks. The individual components of these aspects also scored well generally, though there was a hint of there being too much noise from external sources. The building was perceived as somewhat less satisfactory in terms of temperature and air in winter and summer – too cold and variable in winter and too hot and dry in summer.

The Centre staff did not perceive themselves as having very much control of environmental conditions (the scores were all less than what are a relatively low set of benchmarks, in the 2.0–3.5 range). However, only about a quarter of respondents rated control of heating, cooling, and ventilation important, and even fewer in the case of lighting and noise.

Of the Satisfaction variables (design, needs, comfort overall, productivity, and health), all but needs were better than their respective benchmarks, and at 4.44, even it was well above the scale mid-point of 4.00. Similarly, all but health were higher than the scale mid-point, and even it, at 3.81, was significantly higher than its benchmark value.

Roads staff's perceptions (responses to only ten overall variables were sought in the shorter questionnaire) were mostly lower than those of the office staff. The exceptions were temperature and air which were significantly higher than their corresponding benchmarks and scale mid-points, and much higher than the corresponding values for the office staff. As indicated in Table 6.1, the Roads staff's scores were in fact higher than either the corresponding benchmark or the scale mid-point in virtually every case, and higher than both for temperature, air, and comfort overall.

Users' comments

Overall, some 138 responses were received from Centre staff under the 12 headings where they were able to add written comments – some 32.9 per cent of the 420 potential (35 respondents by 12 headings). Table 6.2 indicates the numbers of positive, balanced, and negative comments overall – in this case, around 27.5 per cent were positive, 12.3 per cent balanced, and 60.2 per cent negative.

Generally speaking, comments about the design were relatively positive from the users of both the ground and the upper floors, but lack of storage was commented upon negatively by both groups.

Noise appeared to be an issue for many users of the upper floor – sounds from the adjacent railway sidings were noted (see also the poor score for noise from outside) and comments were made about sound transmission between floors.

Centre staff on both floors appeared to be affected by odours from the washrooms, and the Roads staff commented negatively on that aspect under both Comfort and Health.

Overall performance indices

The Comfort Index for the Centre staff, based on the comfort overall, noise, lighting, temperature, and air quality scores, works out at +0.22, while the Satisfaction Index, based on the design, needs, health, and perceived productivity scores, is +0.44, both higher than the scale mid-point (noting these indices are scaled from -3 to +3).

The Summary Index, being the average of these, works out at +0.33, while the Forgiveness Factor, calculated to be 1.09 in this instance, indicates that the Centre staff as a whole are likely to be relatively tolerant as far as minor shortcomings in individual aspects such as winter and summer temperatures, air quality, lighting, and noise are concerned (a factor of 1 being the mid-point on a scale that normally ranges from 0.80 to 1.20).

In terms of the Ten-Factor Rating Scale, the building was well within the 'Good Practice' band of the 7-point scale, with a calculated percentage value of 78 per cent. When All-Factors were taken into account the percentage value worked out at 60 per cent, comfortably within the 'Above Average' band.

Applying the same system to the ten factors assessed by the Roads staff, a percentage value of 70 per cent was obtained, at the high end of the 'Above Average' band.

ACKNOWLEDGEMENTS

I must thank Kevin Hanvey of Omicron for helping my understanding of the design of the Administration Centre, together with Engineering Yards Manager E. C. (Ted) Batty for permission to visit the building and survey the users.

REFERENCES

ASHRAE (2001) *ASHRAE Handbook: Fundamentals, SI Edition*, Atlanta, GA: American Society of Heating Refrigerating and Air-Conditioning Engineers.

Bremner, P. (2004) 'Transportation Association of Canada Environmental Achievement Award – City of Vancouver National Works Yard', City of Vancouver Engineering Services, 30 March 2004.

DTI (2005) *Towards a Low-Carbon Society: A Mission to Canada and the USA*, report of a DTI global watch mission, Global Watch Service, Melton Mowbray, June 2005, available at: www.globalwatchonline.com.

Hanvey, K. (2005) Transcript of interview of 9 December 2005, Vancouver.

Omicron (2008) 'City of Vancouver National Works Yard Overview', available at: www.omicronaec.com/gallery07.php (accessed 4 January 2008).

'Outside the Box' (2004) Annual Awards, available at: www.building.ca/outsidethebox/project11.asp (accessed 3 January 2008).

Patterson, J. (2004) 'Showcasing Sustainability – National Public Works Yard Lands Gold', *Canadian Property Management (BC Edition)*, 12(4): 3–7.

7

Liu Institute,
University of British Columbia
Vancouver, Canada

THE CONTEXT

The 1750m² building for the Liu Institute for Global Issues (Figure 7.1) was officially opened in September 2000. Comprised of a conference space and offices designed to accommodate up to 37 staff, it is located within the Point Grey Campus of the University of British Columbia.

The Institute (formerly designated a Centre) 'is a forum for policy-relevant research on emerging issues that demand innovative, interdisciplinary, and impact-oriented responses from the academic community' (Liu Institute, 2007), environmental degradation being one of these issues.

A year or so before the design of the Institute commenced, the University had implemented a sustainable development policy and opened Canada's first Campus Sustainability Office, and was 'committed to developing an environmentally responsible campus' (DTI, 2005).

With that background, it was inevitable that environmental issues would be high on the agenda of the brief for this building, especially as it was coming hard on the heels of the much-lauded C K Choi building (Macaulay and McLennan, 2006), completed in 1996 and located just round the corner.

The Institute is located beside a stand of giant trees on the site of a former student residence, at the north-west corner of the campus. Given its latitude of 49°N, 1 per cent design temperatures of -4.7°C and +23.2°C (ASHRAE, 2001: 27.22–3), and proximity to the sea, it is a prime candidate for natural ventilation.

7.1 General view of the building from the south-east. Caseroom of the Seminar Wing on the left; (short) south and (long) east façades of the Research Wing to the right. Cherry tree in the foreground in winter mode

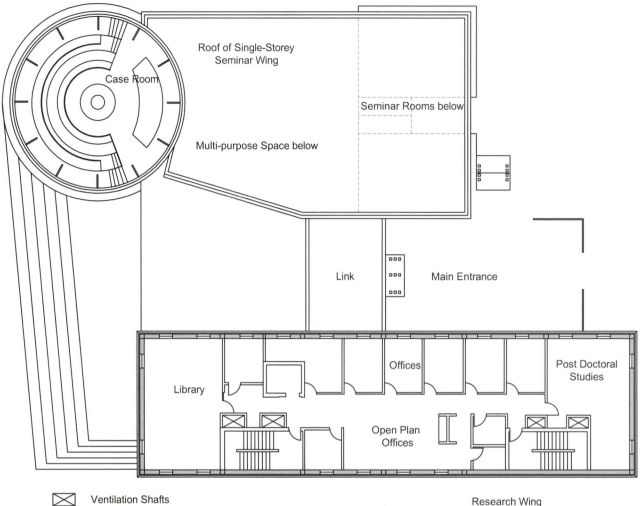

Ventilation Shafts

Research Wing

7.2 Overall plan of the building – at ground level for the single-storey Seminar Wing; at Level 2 for the three-storey Research Wing. Note the pair of vertical natural ventilation ducts at each end of the corridor
Source: Adapted from Architectura

7.3 Section through the Research Wing – note the arrangement and location of the vertical ducts
Source: Adapted from Architectura

0   10   20

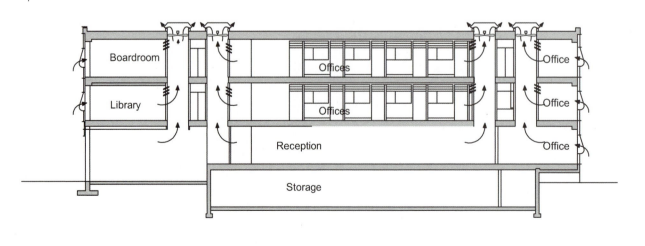

0   10   20

7.4 A typical single office. Note the large opening window with trickle ventilator underneath. A heating terminal unit is located in the cabinet immediately below, with its distribution pipework visible just below. Note too the provision of both roller and Venetian blinds at the upper and lower levels of the fenestration

7.5 Typical corridor in the Research Wing. Note the large transom openings at high level to enable air transfer between the offices and the adjacent corridor

The building has won several awards, including the 1999 Association of Professional Engineers and Geoscientists of BC Environmental Award, the Consulting Engineers of British Columbia Award of Merit, the Architectural Institute of British Columbia Innovation Award, and the Lieutenant Governor's Medal for Excellence in Architecture, all in 2001; and the Building Owners and Managers Association Earth Award in 2002. While the building design was under way before participation in the LEED certification programme was considered, a post-construction assessment suggested that it might have achieved 45 points and possibly a Gold rating (Klopp, 2002).

The design process and architectural outcome have been described elsewhere in some detail (DTI, 2005; Klopp, 2002; Macaulay and McLennan, 2006; McMinn and Polo, 2005). What follows is the briefest of outlines.

THE DESIGN PROCESS

The project was led by the local office of Architectura Planning Architecture Interiors Inc (now Stantec) in collaboration with the world-famous Vancouver-based design architect Arthur Erickson, the latter at

7.6 North end of typical corridor in the Research Wing. Air transfer from the corridor to the vertical exhaust duct (one of four) takes place via the opening just visible at top left of shot. Note too the open panelling on the ceiling that enables access to the thermal mass of the concrete ceiling

7.7 The Seminar Wing – the single-storey multi-purpose space is in the centre of shot (lit up), seminar rooms to the left, and caseroom to the right. The top floor of the three-storey research wing is visible in behind

7.8 One of the two seminar rooms, this one being utilised as a research base at the time. Note the additional mechanical ventilation ducting

the request of the principal donor (Best, 2004). The well-established pan-Canadian firm of Keen Engineering, with their growing reputation and experience in sustainable environmental control systems design (they had been involved in the C K Choi building) was selected as mechanical engineers (Hyde and Sanguinetti, 2004).

This was to be the first project undertaken following the establishment of the University's Campus Sustainability Office. According to Klopp (2002):

At the outset of the Liu Centre project, in January 1998, the University convened a group of 36 stakeholders who took part in a day-long 'project alignment' workshop [led by Freda Pagani, Head of the Sustainability Office and with input from noted sustainable architect Bob Berkebile]. The stakeholder group covered the spectrum of interests in the development, use, and operation of the facility. The result of the workshop was a list of qualitative aspirations and objectives, and a more specific list of 60 sustainable targets, that together defined the common vision for the project. These targets were an important reference for the project team, providing a basis for decision making through all phases of the Liu Centre's development.

The inter-related nature of these targets and the cross-disciplinary design strategies required to achieve them, no doubt helped to reinforce the adoption of integrated design processes.

The concept that emerged was for a building with two separate but parallel wings – a three-storey plus basement Research Wing and a single-storey Seminar Wing (Figures 7.2 and 7.3). A glazed lobby connects the two wings, resulting in the creation of two semi-enclosed courtyards, all in a natural forest setting. This concept enabled the exploitation of natural ventilation, shading, and daylighting strategies in order to minimise energy consumption (a target of 50 per cent of the Canadian Model National Energy Code had been set) while at the same time meeting the University's budget for a conventional office design (Hydes and Creech, 2000).

7.9 The multi-purpose space – note the full-height glazing, the linear grillework of the trench heater immediately underneath, and the openable windows at low level

7.10 Internal view of the circular plan caseroom. Note the high-level windows and the tall trees visible outside; and the low-level air supply grilles from the plenum space under the tiered seating

7.11 Looking down onto the caseroom and multi-purpose room from the Research Wing. Note the high-level glazing around the top of the caseroom, the fresh air inlet grille lower left, and the exhaust air outlets on the roof

THE DESIGN OUTCOME

Building layout, construction, and passive environmental control systems

Rectangular in plan (45m by 12m approximately) and with its long axis orientated approximately north–south (Figure 7.2), the Research Wing contains individual and open offices (Figure 7.4), a reading room and a board room, and all their related facilities on the three above-ground levels, together with service, storage, and locker facilities in the basement. The narrow plan of this wing, with the offices located either side of a central corridor (Figures 7.2 and 7.6), enables daylighting by means of the windows distributed around virtually the entire perimeter, with daylight and occupancy sensors designed to control the artificial lighting as appropriate to ambient conditions.

The natural ventilation system comprises the main openings and trickle ventilators of the perimeter windows functioning as air intakes to the offices (Figure 7.4), transom openings above the doorways enabling air transfer from the offices to central corridor (Figure 7.5), which in turn connect to two pairs of vertical ducts positioned at each end of the corridor to exhaust the air (Figures 7.2 and 7.6). Exhaust fans have been fitted at the top of these ducts for use should the natural stack effect prove insufficient, or for smoke exhaust in the case of a fire. Of course, cross-ventilation is also an option.

The building envelope is reported as having 'high resistance wall and roof insulation and high performance glazing' (Hydes and Creech, 2000), the latter being low-e, argon-filled double glazing, while the exposed concrete inside provides a significant amount of thermal mass. The tall trees to the south provide significant protection from solar radiation.

The single-storey Seminar Wing (Figure 7.7) is designed to accommodate gatherings of various kinds. It is comprised of two 45m^2 seminar rooms (Figure 7.8), a 150m^2 naturally ventilated multi-purpose space (Figure 7.9), and a 100m^2 caseroom (Figure 7.10). The caseroom is circular in plan with glazing at high level all round and displacement ventilation, the latter comprising an air handling unit and supply air plenum under the tiered seating and exhaust vents on the roof (Figure 7.11).

TABLE 7.1

Average scores for each factor and whether they were significantly better, similar to, or worse than the BUS benchmarks

OPERATIONAL FACTORS

Factor	Score	Worse	Similar	Better	Factor	Score	Worse	Similar	Better
Image to visitors	5.43		●		Cleaning	6.29			●
Space in building	3.81		●		Availability of meeting rooms	4.86			●
Space at desk – too little/much[4]	4.33		●		Suitability of storage arrangements	3.53		●	
Furniture	5.14			●	Facilities meet work requirements	4.26		●	

ENVIRONMENTAL FACTORS

Temp and Air in Winter / *Temp and Air in Summer*

Factor	Score	Worse	Similar	Better	Factor	Score	Worse	Similar	Better
Temp Overall	3.20	●			Temp Overall	4.44			●
Temp – too hot/too cold[4]	5.63	●			Temp – too hot/too cold[4]	3.67		●	
Temp – stable/variable[4]	4.95	●			Temp – stable/variable[4]	4.50		●	
Air – still/draughty[4]	3.80		●		Air – still/draughty[4]	3.38		●	
Air – dry/humid[4]	3.35		●		Air – dry/humid[4]	3.50	●		
Air – fresh/stuffy[1]	4.00		●		Air – fresh/stuffy[1]	3.88			●
Air – odourless/smelly[1]	3.25			●	Air – odourless/smelly[1]	3.31			●
Air Overall	3.32	●			Air Overall	3.87		●	

Lighting / *Noise*

Factor	Score	Worse	Similar	Better	Factor	Score	Worse	Similar	Better
Lighting Overall	3.79	●			Noise Overall	2.47	●		
Natural light – too little/much[4]	4.16			●	From colleagues – too little/much[4]	5.42	●		
Sun & Sky Glare – none/too much[1]	3.47			●	From other people – too little/much[4]	5.50	●		
Artificial light – too little/much[4]	3.42		●		From inside – too little/much[4]	5.17	●		
Art'l light glare – none/too much[1]	3.11			●	From outside – too little/much[4]	4.56		●	
					Interruptions – none/frequent[1]	5.33	●		

CONTROL FACTORS [b]

Factor	%	Score	Worse	Similar	Better	Factor	Score	Worse	Similar	Better
Heating	43%	3.37		●		Design	4.00		●	
Cooling	24%	2.47		●		Needs	4.24		●	
Ventilation	14%	3.72		●		Comfort Overall	3.55	●		
Lighting	14%	4.11		●		Productivity %	−13.00	●		
Noise	38%	1.74	●			Health	3.70		●	

SATISFACTION FACTORS (right column above)

NOTES: (a) unless otherwise noted, a score of 7 is 'best'; superscript [4] implies a score of 4 is best, superscript [1] implies a score of 1 is best; (b) the per cent values listed here are the percentages of respondents who thought personal control of that aspect was important.

TABLE 7.2

Numbers of staff offering positive, balanced, and negative comments on 12 performance factors

Aspect	Number of respondents			
	Positive	Balanced	Negative	Total
Overall Design	3	4	9	16
Needs Overall	1	2	9	12
Meeting Rooms	0	1	7	8
Storage	0	0	9	9
Desk/Work Area	2	5	3	10
Comfort	0	2	5	7
Noise Sources	0	0	10	10
Lighting Conditions	0	0	4	4
Productivity	0	1	5	6
Health	0	2	2	4
Work Well	8	–	–	8
Hinder	–	–	17	17
TOTALS (Staff only)	14	17	80	111
PER CENT (Staff only)	12.6	15.3	72.1	100

Active environmental control systems

Heating for the building is supplied via a steam line from the campus district heating system. A heat exchanger in the basement of the Research Wing produces low temperature hot water for distribution to individually controllable heating terminal units under the windows in the Research Wing and trench heaters in the multi-purpose space, and the air handling unit in the plenum space under the tiered seating of the caseroom. Cooling throughout the building is by natural ventilation and the use of thermal mass, with the option of night cooling in the case of the Research Wing, using the exhaust fans at the top of the vertical ducts if necessary.

USERS' PERCEPTIONS OF THE BUILDING

Overall response

For virtually all of the 21 respondents (57 per cent female, 43 per cent male), representing almost all of the occupants at the time of the survey (6–8 December 2005), the building was their normal place of business. They worked 4.1 days per week on average and 7.3 hours per day, of which around 6.7 were spent at their desk or work space and 6.4 at a computer. The ratio of under-30s to over-30s was 48:52 per cent and most (76 per cent) had worked in the building for more than a year at the same desk or work area. The proportions were equally divided between those with a single office, those who shared with one other, and those who shared with two or more colleagues (that is, around one-third of each).

Significant factors

The average score for each of the survey questions is listed in Table 7.1. Table 7.1 also indicates those aspects of the building that the staff perceived as being significantly better, similar to, or worse than the benchmark and/or scale mid-point. In this cases, some ten aspects were significantly better, 14 were significantly worse, while the remaining 21 aspects had much the same score as the benchmark.

In terms of the eight operational factors, this building scores better than the benchmark for cleaning, meeting rooms, and furniture. Most of the other factors are close to or slightly better than either the mid-point of the scale or the benchmark (but not both).

Overall scores for temperature and air in winter were well under their respective benchmarks and the scale mid-point, the main contributor appearing to be a perception that the temperature was too cold and variable. Perceptions of summer temperature and air were very much better, if on the dry side. The air was perceived as odourless in both seasons.

Glare from sun and sky or from the artificial lighting was not perceived to be a problem, and the score for natural lighting was fine. However, there were indications that there was too little artificial lighting, which presumably contributed to lighting overall scoring under the benchmark and scale mid-point.

Noise appeared to be a major issue for a large number of respondents, with all aspects of this factor scoring poorly against their corresponding benchmarks and scale mid-points. This was reinforced under personal control where 38 per cent of respondents rated control of noise as important, but their perception of degree of control was a lowly 1.74, well below the other four aspects considered. In this connection, the *User Guide* (Architectura, 2000) notes that a degree of trade-off between acoustic privacy and the free flow of the air by natural ventilation had been agreed from the outset. More recently, the architects have carried out successful trials of a prototype baffle system designed to 'mitigate the sound transfer between the enclosed office and the adjacent corridor without impeding the flow of natural ventilation'. Once confirmed over a longer period, it is hoped to install this throughout the building (Best, 2008).

In the case of the satisfaction variables, health scored higher than its benchmark, though, in common with many buildings, under the scale mid-point. All the other factors scored less than their benchmarks, but a couple (design and needs) were at or above the scale mid-point.

Users' comments
Overall, some 111 responses were received from staff under the 12 headings where they were able to add written comments – some 44.0 per cent of the 252 potential (21 respondents by 12 headings).

Table 7.2 indicates the numbers of positive, balanced, and negative comments – in this case around 12.6 per cent were positive, 15.3 per cent balanced, and 72.1 per cent negative.

Reinforcing the poor perception scores for noise, all the comments on this aspect were negative, and negative comments were given frequently under the design and hindrances headings too. Heating was also mentioned relatively frequently under hindrances, reinforcing the low scores for temperature and air in winter.

Also in keeping with its low score, storage (or lack of it) attracted entirely negative comments – this appears to be a common issue as the benchmark is relatively low too, and the score here was not significantly different from it. The availability of meeting rooms also attracted mainly negative comment, this time despite a very high score and some positive comments under things that work well.

Overall performance indices
The Comfort Index, based on the comfort overall, noise, lighting, temperature, and air quality scores, works out at -0.90, while the Satisfaction Index, based on the design, needs, health, and perceived productivity scores, is -0.51, noting that the scale mid-point in these instances is zero on a -3 to +3 scale.

The Summary Index, being the average of the Comfort and Satisfaction Indices, works out at -0.71, while the Forgiveness Factor, calculated to be 1.01 in this instance, indicates that staff are likely to be relatively neutral (neither very forgiving or particularly intolerant) of minor shortcomings in individual aspects such as winter and summer temperatures, air quality, lighting, and noise (a factor of 1 being the mid-point on a scale that normally ranges from 0.80 to 1.20).

In terms of the Ten-Factor Rating Scale, the building was 'Average' on the 7-point scale with a calculated percentage value of 44 per cent. When All-Factors were taken into account, the percentage value worked out at 55 per cent – at the borderline between the 'Average' and 'Above Average' bands.

OTHER REPORTED ASPECTS OF PERFORMANCE
From the start, the design team and the client were committed to the assessment of this building. In addition to the commendably full and frank 109-page report (Klopp, 2002) detailing actual performance

against the 60 sustainability targets that had been set following the stakeholder workshop, a web-based survey of the occupants was also carried out. Administered by the Center for the Built Environment at the University of California at Berkeley, it is similar in nature to the Building Use Studies survey instrument, and uses a 7-point scale.

Based on that work, Hydes *et al.* (2004) report an average 'Occupant Satisfaction' score of 3.92 which is less than the corresponding benchmark of 4.78 and under the scale mid-point of 4.00 – 'the Liu Centre was perceived as slightly unsatisfactory and somewhat below average'. This bears comparison with the present survey in which Comfort Overall scored 3.55, against a benchmark average of 4.30; and the Satisfaction Index worked out at -0.51 (on a -3 to +3 scale) which is loosely equivalent to 3.49 on a 1- to 7-point scale.

Referring to both the C K Choi and Liu Institute buildings (both had been surveyed), Hydes *et al.* (2004) also reported that 'Many occupants (100% of respondents) had complaints about acoustic privacy', and that 'Occupants appreciated the uniqueness and aesthetic qualities of the buildings'. In the case of the Liu Institute, he reported that 'The ceilings … which are made of concrete planks with plywood in between, are quite dark in colour, with the result that the rooms feel dark.' These findings closely parallel those of the present survey where all aspects of noise rated poorly, image rated highly, and respondents felt there was too little artificial light (while appreciating the natural light and lack of glare).

Hydes *et al.* (2004) also carried out an audit of the building's energy use in 2001, reporting an energy use index of 195 kWh/m^2.yr, and noting this as less than half the average for college buildings in British Columbia.

ACKNOWLEDGEMENTS

I must express my gratitude to Peggy Ng, Administrator of the Liu Institute for granting permission for me to undertake this survey. Particular thanks go Noel Best of Stantec Architecture, and to Rosamund Hyde and Jennifer Sanguinetti of Keen Engineering for assisting my understanding of the building and its design.

REFERENCES

Architectura (2000) *User Guide: Liu Centre for the Study of Global Issues*, Vancouver: Architectura Inc.

ASHRAE (2001) *ASHRAE Handbook: Fundamentals, SI Edition*, Atlanta, GA: American Society of Heating Refrigerating and Air-Conditioning Engineers.

Best, N. (2004) Transcript of interview held on 27 August 2004, Vancouver, British Columbia.

Best, N. (2008) Personal communication, 17 June 2008.

DTI (2005) *Towards a Low-Carbon Society: A Mission to Canada and the USA*, report of a DTI global watch mission, Global Watch Service, Melton Mowbray, June 2005, available at: www.globalwatchonline.com.

Hyde, R. and Sanguinetti, J. (2004) Transcript of interview held on 25 August 2004, Vancouver, British Columbia.

Hydes, K. R. and Creech, L. (2000) 'Reducing Mechanical Equipment Cost: The Economics of Green Design', *Building Research and Information*, 28(5/6): 403–7.

Hydes, K. R., McCarry, B., Mueller, T. and Hyde, R. (2004) 'Understanding Our Green Buildings: Seven Post-Occupancy Evaluations in British Columbia', in *Proceedings of 'Closing the Loop: Post-Occupancy Evaluation – the Next Steps'*, Windsor, UK, April.

Klopp, R. (2002) *60 Targets: Post-Occupancy Environmental Assessment*, Vancouver: Architectura Inc. p. 107.

Liu Institute (2007) 'About Us', available at: www.ligi.ubc.ca/page121.htm (accessed 1 October 2007).

Macaulay, D. R. and McLennan, J. F. (2006) *The Ecological Engineer*, vol. 1: *Keen Engineering*, Kansas City, MO: Ecotone Publishing.

McMinn, J. and Polo, M. (2005) *41° to 66° – Regional Responses to Sustainable Architecture in Canada*, Waterloo, ON: Cambridge Galleries Design at Riverside, University of Waterloo.

Part 2

Buildings in Medium–Temperate Climates

Chapters 8–18

The following 11 case studies are all located in what could classed broadly as medium–temperate climates, with wintertime design temperatures ranging from -4°C to around zero. Just over half are located in the southern half of England, together with two in Japan, and one each in Ireland, Tasmania, and the South Island of New Zealand. They will be described in the following order:

Seven of these buildings have advanced natural ventilation systems, three have changeover mixed-mode, and one (the Nikken Sekkei Building) is fully air conditioned.

Sun penetration patterns at Gifford Studios

8
Gifford Studios
Southampton, England

THE CONTEXT

The Head Office of consulting engineers Gifford and Partners is located some 10 km west of the centre of the city of Southampton on the south coast of England. The 1600m² Gifford Studios building forms part of the practice's campus there at which most of their staff are based (Figure 8.1).

While the main aim of the brief was the creation of large open-plan design studios, a no less important aim was to demonstrate that it was commercially feasible '[to] construct a building that is more energy efficient and more sustainable at no additional cost compared to a conventional building' (Pettifer, quoted in Coyle, 2004).

Situated at around 51°N Latitude, and with 1 per cent design temperatures of approximately -4°C and +24°C (ASHRAE, 2001:

27.51–2), the building was completed and staff moved in during April 2004, since when its energy performance has been the subject of some in-house study.

The building was designated 'Office Building of the Year' in the 2003 Building Services Awards, won a local 'Sustainable Business Award' in 2004, and the 2005 Institution of Structural Engineers David Alsop Award for sustainable design.

The design process and architectural outcome have been described elsewhere in some detail (Coyle, 2004; Pettifer, 2004). What follows is the briefest of outlines.

8.1 General view of a section of the campus. The east façade of the Studio building and the Reception building are to the left of shot, Carlton House in the centre background, and the North and South Lodges to the right

8.2 View of the cedar-clad south and east façades of the Gifford Studios building and the gable end of the brick-clad Reception building. Note the glazing arrangement on the ground and first floors of the Studios

8.3 Long section indicating the two main office floors and lower ground floor. Note the saw-tooth glazing arrangement and the thermal mass indicated on the underside of all the ceilings
Source: Adapted from Design Engine Architects

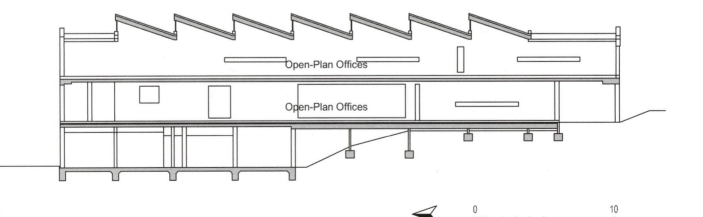

8.4 View of the cedar-clad north and west façades of the Gifford Studios building. Note the dining area at lower ground floor level and the linked Reception building to the left of shot. The separate enclosure to the right of shot contains the outdoor heat-pump equipment

8.5 Exterior view showing the saw-tooth arrangement of the glazing on the roof and the disposition of the view windows on the first floor level of the east façade

THE DESIGN PROCESS

According to Andrew Pettifer (2004), at that time a director of Gifford and Partners and lead building services engineer for the project, 'As funders, owners and users of the building the project gave the practice a unique opportunity to examine the issues surrounding the delivery of a low energy "sustainable" building in a commercial context.' They sought out the small and relatively recently established Winchester-based practice Design Engine Architects, whose philosophy included 'work[ing] closely with other members of the design team to deliver holistic designs in which structure, space and environmental performance are seamlessly integrated' (Design Engine, 2005). Gifford and Partners themselves provided the building services, civil/structural, and environmental engineering input to the design.

The process started with a review of the existing campus which had developed in a somewhat piecemeal fashion over the years and included a number of relatively poor quality temporary buildings as well as a converted former coaching house (Jobson, 2005). The concept that emerged was for a box-like two-and-a-half-storey open-plan studio space with a closely linked reception/exhibition area, located on the campus in relation to the existing retained buildings around a series of interlocking courtyards. This process has continued, with the extension and remodelling of the North Lodge building in 2005 by the same architects.

For the new Gifford Studios building, the aim was to 'maximise the ability of the building envelope to attenuate the impact of the external environment, allowing simple, low intensity and low energy consuming services systems to be employed' (Pettifer, 2004); at the same time making full use of available daylight.

8.6 First floor open-plan office, looking south. Note the sloping sections of the saw-tooth roof above and the perimeter strip of artificial lights

8.7 First floor open-plan office, looking north. Note the north-facing openable glazing in the saw-tooth roof above; the view windows in the façades to left and right; and the artificial lighting arrangement

8.8 View 'down' into part of the ground floor open-plan office. Note the full height glazing arrangement with roller blinds and openable top-lights, as well as the artificial lighting layout

THE DESIGN OUTCOME

Building layout, construction, and passive environmental control systems

The studio building is approximately 40m by 12m in plan. It lies to the east of the campus with its long axis running roughly north–south (Figure 8.2). The ground and first floor levels house the main studio spaces, offices, and meeting rooms, while a smaller lower-ground floor level contains a canteen and other facilities (Figure 8.3). The elongated (18m by 5m approx.) two-storey reception/exhibition building lies alongside, linked to the studio building at the latter's north-east corner (Figures 8.2 and 8.4).

The external skin is comprised of an external cedar rain-screen and a sandwich construction containing 300mm of thermal insulation which give it a U-value of 0.1W/m^2.°C. The concrete slab construction used for most of the floors has been left exposed on the underside to provide thermal mass for the lower floors; while in the case of the first floor, additional layers of high density plasterboard have been fixed to the underside of the north-lights.

The seven rows of saw-tooth north-lights (Figure 8.5) provide daylight over the whole of the first floor, with view windows disposed around the perimeter (Figures 8.6 and 8.7). On the ground floor the strategy was to have four full-height windows providing 'significant pools of natural daylight' (Pettifer, 2004) together with a number of view windows (Figures 8.8 and 8.9). The argon-filled low-E double glazing has a U-value between 1.3 and 1.6W/m^2.°C, and appropriate shading has been provided for all but the north-lights. Overall, 'glazing comprises only 21% of the external envelope' (Pettifer, 2004).

Active environmental control systems

An air-to-water heat pump (38.5kW heating; 51.0kW cooling) located in a compound near the south-west corner of the building serves the studio spaces via pipework in the raised floor system – this has a dual function, acting as an underfloor heating/cooling system, and tempering the air supply to the spaces (see later). A gas-fired 120kW condensing boiler system, located in the lower ground floor, is used to heat conventional radiators in the non-studio spaces as well as serving the domestic hot water system. This allows for the different load patterns and requirements of the two types of spaces.

8.9 General view of the ground floor open-plan office. Note the swirl diffusers, artificial lighting arrangements, and disposition of the glazing

8.10 Detail indicating the methods of natural ventilation and of mechanical air distribution
Source: Adapted from Design Engine Architects

A mixed-mode ventilation strategy is used comprising very low energy mechanical ventilation system and occupant-controlled supplementary natural ventilation. The mechanical system uses low pressure fans mounted in the floor cavity and pulling outside air in through the cedar cladding [Figure 8.10]. The floor voids act as supply air plenums and the fresh air is distributed into the space through floor mounted swirl diffusers [Figure 8.9]. [The 100 per cent fresh] supply air is unfiltered but tempered in the floor void … Occupants are able to open toplights in the ground floor windows and a proportion of the rooflights [Figure 8.7], providing the facility for free additional cooling through natural ventilation in intermediate seasons.

(Pettifer, 2004)

USERS' PERCEPTIONS OF THE BUILDING

Overall response

The building was surveyed during October 2005. For most of the 87 respondents (38 per cent female, 62 per cent male), the building was their normal place of business. They worked 4.7 days per week on average and 8.1 hours per day, of which around 7.2 were spent at their desk or present work space and 6.3 at a computer. The ratio of under-30s to over-30s was 36:64 per cent and most (70 per cent) had worked in the building for more than a year, 53 per cent at the same desk or work area. Around 23 per cent had a single office or shared with one other; 14 per cent shared with two to eight colleagues; and 64 per cent shared with more than eight.

Significant factors

Table 8.1 lists the average scores for each of the survey questions and indicates those aspects of the building that the staff perceived as being significantly better, similar to, or worse than the benchmark and/or scale mid-point. In this case, some 17 aspects were significantly better, 8 were significantly worse, while the remaining 20 aspects had much the same score as the benchmark.

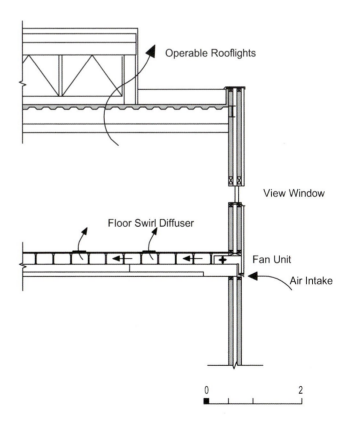

TABLE 8.1

Average scores for each factor and whether they were significantly better, similar to, or worse than the BUS benchmarks

OPERATIONAL FACTORS

Factor	Score	Worse	Similar	Better	Factor	Score	Worse	Similar	Better
Image to visitors	3.06			●	Cleaning	4.99			●
Space in building	5.38			●	Availability of meeting rooms	5.35			●
Space at desk – too little/much[4]	3.84		●		Suitability of storage arrangements	4.26			●
Furniture	5.29			●	Facilities meet work requirements	5.20		●	

ENVIRONMENTAL FACTORS

Temp and Air in Winter

Temp and Air in Summer

Factor	Score	Worse	Similar	Better	Factor	Score	Worse	Similar	Better
Temp Overall	4.64			●	Temp Overall	3.99		●	
Temp – too hot/too cold[4]	4.27		●		Temp – too hot/too cold[4]	3.13		●	
Temp – stable/variable[4]	4.61	●			Temp – stable/variable[4]	4.82	●		
Air – still/draughty[4]	3.83		●		Air – still/draughty[4]	3.47		●	
Air – dry/humid[4]	3.36		●		Air – dry/humid[4]	3.64		●	
Air – fresh/stuffy[1]	4.44		●		Air – fresh/stuffy[1]	4.60		●	
Air – odourless/smelly[1]	3.49		●		Air – odourless/smelly[1]	3.49		●	
Air Overall	4.44			●	Air Overall	4.14			●

Lighting

Noise

Factor	Score	Worse	Similar	Better	Factor	Score	Worse	Similar	Better
Lighting Overall	4.75			●	Noise Overall	4.27		●	
Natural light – too little/much[4]	3.93			●	From colleagues – too little/much[4]	4.45	●		
Sun & Sky Glare – none/too much[1]	3.61			●	From other people – too little/much[4]	4.44		●	
Artificial light – too little/much[4]	3.86		●		From inside – too little/much[4]	4.16		●	
Art'l light glare – none/too much[1]	2.68			●	From outside – too little/much[4]	3.38	●		
					Interruptions – none/frequent[1]	3.29		●	

CONTROL FACTORS [b]

SATISFACTION FACTORS

Factor	%	Score	Worse	Similar	Better	Factor	Score	Worse	Similar	Better
Heating	23%	1.68	●			Design	5.23			●
Cooling	24%	1.95	●			Needs	5.53			●
Ventilation	41%	2.99		●		Comfort Overall	4.73			●
Lighting	30%	2.35	●			Productivity %	+2.80			●
Noise	24%	1.44	●			Health	3.91		●	

NOTES: (a) unless otherwise noted, a score of 7 is 'best'; superscript [4] implies a score of 4 is best, superscript [1] implies a score of 1 is best; (b) the per cent values listed here are the percentages of respondents who thought personal control of that aspect was important.

TABLE 8.2

Numbers of respondents offering positive, balanced, and negative comments on 12 performance factors

Aspect	Number of respondents			
	Positive	Balanced	Negative	Total
Overall Design	16	7	16	39
Needs Overall	5	1	18	24
Meeting Rooms	3	8	10	21
Storage	3	3	24	30
Desk/Work Area	5	12	24	41
Comfort	13	2	10	25
Noise Sources	2	2	26	30
Lighting Conditions	14	6	14	34
Productivity	4	14	8	26
Health	3	6	14	23
Work Well	42	–	2	44
Hinder	–	–	61	61
TOTALS	110	61	227	398
PER CENT	27.6	15.3	57.1	100.0

In terms of the seven operational aspects, this building scores significantly better than the benchmark on all counts but two; it appears that the amount of desk space is perceived to be too little, despite space in the building scoring relatively well; and the score for facilities, while well above the scale mid-point, is just under the benchmark. Image, with a score of 6.06, is the highest.

Temperature overall and air overall scored higher than both the corresponding benchmarks and the scale mid-point in winter. The corresponding summer scores were lower, but still better than the corresponding benchmarks, if not the scale mid-point in the case of temperature. While temperatures were perceived to be excessively variable in both winter and summer, most of the other factors were either greater than the benchmark (but not the scale mid-point) or equal to it.

Lighting scores reasonably well overall (at 4.75) and in terms of the amount of daylight and relative lack of glare from natural and artificial lighting sources. However, there is a perception of there being too little artificial lighting.

Too much noise from colleagues, as well as from other people and internal sources resulted in an overall score around the same as the benchmark, though still better than the scale mid-point. It appeared that there was too little noise from outside sources.

Of the five control aspects, ventilation, with the highest number of occupants deeming it important, scored the best at around the benchmark value. All the others were well below their respective benchmarks, but were considered important by between 23 and 30 per cent of participants.

In the case of the satisfaction variables, all five scored significantly higher than their respective benchmarks and, with the exception of health, their scale mid-points.

Users' comments

Overall, some 398 responses were received from staff under the seven headings where they were able to add written comments – some 38.1 per cent of the 1044 potential (87 respondents by 12 headings). Table 8.2 indicates the numbers of positive, balanced, and negative comments – in this case, around 27.6 per cent were positive, 15.3 per cent balanced, and 57.1 per cent negative.

Of the specific categories, design and desk/work area attracted by far the most comments (each at around 10 per cent of the total number received), followed by storage, noise, and lighting. Over half the comments on desk/work area were negative and most of these were about insufficient space, a factor which had also scored on the low side. Comments on storage were predominantly negative, with around 80 per cent of those commenting on this aspect finding there was not enough.

Design, comfort overall, and lighting overall attracted almost equal numbers of positive and negative comment. No common issues emerged other than the occurrence of glare in the early morning and late afternoon, but some of that appeared to have been mitigated by the installation of blinds, according to some of the comments.

Nearly 90 per cent of the comments about noise were negative – issues included other people conversing with each other and on the telephone, cell phones ringing, noise from adjacent breakout areas and kitchen, and footfalls on the wooden internal stairs – for those nearby. In this connection, it should be noted that the scores for noise were all on the low side too.

Nearly half of the participants had made comments about things that worked well in the building, and around half of these comments related to the respondents' enhanced ability to readily interact and communicate with colleagues. Over 70 per cent of participants noted various hindrances – both noise and workspace issues were raised most frequently here too, reinforcing the comments already made under these particular headings, and their respective scores. Glare from direct sunlight was again mentioned, echoing the comments on this aspect, though not the score; while lack of temperature control was also noted, in this case, echoing the scores for temperature variability in both winter and summer.

Overall performance indices

The Comfort Index, based on the comfort overall, noise, lighting, temperature, and air quality scores, works out at +0.51; while the Satisfaction Index, based on the design, needs, health, and perceived productivity scores, is +0.94, noting that the scale mid-point in these instances is zero on a -3 to +3 scale.

The Summary Index, being the average of the Comfort and Satisfaction Indices, works out at +0.73, while the Forgiveness Factor, calculated to be 1.08 in this instance, indicates that staff are likely to be relatively tolerant of minor shortcomings in individual aspects such as winter and summer temperatures, air quality, lighting, and noise (a factor of 1 being the mid-point on a scale that normally ranges from 0.80 to 1.20).

In terms of the Ten-Factor Rating Scale, the building was 'Exceptional' on the 7-point scale with a calculated percentage value of 94 per cent. When All-Factors were taken into account, the percentage value worked out at 68 per cent – at the upper end of the 'Above Average' band.

ACKNOWLEDGEMENTS

I must express my particular gratitude to Andrew Pettifer, former director of Gifford and Partners, for granting permission for me to survey the building; and to both him and Richard Jobson of Design Engine Architects for assisting my understanding of the building and its design.

REFERENCES

ASHRAE (2001) *ASHRAE Handbook: Fundamentals, SI Edition*, Atlanta, GA: American Society of Heating Refrigerating and Air-Conditioning Engineers.

Coyle, D. (2004) 'Building Analysis', *Building Services Journal*, 26(4): 22–6.

Design Engine (2005) 'Practice', available at: www.designenginearchitects.com/practice.html (accessed 11 April 2008).

Jobson, R. (2005) Transcript of interview held on 25 October 2005, Winchester, England

Pettifer, A. (2004) 'Gifford Studios: A Case Study in Commercial Green Construction', in A. A. M. Sayigh (ed.) *Proceedings of the World Renewable Energy Conference VIII*, Elsevier, Denver, CO, September.

9

Arup Campus
Solihull, England

with Barry Austin and Alexander Wilson

THE CONTEXT

The Midlands headquarters of consultants Ove Arup and Partners Ltd is located in a business park roughly equidistant from the English cities of Birmingham and Coventry. This new development of close to 6000m², designed to consolidate the workforce from the company's former offices in these two cities, was planned to house around 350 staff, but allow for future expansion on the site. Situated at around 52.5°N latitude, and with 1 per cent design temperatures of approximately -4.2°C and +23.9°C (ASHRAE, 2001: 27.51–2), the site is adjacent to the M42 motorway and slopes down gently to the north-west.

The firm has been involved in the design of many sustainable buildings around the world over a long period of time. With such a background it was to be expected that 'The intent … was to set an example of sustainability. The meta-goals were to minimise carbon emissions and to maximise worker productivity' (Kwok and Grondzik, 2007).

In the words of Arup Director Terry Dix (2006a), the brief was to provide 'style, comfort and running efficiency [and a] pleasant and productive environment' thus 'to say to the world that, when we define our own space, this is what we are proud to achieve'.

The twin pavilion two-storey building (Figure 9.1) was completed and staff moved in at the beginning of 2001, since which time its performance has been the subject of intense study and documentation, with the results readily available in the public domain.

9.1 General view of the building from the south. The south-east façade of the lower pavilion is on the left, the south-west gable end of the upper pavilion is on the right, and the link block with the main entrance is in the centre. The daylighting/ventilation pods are prominent on the ridge lines

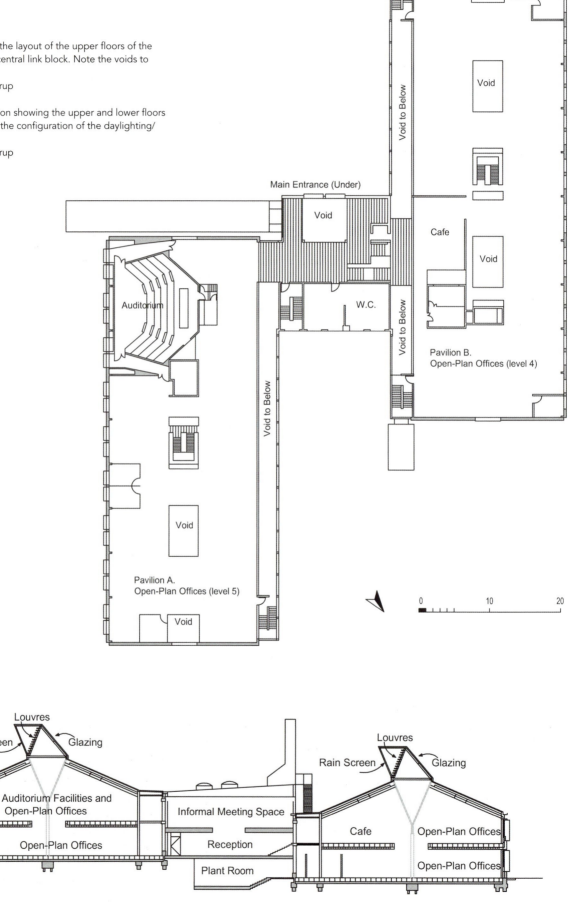

9.2 Plan view indicating the layout of the upper floors of the two pavilions with their central link block. Note the voids to the lower floors
Source: Adapted from Arup

9.3 Indicative cross-section showing the upper and lower floors of the two pavilions and the configuration of the daylighting/ventilation pods
Source: Adapted from Arup

Main Entrance (Under)

Void

Void to Below

Cafe

Void

W.C.

Void to Below

Pavilion B.
Open-Plan Offices (level 4)

Auditorium

Void to Below

Void

Void

Pavilion A.
Open-Plan Offices (level 5)

Void

0   10   20

Louvres

Rain Screen   Glazing

Auditorium Facilities and
Open-Plan Offices

Open-Plan Offices

Louvres

Rain Screen   Glazing

Informal Meeting Space

Cafe   Open-Plan Offices

Reception

Open-Plan Offices

Plant Room

0   10   20

9.4 General interior view of the upper-level open-plan office of a pavilion. Note the penetrations to the floor below, the daylighting/ventilation pod above, and the concrete slab ceiling

9.5 Interior view of the central area of the lower floor of a pavilion. Note the penetration to the upper floor

The design process and architectural outcome, as well as the results of extensive performance surveys, have been described elsewhere in some detail (Kwok and Grondzik, 2007; Phillips, 2004; Powell, 2002; Wilson and Austin, 2004). What follows is the briefest of outlines.

THE DESIGN PROCESS

There are no prizes for guessing that Arup Associates was the design team for this project, responsible for the architecture, structural and services engineering, and quantity surveying. An integrated multi-disciplinary practice that had been operating for almost four decades, led in this project by architect Daniel Wong, they had established a reputation for 'innovation and seriousness, the latter reflecting a concern for the social aspect of design' (Powell, 2002).

The team's response to the brief was to specify a '2 to 3 storey building [with a] coherent office layout, big volume with "mezzanine feel", interactive social spaces, cohesive campus atmosphere, natural ventilation, well daylit, natural materials, flexible space, [and last but not least] commercially viable' (Dix, 2006a).

The design concept that emerged was for twin two-storey pavilions linked by a common entrance and reception area (with allowance on site for a future third pavilion).

THE DESIGN OUTCOME

Building layout, construction, and passive environmental control systems

The two 24m by 60m pavilions lie one 'above' the other, parallel to the site contours, with their long axes orientated south-west to north-east (Figure 9.2). While the lower of the two levels of each pavilion has a floor-to-ceiling height of around 3m, the central ridge of the pitched roof over the upper level rises to around 7m above its floor plate (Figure 9.3). The pavilion spaces contain predominantly open-plan offices (Figures 9.4 and 9.5), with the occasional partitioned office or meeting space, and a small raked auditorium taking up part of the upper floor of one pavilion.

9.6 Interior view of the south-east façade of the lower pavilion taken from the upper floor. Note the full-height void enabling air transfer between floors. The various window-opening and shading controls can be seen, as well as the heating terminal units at high and low levels

9.7 Exterior view of the south-east façade of the lower pavilion. Note the large sash windows, some with their sets of retractable external louvres deployed; the horizontal grillework of the trickle/night ventilation openings; and the daylighting/ventilation pods on the ridge line. Note too the mini weather station and boiler chimney protruding above the link block

9.8 Interior view of a typical window arrangement on the south-east-facing façade of the upper pavilion. Note the winding mechanisms – the one on the right for the sash windows, the one in the centre for the external wooden shutters. Note too the heating terminal unit under the window and the trickle/night ventilation grille above

9.9 The south-east façade of the upper pavilion. Note the exterior shutters in various positions on the upper and lower levels, the fixed horizontal shades on the south-west-facing gable end window. Note too the absence of any glazing on the south-facing sides of the daylighting/ventilation pods

9.10 Internal detail of a typical daylighting/ventilation pod. The glazed areas (to the left of the shot) face north and north-west; the ventilation openings (all the louvres are currently shut) are on the right, with an access door just visible towards the bottom of the shot

9.11 'Back-of-house' view with the three-storey link in the centre (boiler house chimney prominent); gable end of lower pavilion to the right with pods above; and the north-west façade of the upper pavilion to the left

The floor plate has a number of penetrations and these, in combination with openable perimeter windows on both levels and a set of three pods spaced along the ridgeline (Figures 9.6, 9.7, 9.8, and 9.9), make up the natural ventilation system. The pods (Figures 9.7, 9.9, and 9.10) and perimeter windows, the latter concentrated on the north-west façades (Figure 9.11), are also designed to provide daylight to the offices. Dependent on orientation, the south-facing windows are equipped externally with retractable horizontal louvres, adjustable vertically-hinged wooden shutters, or fixed horizontal louvres (Figures 9.7 and 9.9). The pre-cast concrete floor plate and (relatively unusually) ceiling panels provide thermal mass (Figures 9.4 and 9.5).

The link between the two pavilions has three levels (Figures 9.1, 9.3, and 9.11) – the middle floor houses the reception area, with an informal meeting area above, and mechanical plant space below.

Active environmental control systems

Four 120kW gas-fired condensing boilers supply a conventional low temperature hot water radiator system (each terminal unit thermostatically valved), the heater batteries of the auditorium air handling unit, and the central domestic hot water storage calorifiers. A 100kW air cooled central chiller supplies the cooling coils in the auditorium air handling unit and fan coil units in various specialist areas.

While the focus of the design has been on achieving good natural ventilation, the raised access floor system on the lower level incorporates user-controlled fan terminals linked to floor-mounted swirl diffusers – intended for use during hot calm conditions (Waterloo, 2004). However, under most conditions,

The majority of the building is naturally ventilated through a mix of automatic control of openings through the BMS [Building Management System] and manual control on a 'when needed' basis by the occupants. The principal driving force is created by the roof top pods through buoyancy effects although the building can also make use of wind forces to supplement this effect … There are automatic louvres located above the windows along each of the pavilion facades … These automatic louvres are operated for minimum fresh air requirements in winter or

TABLE 9.1

Average scores for each factor and whether they were significantly better, similar to, or worse than the BUS benchmarks

OPERATIONAL FACTORS

Factor	Score	Worse	Similar	Better
Image to visitors	5.60			•
Space in building	5.09			•
Space at desk – too little/much[4]	3.79		•	
Furniture	4.86			•

Factor	Score	Worse	Similar	Better
Cleaning	5.01			•
Availability of meeting rooms	4.29	•		
Suitability of storage arrangements	4.09			•

ENVIRONMENTAL FACTORS

Temp and Air in Winter

Factor	Score	Worse	Similar	Better
Temp Overall	4.01		•	
Temp – too hot/too cold[4]	4.66	•		
Temp – stable/variable[4]	4.95	•		
Air – still/draughty[4]	4.08		•	
Air – dry/humid[4]	3.38		•	
Air – fresh/stuffy[1]	3.79			•
Air – odourless/smelly[1]	2.96			•
Air Overall	3.96		•	

Temp and Air in Summer

Factor	Score	Worse	Similar	Better
Temp Overall	4.42			•
Temp – too hot/too cold[4]	3.53		•	
Temp – stable/variable[4]	4.39	•		
Air – still/draughty[4]	4.05			•
Air – dry/humid[4]	3.94			•
Air – fresh/stuffy[1]	3.85			•
Air – odourless/smelly[1]	3.22			•
Air Overall	4.58			•

Lighting

Factor	Score	Worse	Similar	Better
Lighting Overall	4.71			•
Natural light – too little/much[4]	3.77		•	
Sun & Sky Glare – none/too much[1]	4.16	•		
Artificial light – too little/much[4]	4.05			•
Art'l light glare – none/too much[1]	4.11	•		

Noise

Factor	Score	Worse	Similar	Better
Noise Overall	4.69			•
From colleagues – too little/much[4]	4.19		•	
From other people – too little/much[4]	4.35		•	
From inside – too little/much[4]	4.32	•		
From outside – too little/much[4]	3.76		•	
Interruptions – none/frequent[1]	3.82		•	

CONTROL FACTORS[b]

Factor		Score	Worse	Similar	Better
Heating	56%	1.81	•		
Cooling	49%	2.44		•	
Ventilation	57%	3.22		•	
Lighting	53%	2.24	•		
Noise	38%	1.94		•	

SATISFACTION FACTORS

Factor	Score	Worse	Similar	Better
Design	5.38			•
Needs	5.33			•
Comfort Overall	4.93			•
Productivity %	+4.47			•
Health	4.16			•

NOTES: (a) unless otherwise noted, a score of 7 is 'best'; superscript [4] implies a score of 4 is best, superscript [1] implies a score of 1 is best; (b) the per cent values listed here are the percentages of respondents who thought personal control of that aspect was important.

TABLE 9.2

Numbers of respondents offering positive, balanced, and negative comments on 12 performance factors

Aspect	Number of respondents			
	Positive	Balanced	Negative	Total
Overall Design	58	16	74	148
Needs Overall	15	9	60	84
Meeting Rooms	–	–	–	–
Storage	–	–	–	–
Desk/Work Area	–	–	–	–
Comfort	11	9	19	39
Noise Sources	8	13	48	69
Lighting Conditions	12	21	59	92
Productivity	22	21	14	57
Health	9	21	24	54
Work Well	–	–	–	–
Hinder	–	–	–	–
TOTALS	135	110	298	543
PER CENT	24.9	20.3	54.8	100

NOTE: Respondents were asked to comment on seven factors only during the survey rather than the 'standard' set of 12.

for night time cooling in summer. The dampers located in the ventilation pods are also automatically controlled with zonal thermostats to minimise excessive temperature swings.

(Wilson and Austin, 2004)

The thermal mass of the building is also incorporated into the control system, with temperature sensors in the pre-cast concrete floors and ceiling panels. These are used to control the amount of night-time cooling. Following fine tuning of the system it was found that a temperature of around 17°C was about as low as the slab could be taken before occupants began to experience the discomfort effects of cold radiation (Dix, 2006b; Wilson and Austin, 2004).

USERS' PERCEPTIONS OF THE BUILDING

This survey was carried out during September 2002 by Arup Research and Development (Wilson and Austin, 2004) to whom I am most grateful for allowing me full access to the results of the BUS Ltd analyses. Their paper describes their interpretation of these analyses in detail, together with the results of subsequent monitoring of conditions in the building. In this particular instance, the questionnaire was distributed electronically via their corporate network.

Overall response

For most of the 197 respondents (20 per cent female, 80 per cent male), the building was their normal place of business. They worked 4.6 days per week on average and 8.8 hours per day, of which around 7.4 were spent at their desk or present work space and 6.5 at a computer. The ratio of under-30s to over-30s was 33:67 per cent and most (75 per cent) had worked in the building for more than a year, 47 per cent at the same desk or work area. Around 32 per cent had a single office or shared with one other; 20 per cent shared with two to four colleagues; and 48 per cent shared with five or more.

Significant factors

Table 9.1 lists the average scores for each of the survey questions and indicates those aspects of the building that the staff perceived as being significantly better, similar to, or worse than the benchmark and/or scale mid-point. In this case, some 22 aspects were significantly better, six were significantly worse, while the remaining 16 aspects had much the same score as the benchmark.

In terms of the seven operational aspects, this building scores significantly better than the benchmark on all counts but one; it appears that the amount of desk space is perceived to be too little, despite space in the building scoring relatively well. Image, with a score of 5.60, is highest.

In summer, temperature overall and air overall scored very well, as did most of the more detailed aspects of these parameters. The picture was not quite so good in winter – while the air was perceived to be relatively fresh and odourless, the temperature was perceived to be too cold and variable. Nevertheless, as noted earlier, the overall wintertime scores for air and temperature were not significantly different from the corresponding benchmarks and (at 3.96 and 4.01 respectively) very close to the scale mid-point.

Lighting overall scores reasonably well (at 4.71) with just about the right amount of artificial lighting. However, there is a perception of there being too little natural light and a suggestion of some glare from sun and sky.

Noise overall scored reasonably well too (at 4.69), significantly better than the benchmark and the scale mid-point, but with most of its components just less than ideal.

On average, around half of the respondents thought that personal control was important, but perceptions of the amount of control available were lower than the scale mid-point in all cases. However, ventilation scored higher, while cooling and noise were about the same as their respective benchmarks.

In the case of the satisfaction variables, all five scored significantly higher than the benchmark and scale mid-point.

Users' comments

Overall, some 543 responses were received from staff under the seven headings where they were able to add written comments – some 39.4 per cent of the 1379 potential (197 respondents by seven headings). Table 9.2 indicates the numbers of positive, balanced, and negative comments – in this case, around 24.9 per cent were positive, 20.3 per cent balanced, and 54.8 per cent negative.

Of the specific categories, design attracted by far the most comments, with 75 per cent of respondents (representing around 27 per cent of the total number received) making some comment on this aspect. The proportions of positive:balanced:negative comments were 39:11:50 per cent for this factor.

On the positive side, the predominant comments referred to the pleasant, spacious, airy nature of the space and how well it was working overall; while on the negative side the temperatures in the space and the operation of the blinds and lighting controls, and to a lesser extent the design of the stairs, came in for some criticism. The external appearance of the building also came in for some comment, with negative outnumbering positive roughly 3:1. However, virtually all the comments about the internal appearance were positive, including several respondents who had been negative about the exterior.

No particularly dominant themes emerged under needs, but inadequate parking, problems with the meeting areas, and the lack of food warming facilities were all commented upon by several respondents; and the need for better facilities for cyclists and a medical room noted by a few.

Lighting conditions also attracted a good number of comments, some 67 per cent of which were negative. While a number of issues were canvassed under this heading, the dominant ones related to glare and the operation of the artificial lighting controls.

Noise too attracted predominantly (around 70 per cent) negative comments. Three issues dominated – the ring tones of (frequently unanswered) office and mobile phones (especially the latter); the disturbance resulting from the use of the break-out area adjacent to the auditorium; and the irritation of equipment noises and intrusive conversations.

In surveys such as these, it can be relatively rare to find the positive comments outweighing the negative, but such was the case with productivity where the roughly equal numbers of positive and balance comments constituted some 76 per cent of the total.

Overall performance indices

The Comfort Index, based on the comfort overall, noise, lighting, temperature, and air quality scores, works out at +0.67; while the Satisfaction Index, based on the design, needs, health, and perceived productivity scores, is +1.25, noting that the scale mid-point in these instances is zero on a -3 to +3 scale.

The Summary Index, being the average of the Comfort and Satisfaction Indices, works out at +0.96, while the Forgiveness Factor, calculated to be 1.12 in this instance, indicates that staff are likely to be relatively tolerant of minor shortcomings in individual aspects such as winter and summer temperatures, air quality, lighting, and noise (a factor of 1 being the mid-point on a scale that normally ranges from 0.80 to 1.20).

In terms of the Ten-Factor Rating Scale, the building was 'Exceptional' on the 7-point scale with a calculated percentage value of 95 per cent. When All-Factors were taken into account, the percentage value worked out at 79 per cent – around the middle of the 'Good Practice' band.

OTHER REPORTED ASPECTS OF PERFORMANCE

In addition to the questionnaire survey, Wilson and Austin (2004) monitored air and slab temperatures in winter and summer, carbon dioxide levels in winter, and annual energy use during 2002/2003.

During the winter it was found that the temperature of the slab lagged that of the air by about 2°C. 'It was evident from this that buildings with high thermal mass cannot be allowed to drop below say 17 °C otherwise preheat will not deliver acceptable comfort conditions by the take up of occupancy.'

In summer, it was found that the air temperature on the upper level averaged around 0.5°C higher than the lower. It was concluded that 'Extremes are dealt with well by the passive control measures of shading, insulation, thermal mass and night cooling' and the indications were that the inside temperature would rise above 25°C for only 8 per cent of occupied hours. As a result of the monitoring, the night cooling regime evolved to enable it to take place between

21.00 and 06.30hrs, provided the outside temperature was less than 21°C. Carbon dioxide measurements on a winter day indicated 'that ventilation rates were sufficient to hold the CO_2 to levels between 800 and 1000ppm on level 4 [an upper floor] and between 500 and 750ppm on level 2 [a lower floor] under full occupancy' with 450ppm outside. 'In terms of energy consumption the building performs well on gas usage and meets a good practice standard of 76kWh/m² for a naturally ventilated building … Its [total] annual electricity usage is 157kWh/m²' (Wilson and Austin, 2004).

ACKNOWLEDGEMENTS

I must express my particular gratitude to Barry Austin, Associate Director of Arup Research and Development for granting permission for me to access the analyses of the survey undertaken at the building and to Terry R. Dix, Director of Ove Arup and Partners Ltd for assisting my understanding of the building and its design.

REFERENCES

ASHRAE (2001) *ASHRAE Handbook: Fundamentals, SI Edition*, Atlanta, GA: American Society of Heating Refrigerating and Air-Conditioning Engineers.

Dix, T. R. (2006a) 'Arup Campus', PowerPoint presentation.

Dix, T. R. (2006b) Transcript of interview held on 2 November 2005, Arup Campus, Solihull, England.

Kwok, A. G. and Grondzik, W. T. (2007) *The Green Studio Handbook: Environmental Strategies for Schematic Design*, Oxford: Elsevier Architectural Press, pp. 267–73.

Phillips, D. (2004) 'Arup Campus, Solihull', in *Daylighting: Natural Light in Architecture*, Oxford: Architectural, 90–3.

Powell, K. (2002) 'Candid Campus', *The Architects' Journal*, 215(7): 24–33.

Waterloo (2004) 'Waterloo's Diffusers Boost Airflow at the Touch of a Button', available at:www.waterloo.co.uk/news_arup.htm (accessed 17 November 2004).

Wilson, A. and Austin, B. (2004) 'Post Occupancy Evaluation Case Study – Advanced Naturally Ventilated Office', in *Proceedings of 'Closing the Loop: Post Occupancy Evaluation Conference – The Next Steps'*, Cumberland Lodge, Windsor, United Kingdom, 29 April–2 May.

Atrium façade of the ZICER Building

10

ZICER Building,
University of East Anglia
Norwich, England

THE CONTEXT

The five-storey, 2883m^2 building housing the Zuckerman Institute for Connective Environmental Research (the ZICER Building) at the University of East Anglia, England, was opened in 2003 (Figure 10.1). An Institute within the University's School of Environmental Sciences, it houses several research centres, including the Tyndall Centre for Climate Change Research, the Climatic Research Group, and the Centres for Social and Economic Research on the Global Environment, for Economic and Behavioural Analysis Risk and Decision, and for Environmental Risk.

The University has a reputation for innovative buildings by architects such as Sir Norman Foster and Sir Denys Lasdun, the ZICER Building

being connected to the centre of the1960s teaching spine designed by the latter, and just a short distance along Chancellor's Drive from the low-energy Elizabeth Fry Building.

With such a background and given the aims of the Institute, it will be evident that sustainability would be a high priority for the University, and given the relatively temperate climate of this part of England (with winter and summer 1 per cent design temperatures of around -1°C and +22°C respectively – ASHRAE, 2001, 27.50–1), some attempt to incorporate natural ventilation was inevitable.

The building has won several awards, including the 2004 European Association for Renewable Energy Award for solar architecture, a high commendation for sustainability in the 2005 Royal Institute

10.1 General view of the south façade showing the window arrangement on Levels 01, 0, and 1. Note the building-integrated photo-voltaic installation on Level 2 (the uppermost floor); the glazed link at Level 0 (to the right of shot); and the entrance to the basement (Level 02) bicycle storage area (bottom right). The tall chimneys in the background are from the CHP plant

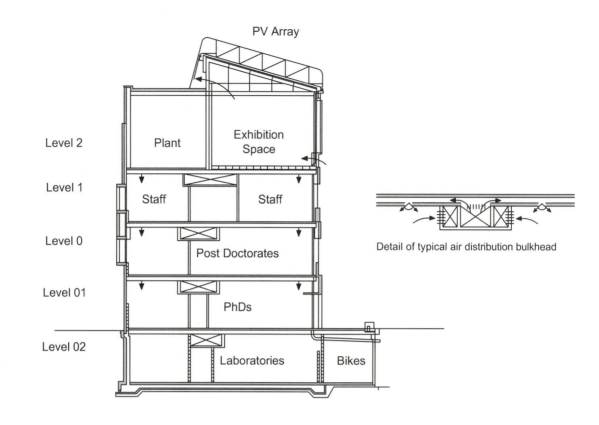

Level 2   Plant   Exhibition Space

Level 1   Staff   Staff

Level 0   Post Doctorates

Level 01   PhDs

Level 02   Laboratories   Bikes

PV Array

Detail of typical air distribution bulkhead

0   10

10.2 Cross-section indicating the designations and main functions
of the five levels of the building. Note the air distribution
bulkheads above the central passage-ways and the features of the
Exhibition Space
Source: Adapted from RMJM

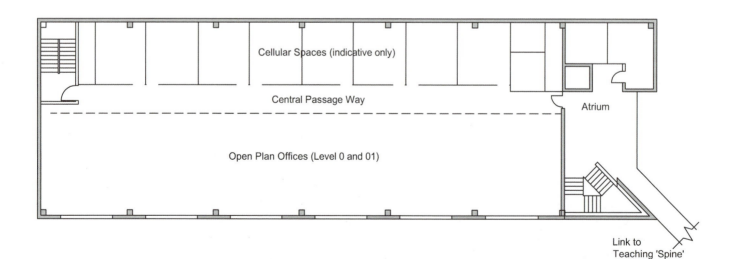

Cellular Spaces (indicative only)

Central Passage Way

Open Plan Offices (Level 0 and 01)

Atrium

Link to
Teaching 'Spine'
at Level 0

10.3 Overall plan of the building indicating the principles
underlying the layout of Levels 0 and 01. Note the main vertical
circulation Atrium at the east end with its link to the teaching spine
of the campus at Level 0
Source: Adapted from RMJM

0   10

10.4 General view of the north façade. Note the high-level window arrangement of Level 01 and the mid-level windows of Levels 0 and 1, all designed to provide daylight and natural ventilation to the mainly cellular offices on that side of the building

10.5 The Exhibition Space on Level 2 with building-integrated photovoltaic panels forming the roof and much of the south façade. Natural ventilation grilles are located at sill level on the south façade and at the top of both walls. Exposed concrete panels are suspended at high level between the steel beams providing thermal mass to what would otherwise be a relatively thermally 'lightweight' space. The Seminar Room is beyond the far wall and the main plant room is behind the wall on the right

of Chartered Surveyors regional awards, and the 2005 *Building Magazine* Low Energy Building of the Year Award.

The design process and architectural outcome have been described elsewhere in some detail (EcoTech, 2003). What follows is the briefest of outlines.

THE DESIGN PROCESS

The project was led by the Cambridge office of the multi-disciplinary practice Robert Matthew Johnston-Marshall (RMJM) – responsible for the architecture and building services – working with structural engineers Whitby Bird and Associates and others.

With a client and brief of this nature, the RMJM team were able to apply their well-practised in-house interdisciplinary approach to the design (Baird, 2001; Williams, 2005). The concept that emerged was for a five-storey building (Figure 10.2) with a full-height atrium/lobby

at its east end linked at Level 0 to the main teaching spine of the campus by a glazed walkway (Figure 10.3). The main research centres are housed in the three middle floors of the building, sandwiched between a large exhibition space and seminar room on the top floor and facilities for the Social Science for the Environment, Virtual Reality and Experimental Laboratories in the basement. 'The Institute was designed to make a strong statement about sustainability by exploiting the technology surrounding high thermal mass, natural ventilation, photovoltaic electricity and recycled construction' (EcoTech, 2003). To achieve a reasonable measure of natural ventilation, a partial open-plan layout was utilised on some of the floors.

The fact that most of the staff to be housed in the Institute were already on campus, but scattered around different locations and

10.6 The Seminar Room on Level 2. Note the air supply grilles on the floor and the ceiling arrangement of concrete panels and adjustable louvres which provide some environmental control – the building-integrated photo-voltaic roof is immediately above

10.7 An administration staff group housed in a south-facing office on Level 1. Note the row of ceiling-mounted air supply diffusers

10.8 High-level view (looking westwards) of the open-plan floor of Level 0, housing the postdoctoral and contract researchers. Note the row of ceiling-mounted air supply diffusers (upper left of shot) and the linear extract grille on the ventilation bulkhead (upper right). Note also the partitioning system used here and the window arrangement

in accommodation of variable quality, posed particular issues. In some instances, researchers would now have a personal space, albeit in a modern open-plan layout, rather than having to share a workplace. In other cases, researchers were moving from cellular offices in older buildings with only one or two occupants to an open-plan environment, albeit with adjacent break-out spaces and meeting rooms. This has proved problematical for some of the research staff (Turner, 2005), but with the trialling of different layouts and screening arrangements, it is hoped that a reasonably satisfactory arrangement will be reached from the point of view of the occupants, while at the same time achieving the environmental objectives of the design.

THE DESIGN OUTCOME

Building layout, construction, and passive environmental control systems

Rectangular in plan (around 47m by 14m) and with its long axis oriented approximately east–west (Figure 10.3), the Institute has four levels above ground (Figure 10.4) and a basement level. The uppermost level (designated Level 2 in conformity with the campus-wide datum) contains a large exhibition area (Figure 10.5), seminar space (Figure 10.6), and plant room. Level 1 immediately below houses academic and administrative staff in mainly cellular offices designed for single occupants or small groups of staff (Figure 10.7). Levels 0 and 01 immediately below house, respectively, postdoctoral fellows (Figure 10.8) and PhD candidates (Figure 10.9) in predominantly open-plan offices in the southerly two-thirds of the space, with cellular spaces along the northern perimeter, the latter accommodating meeting rooms, staff rooms, research library, etc. The basement (Level 02) accommodates the virtual laboratory space and ancillary offices, together with a space for bike storage.

Particular emphasis was placed on achieving a high level of airtightness and good levels of thermal resistance for the various elements of the building envelope. Of particular note is the use of triple-glazed windows with integral adjustable blinds (Figure 10.11). These measures, in combination the thermal mass of the exposed concrete ceiling structure (or element in the case of the Exhibition

10.9 High-level view (looking eastwards) of the open-plan floor of Level 01, housing the PhD candidates. Note the row of ceiling-mounted air supply diffusers (upper right of shot) and the linear extract grille on the ventilation bulkhead (upper left). Note also the partitioning system used here and the window arrangement

10.10 Exterior view of the window arrangement on the south façade. Note the internal and external shading on levels 1 and 0; and the full height French doors on Level 01. The two upstands at ground level provide light and ventilation to the bicycle storage area

10.11 Close-up interior view of the openable windows on the south façade (Levels 1 and 0). Note the between-pane Venetian blinds – fully open on the left; fully closed on the right

and a 'suspended ceiling' of pre-cast concrete to provide some thermal mass (Figures 10.1 and 10.5).

USERS' PERCEPTIONS OF THE BUILDING

Overall response

The building was surveyed in October 2005. For most (some 96 per cent) of the 67 respondents (51 per cent female, 49 per cent male), representing almost all of the occupants at the time of the survey, the building was their normal place of business. They worked 4.6 days per week on average and 8.2 hours per day, of which around 7.1 were spent at their desk or present work space and 6.7 at a computer. The ratio of under-30s to over-30s was 28:72 per cent and most (85 per cent) had worked in the building for more than a year, 72 per cent at the same desk or work area. The proportions were approximately equally divided between those with a single office or who shared with one other; those who shared with two to eight colleagues; and those who shared with more than eight, i.e. around one-third of each.

Significant factors

Table 10.1 lists the average scores for each of the survey questions and indicates those aspects of the building that the staff perceived as being significantly better, similar to, or worse than the benchmark and/or scale mid-point. In this case, some 13 aspects were significantly better, 16 were significantly worse, while the remaining 16 aspects had much the same score as the benchmark.

In terms of the eight operational aspects, this building scores significantly better than the benchmark for space at desk, furniture, cleaning, and storage. Image, facilities, and meeting rooms scored around the same or less than their benchmarks, but better than the scale mid-point, while space in building, at 3.50, scored less than both criteria.

With the exception of summer temperature which scored on the hot side (though still better than the benchmark), overall scores for temperature and air in summer and winter were well over their respective benchmarks and the scale mid-point. In both seasons, temperatures were judged to be on the stable side and the air slightly dry, on average. Air overall scored well and it was considered to be relatively odourless in both summer and winter. At the same time, the scores indicated that the air was on the relatively still and stuffy side of the relevant scales.

With an average value of 3.80, the score for lighting overall was under both the benchmark and the scale mid-point. Users assessed the building as having too much artificial lighting and too little daylighting – perhaps as a consequence, glare was less of an issue with the scores indicating conditions on the satisfactory side of the scale.

The score for noise overall was around the same as the benchmark and higher than the scale mid-point. However, there appeared to be issues with too much noise from colleagues and from other people.

Responses to the personal control questions reflected some of these concerns with lighting and noise, some 46 per cent of respondents rating control of these as important, while their perception of degree of control scored only 2.61 and 2.06 respectively. Control of ventilation was also rated important by some 36 per cent of the occupants, but scored only 2.18.

In the case of the satisfaction variables, needs, comfort, and health scored around the same as the benchmark, while design and productivity were significantly lower.

Users' comments

Overall, some 407 responses were received from staff under the 12 headings where they were able to add written comments – some 50.6 per cent of the 804 potential (67 respondents by 12 headings). Table 10.2 indicates the numbers of positive, balanced, and negative comments – in this case, around 20.1 per cent were positive, 14.0 per cent balanced, and 65.7 per cent negative – from the building as a whole.

Reinforcing the relatively low perception scores for lighting, noise, and design, the largest numbers of negative comments related to these three aspects. Noise and lighting issues were also predominant in the things that hinder category (around 46 and 27 per cent respectively). Computing facilities and the work space were mentioned relatively frequently among the things that work well, by the PhD candidates and by the postdoctoral researchers on Levels 01 and 1 respectively.

Given the three groups of building users and the configuration of their respective floors (Level 1 – academic and administration staff; Level 0 – postdoctoral and contract researchers; Level 01 – PhD candidates), it was of interest to see if different issues were being raised. As it turned out, the comment rates were very close to the overall response rates – 27.7, 41.2, 31.1 as against 29.9, 37.3, 32.8 per cent for Levels 1, 0, and 01 respectively – in other words, the comments were not dominated by the occupants of any particular floor. While balanced comments were around 14 per cent for all three floors, the proportion of negative comments trended upwards as one moved higher in the building (61.4, 64.3, and 73.4 for Levels 01, 0, and 1 respectively); while conversely the positive comments trended downwards (25.2, 20.2, and 14.2 respectively).

In the case of Level 1, lighting and design issues attracted some negative comment – more than half of those felt there was not enough natural light, and there were several comments relating to the difficulty of easy interaction with the researchers as a result of their being on different and open-plan floors.

On Level 0, the main negative issues raised related to design and noise, more than half of the respondents opining that the open-plan layout was not conducive to research, and noting the difficulty of holding conversations (for both the speakers and the inadvertent listeners). Lighting appeared to be less of an issue (the artificial lighting layout had recently been modified to align with the workspaces) but it still, along with noise, received frequent mention among the hindrances.

Lighting and noise issues appeared to dominate the comments from the users of Level 01. The main comment related to the lack of daylight and the need for the artificial lighting to be on most of the time, while conversations and telephones (other people's) were a distraction.

Compounding the dilemma, several comments from users of both Levels 0 and 01 noted that the open-plan spaces could also be oppressively quiet and inhibiting of conversations at times.

Overall performance indices

The Comfort Index, based on the comfort overall, noise, lighting, temperature, and air quality scores, works out at +0.73; while the Satisfaction Index, based on the design, needs, health, and perceived productivity scores, is -0.58, noting that the scale mid-point in these instances is zero on a -3 to +3 scale.

The Summary Index, being the average of the Comfort and Satisfaction Indices, works out at +0.07, while the Forgiveness Factor, calculated to be 0.95 in this instance, indicates that staff are likely to be relatively intolerant of minor shortcomings in individual aspects such as winter and summer temperatures, air quality, lighting, and noise (a factor of 1 being the mid-point on a scale that normally ranges from 0.80 to 1.20).

In terms of the Ten-Factor Rating Scale, the building was 'Above Average' on the 7-point scale with a calculated percentage value of 60 per cent. When All-Factors were taken into account, the percentage value worked out at 58 per cent – again just inside the 'Above Average' band.

ACKNOWLEDGEMENTS

I must express my gratitude to Professor R. Kerry Turner, Director of the Centre for Social and Economic Research on the Global Environment, and Martyn Newton, Assistant Director of Estates (Facilities) at the University of East Anglia for granting permission for me to undertake this survey. Particular thanks go to project architect Peter Williams and to Drew Elliot of RMJM for assisting my understanding of the building and its design. I must also thank PhD candidate Charlotte Turner for her assistance during the time of the survey.

REFERENCES

ASHRAE (2001) *ASHRAE Handbook: Fundamentals, SI Edition*, Atlanta, GA: American Society of Heating Refrigerating and Air-Conditioning Engineers.

Baird, G. (2001) *The Architectural Expression of Environmental Control Systems*, London: Spon Press, Chapters 9 and 16.

EcoTech (2003) 'Building – "Eastern Promise. EcoTech"', *Sustainable Architecture Today*, 8: 14–18.

Turner, R. K. (2005) Transcript of interview held on 31 October 2005, Norwich, England.

Williams, P. (2005) Transcript of interview held on 1 November 2005, Cambridge, England.

Inter-floor opening at the RES Building

11
Renewable Energy Systems (RES) Building
Kings Langley, England

THE CONTEXT

The world headquarters of Renewable Energy Systems (RES) Ltd is located on the site of a former Ovaltine egg farm on the outskirts of the village of Kings Langley. Situated on the northern fringes of London at around 52°N Latitude, and with 1 per cent design temperatures approximately -3.3°C and +24.2°C (ASHRAE, 2001: 27.51–2), the site is bounded by a trunk railway line to its west and the busy M25 motorway to its south-east.

Founded in the 1980s, RES Ltd is now involved in the development, construction, and operation of wind farms worldwide. Given the company's mission it is perhaps not surprising that the brief for their new headquarters called for it to be carbon-neutral and self-sustaining in terms of electricity generation and thermal environmental control, while at the same time being commercially viable (Cameron, 2006). More than that, the complex was to include a visitor centre as well as the office accommodation, and utilise the existing heritage-listed buildings. In addition and from the outset, the client was determined that the building would be a test bed for the demonstration of a range of renewable energy technologies.

The two-storey 2700m² conversion was completed and staff moved in towards the end of 2003, since when it has won several regeneration and sustainability awards. These include the 2004 British Council for Offices Award for Best Refurbishment in South England and South Wales, the 2004 Business Commitment to the Environment Award, the 2005 East of England RICS Award for Sustainability, the 2005 Queen's Award for Enterprise (Sustainable Development Category), and an 'Excellent' Design Stage BREEAM rating in 2006.

The design process and architectural outcome, as well as the results of extensive performance monitoring of the various energy systems, have been described elsewhere in some detail (Bunn, 2004; Beaufort Court Seminars, 2005; Tweddell and Watts, 2005; Watts, 2005; Bristow and Tweddell, 2006; Beaufort Court website). What follows is the briefest of outlines.

THE DESIGN PROCESS

Environmental design for the building was a close collaboration between two of the UK's leading exponents of integrated low energy building design – Studio E Architects and consulting engineers

Max Fordham, both based in London. These firms had extensive experience and well-established reputations in the field of low energy and sustainable design and had worked together previously.

Selected for the project following an interview process (Lloyd-Jones, 2006; Watts, 2006), the brief required the team to do the following:

- Meet the commercial needs and conditions of the property market.
- Provide approx. 2670m² net of high quality head office space.
- Provide exhibition, conference and associated spaces for the use of visitors to the Centre as well as RES.
- Deliver a building that minimises energy consumption and the use of scarce resources and that contributes positively to the local economy and community needs.
- Provide all the Centre's energy needs from on-site renewable energy sources.
- Integrate seamlessly the social, technical and aesthetic aspects of the project.

(Lloyd-Jones, Beaufort Court Seminars, 2005)

While it was to be expected that RES would wish to use a wind turbine as one of its on-site renewable energy sources, the farm site had also been purchased with a view to growing biomass. In addition, the design team also had available a major European Commission grant to demonstrate the feasibility of using combined solar thermal and photo-voltaic panels in conjunction with seasonal heat storage. The client was pleased to provide a vehicle for that system as well as for the use of ground source cooling suggested by the engineers – one of the benefits of a highly motivated client with a genuine interest in the exploration and demonstration of renewable energy systems (Watts, 2006). As succinctly phrased by Bunn (2004):

Take a client who trades in renewable energy systems, add an environmentally sound architect and building services engineer, liberally dust with a EU renewable energy grant, and what do you get? Answer: an office building fairly simmering with green technologies.

11.1 View into the 'horseshoe'. Note the two levels of offices; the continuous strip of windows near the ridge; and of course the wind turbine

11.2 Cross-section indicating the two-level arrangement of the offices and some of the methods of thermal environmental control and ventilation
Source: Adapted from Studio E Architects

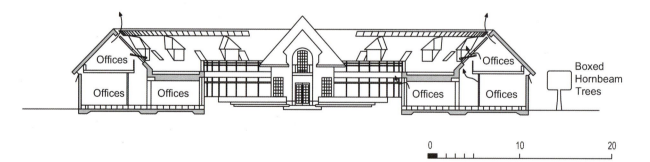

11.3 A ground-floor external perimeter office space. Note the chilled beam convectors at high level on both sides of the structural beams and parallel to the window

11.4 Office layout on the upper floor – workstations to the right and circulation on the left. The sun pattern on the rafters is from the strip of windows near the ridge, while the dark patches are due to movable horizontal shades resting on the rafters. One of the openings which enable air transfer between floors is located to the left of the railings

11.5 Some of the shading arrangements on the south-western façade. Note the combination of boxed hornbeam trees and fixed glass solar shading on the exterior, and roller blinds internally (see also Figure 11.3)

So what of the building itself?

THE DESIGN OUTCOME

Building layout, construction, and passive environmental control systems

The original buildings comprised a two-storey coach house and a chicken-rearing house with a distinctive U-shaped plan (termed the horseshoe building) and it was a requirement of the local planning authority that their external appearance be retained. Conversion of the former was relatively straightforward, but the latter required extensive demolition, reconstruction, and extension to achieve the required configuration for two levels of office accommodation (Figures 11.1 and 11.2) and a visitor centre (see Beaufort Court website).

11.6 View out northwards from the horseshoe. Note the continuous strip of windows at high level, one in three of which is automated. Note too the grassed roof of the ground floor office 'extension'. The new glazed link between the two arms of the horseshoe is on the extreme left of the shot

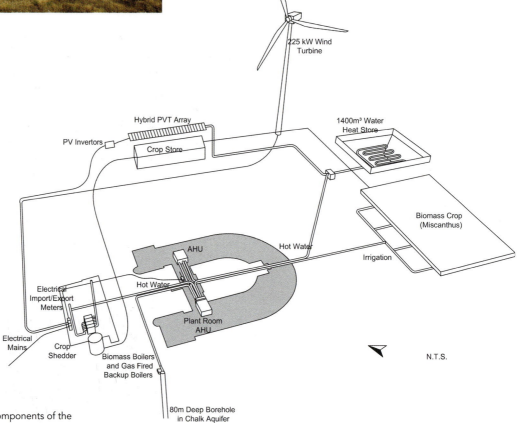

225 kW Wind Turbine

Hybrid PVT Array

1400m³ Water Heat Store

PV Invertors

Crop Store

Biomass Crop (Miscanthus)

AHU

Hot Water

Electrical Import/Export Meters

Hot Water

Irrigation

Plant Room AHU

Electrical Mains

Crop Shedder

Biomass Boilers and Gas Fired Backup Boilers

80m Deep Borehole in Chalk Aquifer

N.T.S.

11.7 Schematic indicating the key components of the renewable energy systems used in this project. Note the wind turbine; the solar array and heat store; the *Miscanthus* crop, store, shredder, and boiler; the chilled water borehole; and the main air handling units
Source: Adapted from Max Fordham

11.8 The solar array which also forms the roof of the *Miscanthus* biomass store consists of 54m² of combined photo-voltaic and thermal panels and 116m² of thermal panels. Horizontal strip glazing just below the ridge provides daylighting to the space

11.9 The upper surface of the heat store, with stones covering the insulating layer that floats on top of the 1400m³ volume of water. Note the absence of openable windows on this façade of the horseshoe building which faces towards the trunk railway line

11.10 The biomass shredder is on the left with a horizontal feed to the boiler house located in the coach-house building

11.11 Interior of one of the two main AHU plant rooms. Note the triangular shape of the air intake plenum and the pipework connecting to the three separate heat exchangers

The open end of the horseshoe building is orientated towards the north-west, with a new single-storey link across the opening serving as its main entrance. The lower floor has a central corridor with offices of various sizes distributed along each side (Figure 11.3). The upper floor, which is entirely within the pitch of the roof structure, is in the form of a narrow continuous space with workstations against the outer wall of the horseshoe, and a walkway on the inner side (Figure 11.4). A concerted effort was made to achieve high thermal insulation, low air infiltration, good solar control and natural light, and a measure of natural ventilation, despite the constraints imposed by the original layout and construction, and the proximity to major road and rail arteries.

Externally, various means of solar shading have been utilised, ranging from fixed glass or aluminium screens to the deciduous boxed hornbeam trees along the south-western façades (Figure 11.5). While the relatively narrow plan lent itself to natural ventilation systems being deployed on both levels, this was precluded by the noise disturbance from the arterial routes – opening windows are confined to the inner façades of the horseshoe or façades facing away from these routes (Figure 11.6).

Active environmental control systems

Four main systems were used to meet the client's objective of providing all the buildings energy needs from on-site renewable energy sources (Figure 11.7). Prime among these was a 225kW wind turbine supplying electricity to the building or to the grid via an appropriate metering system (Figure 11.5). A solar array (Figure 11.8) with 54m² of combined photo-voltaic and thermal panels, and 116m² of thermal panels (forming the roof of the biomass store) provided additional electrical energy and a hot water supply for heating the 1400m³ water volume designed to act as a seasonal heat store (Figure 11.9). The intended biomass is *Miscanthus* (elephant grass) grown on site and eventually burned in a 100kW biomass boiler (Figure 11.10), with gas-fired condensing boilers as back-up. Cooling is obtained from a 75m borehole on site producing water at around 11°C.

Air handling units located at ground level towards the end of each arm supply fresh air to the offices in the horseshoe building (Figure 11.11). As the various energy systems have been kept separate for

TABLE 11.1

Average scores for each factor and whether they were significantly better, similar to, or worse than the BUS benchmarks

OPERATIONAL FACTORS

Factor	Score	Worse	Similar	Better	Factor	Score	Worse	Similar	Better
Image to visitors	6.75			●	Cleaning	6.01			●
Space in building	5.47			●	Availability of meeting rooms	5.44			●
Space at desk – too little/much⁴	4.95	●			Suitability of storage arrangements	4.89			●
Furniture	5.41		●		Facilities meet work requirements	5.81			●

ENVIRONMENTAL FACTORS

Temp and Air in Winter	Score	Worse	Similar	Better	Temp and Air in Summer	Score	Worse	Similar	Better
Temp Overall	4.44		●		Temp Overall	4.03		●	
Temp – too hot/too cold⁴	4.89	●			Temp – too hot/too cold⁴	3.05		●	
Temp – stable/variable⁴	4.51	●			Temp – stable/variable⁴	4.36	●		
Air – still/draughty⁴	3.44		●		Air – still/draughty⁴	3.06		●	
Air – dry/humid⁴	3.13		●		Air – dry/humid⁴	3.57		●	
Air – fresh/stuffy¹	2.97			●	Air – fresh/stuffy¹	3.71			●
Air – odourless/smelly¹	2.31			●	Air – odourless/smelly¹	2.64			●
Air Overall	4.65			●	Air Overall	4.40			●

Lighting	Score	Worse	Similar	Better	Noise	Score	Worse	Similar	Better
Lighting Overall	5.51			●	Noise Overall	4.48		●	
Natural light – too little/much⁴	4.45	●			From colleagues – too little/much⁴	4.38		●	
Sun & Sky Glare – none/too much¹	3.99		●		From other people – too little/much⁴	4.21		●	
Artificial light – too little/much⁴	4.07			●	From inside – too little/much⁴	4.00			●
Art'l light glare – none/too much¹	2.83			●	From outside – too little/much⁴	3.63	●		
					Interruptions – none/frequent¹	3.89		●	

CONTROL FACTORS[b]		Score	Worse	Similar	Better	SATISFACTION FACTORS	Score	Worse	Similar	Better
Heating	24%	2.47		●		Design	5.98			●
Cooling	27%	2.20	●			Needs	5.95			●
Ventilation	25%	2.67	●			Comfort Overall	5.41			●
Lighting	23%	2.70	●			Productivity %	+5.77			●
Noise	22%	2.09	●			Health	4.72			●

NOTES: (a) unless otherwise noted, a score of 7 is 'best'; superscript ⁴ implies a score of 4 is best, superscript ¹ implies a score of 1 is best; (b) the per cent values listed here are the percentages of respondents who thought personal control of that aspect was important.

TABLE 11.2

Numbers of respondents offering positive, balanced, and negative comments on 12 performance factors

Aspect	Number of respondents			
	Positive	Balanced	Negative	total
Overall Design	22	5	13	40
Needs Overall	5	2	17	24
Meeting Rooms	2	5	19	26
Storage	3	2	20	26
Desk/Work Area	14	1	15	30
Comfort	7	2	7	16
Noise Sources	1	8	21	30
Lighting Conditions	7	4	9	20
Productivity	3	5	7	15
Health	9	2	3	14
Work Well	45	–	–	45
Hinder	–	–	54	54
TOTALS	118	36	185	339
PER CENT	34.8	10.6	54.6	100

pragmatic reasons, these AHUs are fitted with three heat exchangers – one fed from the solar thermal heat store system, the second from the boiler system, and the third from the borehole system. Zone control is via heater batteries in the under-floor ducting system and ceiling mounted convectors (Figure 11.3), for heating and cooling respectively. Large openings between the floors, spaced around the corridors at regular intervals (Figure 11.4), allow vertical air transfer, the air being exhausted eventually via automated windows at high level along the ridge of the upper floor (Figure 11.6).

USERS' PERCEPTIONS OF THE BUILDING

Overall response

The building was surveyed in August 2006. For most (some 95 per cent) of the 83 respondents (34 per cent female, 66 per cent male), representing almost all of the occupants at the time of the survey, the building was their normal place of business. They worked 4.5

days per week on average and 8.6 hours per day, of which around 7.4 were spent at their desk or present work space and 6.7 at a computer. The ratio of under-30s to over-30s was 30:70 per cent and most (70 per cent) had worked in the building for more than a year, 48 per cent at the same desk or work area. Around 22 per cent had a single office or shared with one other; 42 per cent shared with two to five colleagues; and 36 per cent shared with more than five.

Significant factors

Table 11.1 lists the average scores for each of the survey questions and indicates those aspects of the building that the staff perceived as being significantly better, similar to, or worse than the benchmark and/or scale mid-point. In this case, some 23 aspects were significantly better, eight were significantly worse, while the remaining 14 aspects had much the same score as the benchmark.

In terms of the eight operational aspects, the building scores significantly better than the benchmark on all counts but one; it

Different angles on the London City Hall

12
City Hall
London, England

THE CONTEXT

City Hall, located on the River Thames near Tower Bridge, is the headquarters of the Mayor of London and the Greater London Authority (GLA). Created in 2000, the GLA has responsibility for the UK capital's transport, policing, fire and emergency services, economic development, planning, culture, and environment.

The ten-storey building, which is part of a much more extensive development designated More London (Figure 12.1) for which some nine buildings were planned, was the first to be constructed on this 5.26-hectare site. With a gross floor area of around 18,000m² on its ten levels plus basement, it accommodates a debating chamber, committee rooms, and office space for the 600 or so staff that are based there.

Situated at around 51.5°N latitude, and with 1 per cent design temperatures of approximately -2.3°C and +25.7°C (ASHRAE, 2001: 27.52-3), the building was completed and staff moved in during July 2002.

The building achieved an 'Excellent' BREEAM rating for both its design and its operation and maintenance, and received the Institution of Civil Engineers London Association Merit Award in 2003.

The design process and architectural outcome have been described elsewhere in some detail (Foster *et al.*, 2002; Hart, 2003; Marmot, 2004; Marriage and Curtain, 2004; Merkel, 2003; Powell, 2002; Turpin, 2003). What follows is the briefest of outlines.

12.1 The building in context viewed from the north-east around the middle of an autumn day. Note the surrounding developments, the immediately adjacent amphitheatre (dubbed 'the Scoop') to the right, and the River Thames in the foreground

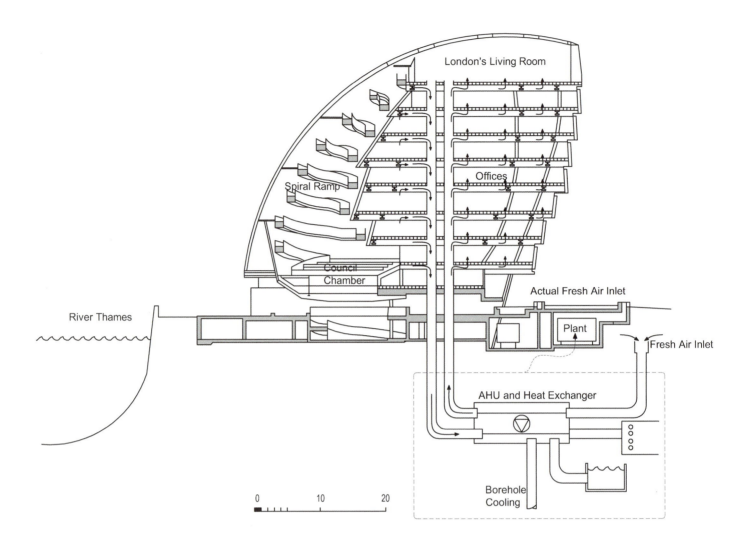

12.2 North–south section, as viewed from the west. Note the distinctive modified-spherical shape, the self-shading on the south façade, and the disposition of the assembly chamber, spiral ramp, and office floors. The schematic illustrates the strategy for air distribution, heat recovery, and the utilisation of borehole water for cooling
Source: Adapted from Foster and Partners

12.3 Plan at Level 6 which accommodates offices for the members of the GLA as well as extensive open-plan areas. Other floors have a variety of arrangements, but are mainly open plan in character
Source: Adapted from Foster and Partners

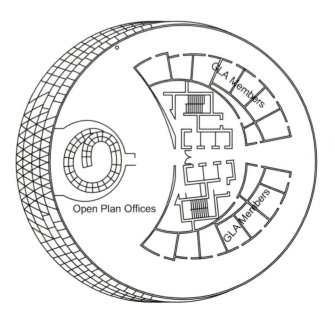

12.4 Internal view of an office space with the spiral ramp visible through the glazing on the right. Note the circular air supply diffuser on the floor and the ceiling-mounted grilles integrated with the luminaires

12.5 View from the north-west with the structure and spiral ramp visible through the clear north-facing glazing over the assembly chamber

THE DESIGN PROCESS

The process leading to the building of City Hall commenced two years or so before the creation of the GLA. From the 55 potential buildings and sites initially put forward in a developer–architect competition, seven were selected from which two were further explored, one a refurbishment, the other and eventual winner (and the public's preference) a new build. The design team for the building comprised architects Foster and Partners with Arup as structural, services, and façade engineers. This building was seen to be a catalyst for the development of the entire site.

According to project architect Curtain (2006), Fosters worked closely with Arup, exploring a range of options for all aspects of the design. Implicit in the brief (Thonger, 2006) was the need for the building to be sustainable and energy-efficient and 'One of the primary goals of the building design was to reduce the heating and cooling requirements' (Arup, 2007), resulting in the use of highly insulated panels combined with high performance glazing.

The outcome was a 45m-high building with a distinctive modified-spherical shape housing flexible open-plan space and cellular offices on Levels 3 through 8 (Figure 12.2). The main assembly chamber takes up part of Levels 1 and 2 and is open right up to Level 9 (an open space dubbed 'London's Living Room'), with a unique spiralling

ramp connecting the two. The ground and basement levels contain the main entrance, exhibition area, committee rooms, cafeteria, and mechanical and electrical services.

THE DESIGN OUTCOME

Building layout, construction, and passive environmental control systems

Approximately 45m diameter in plan (Figure 12.3) and with useable floor areas ranging from 1282 to 259m² as one moves up the levels, the building tilts forwards towards the south (Figure 12.2). Compared

12.6 Exterior detail of the glazing (west façade, Level 3). Note the opaque lower panel and the transparent upper panel, the latter with manually adjustable horizontal louvres. The outer pane of each panel is top-hinged for access

12.7 Exterior glazing with hinged pane of upper panel open for cleaning using dedicated cherry-picker

12.8 View looking down the inner side of the north façade. The horizontal structure incorporates smaller internal heating pipes to mitigate the possibility of cold downdrafts

to a rectangular building containing the same volume, the modified-spherical shape has the effect of reducing the area of the envelope exposed to heat loss and solar gain. The latter is also reduced on the south façade with successive floors overlapping the ones below and providing a degree of self-shading, though this is less pronounced at higher levels.

Office spaces predominate on the east, south, and west façades (Figure 12.4), with the assembly chamber and spiralling ramp on the north side (Figure 12.5). Two main glazing systems reflect this arrangement. The office façades (Figures 12.6 and 12.7) have 'a series of storey-height, triple-glazed and insulated cladding panels' (Dawson, 2002). Each panel (approximately 1.5m wide, but all with slightly different geometry) has an outer set of hinged glass rain-screens with a ventilated cavity behind; the upper half of the inner layer is double-glazed with adjustable horizontal louvres between the panes, while the lower half is an insulated aluminium panel. The north façade has transparent triangular glazing panels which provide daylight to the assembly chamber (Figure 12.5). Overall, around 25 per cent of the of the envelope is glazed and the average U-value is stated to be around 0.75 W/m^2.$^\circ$C.

Active environmental control systems

Two 600kW gas-fired boilers located in a basement area plant room provide hot water for the heater batteries in the air handling units, the convectors and trench heaters in the offices, and heating pipes inside the 300mm-diameter horizontal members of the structure (Figure 12.8) above the assembly chamber (the last of these to mitigate the possibility of cold downdrafts from the extensive north-facing glazing).

Cooling is derived from two 130m-deep boreholes under the building from which water at around 12–14°C is obtained. This is used both directly in the cooling coils of the air handling units and indirectly via a heat exchanger, before being distributed to ceiling-mounted passive chilled beams (Figure 12.9) in the offices. Following this, the water is stored for toilet flushing, with any surplus being discharged into the River Thames.

The ventilation system is mixed-mode in nature. In the case of the mechanical ventilation system, fresh air is taken in near ground level to the basement plant room and conditioned in six major air

12.9 Close-up of the passive chilled beams above a ceiling grille; these ones located in the Library on Level 2

12.10 Inner side of the south façade (Library area) showing natural ventilation flaps in the open position. Note also the grille strip for the trench heaters at floor level and the grillework in the ceiling allowing air to circulate around the passive chilled beams

handling units, ranging in capacity from 3.5 to 7.3m^3/s capacity. It is then distributed to the various levels via diffusers in the raised floor. Return air is taken out at ceiling level and returned to the plant room for heat recovery using thermal wheels, before being discharged to the outside. Natural ventilation is provided via a manually operated vent (Figure 12.10) located between the upper and lower halves of each of the cladding panels – opening this vent also actuates a motorised vent at high level and simultaneously turns off any local heating or cooling terminal units.

It was predicted that 'the annual energy consumption for the building's mechanical systems will be approximately a quarter of that required for a typical high-specification air-conditioned office building' (Foster *et al.*, 2002).

USERS' PERCEPTIONS OF THE BUILDING

Overall response

The building was surveyed in September 2006. For most of the 330 respondents (53 per cent female, 47 per cent male), the building was their normal place of business. They worked 4.8 days per week on

TABLE 12.1

Response rates for various floors of City Hall, London

Floor level	Number of respondents	Percentage of respondents
2	17	5.2
3	56	17.0
4	76	23.0
5	64	19.4
6	50	15.1
7	43	13.0
8	24	7.3
Total	330	100

Balcony and louvres at the Eden Foundation Building

13

The Foundation Building, Eden Project
St Austell, Cornwall, England

Sue Turpin-Brooks

THE CONTEXT

The Eden Project near St Austell is owned by the Eden Trust, a UK-registered charity. The world famous Biomes, landscaping, educational resources, and ancillary buildings provide a unique complex of educational and entertainment facilities within the heart of the 60m-deep disused Bodelva (china clay) Pit (Smit, 2001). 'The core statement of the charitable aims of the Eden Trust is "to promote public education and research in flora, fauna and other aspects of the natural environment"' (Eden Project, 2007). The education and research aspects include consideration of renewable energy and the protection and improvement of land and buildings.

Completed in December 2002, the 1800m² two-storey Foundation Building represents the third phase of the Eden Project and housesthe main administration offices and library at the northern edge of the clay pit.

The Eden Project has adopted a philosophy of undertaking sustainable development with all its buildings and at the time of its construction the Foundation Building was provided as a base for many of its staff. Subsequently, a further staff centre has been developed nearby and an innovative Educational Research Centre (known as the Core) was completed in 2006.

Located at around 50°N latitude, the local 1 per cent winter and summer design temperatures (these are for nearby Plymouth) are around -0.3°C and +22.1°C respectively (ASHRAE 2001: 27.52–3).

13.1 Cedar-clad west façade. Note the fixed aluminium louvred screen and the balcony extension in the centre

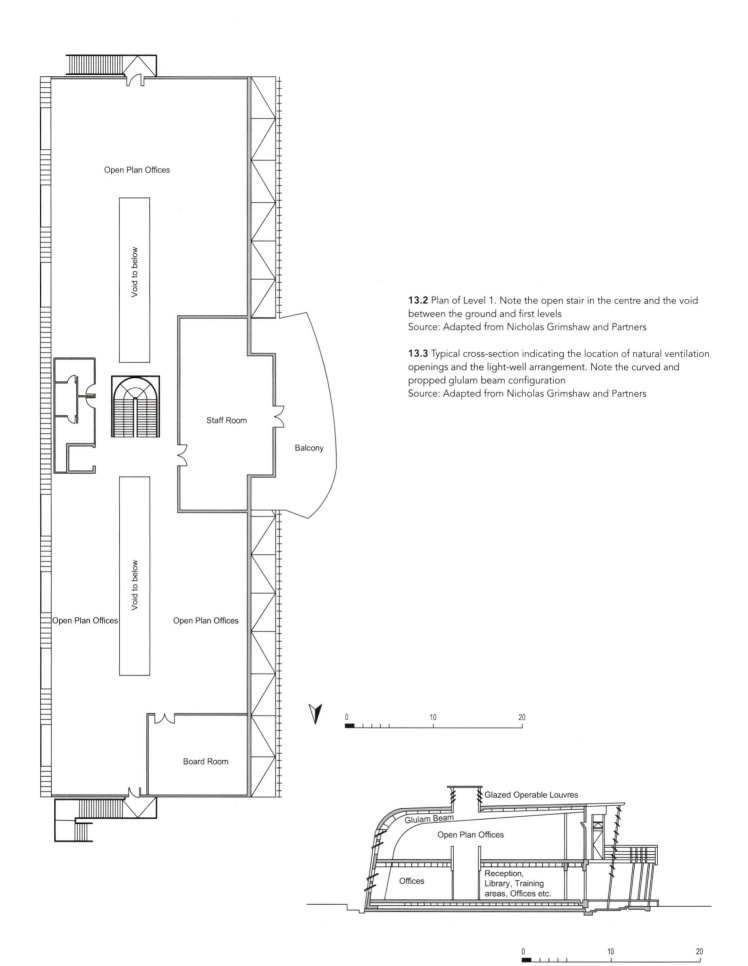

Open Plan Offices

Void to below

Staff Room

Balcony

Open Plan Offices

Void to below

Open Plan Offices

Board Room

13.2 Plan of Level 1. Note the open stair in the centre and the void between the ground and first levels
Source: Adapted from Nicholas Grimshaw and Partners

13.3 Typical cross-section indicating the location of natural ventilation openings and the light-well arrangement. Note the curved and propped glulam beam configuration
Source: Adapted from Nicholas Grimshaw and Partners

0   10   20

Glazed Operable Louvres

Glulam Beam

Open Plan Offices

Offices

Reception, Library, Training areas, Offices etc.

0   10   20

13.4 Cedar-clad north-facing gable end and aluminium-clad east façade and roof. The banking and trees to the left, but out of shot, provide some shading to the east-facing glazing. Note the row of rooflights just visible on top

13.5 Main ground floor reception area with the library area immediately beyond (in April 2004)

THE DESIGN PROCESS

Architects Nicholas Grimshaw and Partners had been appointed for the entire Eden Project, and given its aims and context it was to be expected that the design of the administration building would embody the scheme's overall environmental philosophy. Environmental and M&E consultants BDSP Partnership and structural engineers Anthony Hunt Associates completed the design team.

According to the architects, the project was designed to achieve the following:

> to be naturally ventilated (with the exception of the shower rooms and similar spaces where a degree of mechanical ventilation is essential); to be naturally lit as far as possible; to substantially increase levels of planting in the immediate site area; to incorporate water saving measures; to benefit from passive solar gain; to shelter the building by using planted shelter belts and reduced amounts of glazing in the north and east elevations; to use low embodied energy materials, where possible from a local source; to minimize the use of concrete; to use low energy appliances throughout; to exceed minimum insulation requirements by a significant margin; to

buy electricity from a green supplier; [and] to use recycled or recyclable materials as extensively as possible in the construction of the building.

> (Grimshaw and Partners Limited, 2002: 16)

This was the first project in which Grimshaws had formally used their in-house environmental management system – Environmentally Viable Architecture or EVA for short (Pawlyn, 2006). EVA enables the environmental impact of a project to be scored against a set of 12 indicators (broadly speaking, best practice scores +2; good practice +1; minimum standard 0; and substandard -1) (Grimshaw and Partners Limited, 2002: 5 and Appendix A). At practical completion, the Foundation Building had maintained a score of 16 out of a possible

13.6 Busy open-plan office area at the south end of the ground floor behind the library area – shot taken on a dull wet day in October 2005 with all artificial lighting in operation

13.7 Looking north along the central corridor of the northern half of the ground floor – meeting rooms and offices on either side. Note the air transfer grilles at ground floor ceiling level to enable air movement from these rooms, via the opening above and the louvred openings of the high-level rooflights, to outside

13.8 View from the northern half of Level 1 past the central area towards the southern end of that floor. Note the opening to the ground floor below and to the light-well above

24, or 67 per cent. The building also achieved an 'Excellent' rating in the BREEAM for Offices system.

The design process and architectural outcome have been described elsewhere in some detail (Birch, 2003; Grimshaw website; Turpin-Brooks and Viccars, 2006). What follows is the briefest of outlines.

THE DESIGN OUTCOME

The finished building has an aluminium-louvred front façade to the west and a centrally placed balcony at first floor level, extending the staff recreation space from the interior rest room and kitchen (Figure 13.1). Additionally, timber-decked terraces run along the 58m length of the building at this elevation. The building is raised off the ground on timber columns (on concrete pads) to avoid further excavation and concrete site slab work. The external breathable wall has achieved much better insulation standards than required under UK Building Regulations at the time, $0.13W.m^{-2}.K^{-1}$ (or an R-value of nearly $8m^2.°C/W$).

The structure comprises a 6m by 14m grid with a series of ten propped softwood glulam beams, creating high and open spaces (Figures 13.2 and 13.3). The timber used for the glulam is Swedish Whitewood, obtained from a sustainable source with the appropriate Chain of Custody. With the exception of the hidden ground floor glulam, the timber is left in its natural state. The exterior cladding uses durable western red cedar from Canada (Figures 13.1 and 13.4).

The ethos of the building was to provide a low embodied energy building with minimum energy in use, incorporating natural ventilation, natural light, and high levels of insulation using mainly Warmcel recycled newspaper, but with Rockwool slabs in less accessible places. The roof is shielded with Kalzip – a specialist aluminum sheeting which is mainly produced using non-fossil fuels or recycled material (Figure 13.4). The building aims to provide good air quality and views to the outside in all habitable rooms, and to provide a pleasant and healthy space for occupants.

The compartmentalisation of the building is achieved at the lower level and around key hazard areas such as the kitchen, with the majority of spaces being open plan. The ground floor houses the reception area, library, and an open-plan office in its southern half (Figures 13.5 and 13.6), with cellular offices and meeting rooms

13.9 Typical double-glazed wood-framed doors and windows – these are to a ground floor meeting room – indicating the range of opening sizes available and the provision of a trickle ventilator. Note the external walkway and fixed aluminium louvres, and the trench heater fitted at the inside perimeter

13.10 Exterior close-up of the rooflights

13.11 Interior close-up of a rooflight – Note the translucent top with interior Venetian blind arrangement, together with the translucent horizontal louvres and their actuators, and the heating pipe to mitigate the effect of potential downdrafts

accessed off a central corridor in the northern half (Figure 13.7). Upstairs, the space is mostly open-plan office areas, with WCs, staff rest room, kitchen, and balcony accessed centrally (Figure 13.8).

Large double-glazed windows (Figure 13.9) and openable roof lights let natural light into the building and enable natural ventilation to take place (Figure 13.10, as well as 13.7 and 13.8). There are automatic opening devices for the louvres in the high-level roof lights to permit ventilation (Figure 13.11). The artificial lighting system uses motion sensors to conserve energy.

The central heating system is a conventional low pressure hot water system, originally heated by a gas-fired condensing boiler, but since converted to biomass. Heat is distributed in the building via thermostatically valved radiators and trench heaters (Figure 13.9).

The ventilation system is controlled by three sensors on each floor that operate a series of louvres in the roof lights above the central atrium. When the set temperature is reached, the louvres are opened to allow hot air out and cooler air in. Sensors outside the building detect the wind direction and actuate the louvres on the opposite side of the rooflights to the wind direction.

USERS' PERCEPTIONS OF THE BUILDING

Two surveys were carried out in this building, the first in early 2004 after the building had been occupied for just over a year, the second in late 2006. During that period a number of changes had been made to the workspaces – specifically the number of people housed in the building had increased in line with the Eden Project's phenomenal growth, and furnishings were updated.

Overall response

For all of the 31 or so respondents in the 2004 survey (81 per cent female, 19 per cent male), the building was their normal place of business, working on average 4.8 days per week and 7.9 hours per day, of which around 6.9 were spent at their desk and 6.0 at a computer. The ratio of under-30s to over-30s was 23:77 per cent and over half (61 per cent) had worked in the building for more than a year at more or less the same desk or work area. Some 32 per cent worked with more than eight others, 58 per cent with from two to

Academic Towers

Offices

Double Height Space

Offices

Double Height Space

Offices

Double Height Space

Core

Atrium

Core

Plant

Plant

Tutorial Rooms

Teaching Block

14.1 Plan of Level 2
Source: Adapted from Architectus

14.2 Short cross-section
Source: Adapted from Architectus

0   10   20

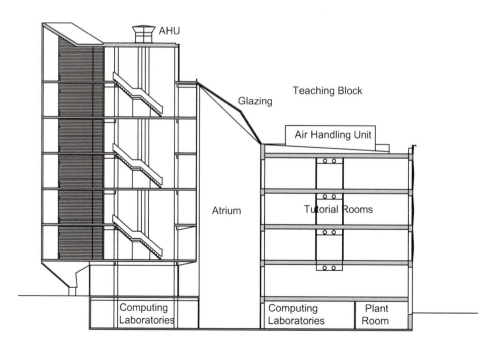

Academic Towers

AHU

Glazing

Teaching Block

Air Handling Unit

Atrium

Tutorial Rooms

Computing Laboratories

Computing Laboratories

Plant Room

14.3 The three Academic Towers viewed from the north

14.4 One of the double height spaces in an Academic Tower – note the vertical air supply and extract ducting and ventilation unit

14.5 Four-storey Teaching Wing to the right, north end services tower in the centre and one of the Academic Towers to the left of the shot

its flanking circulation towers runs the entire length of the building, links the two wings visually. Its sloping glazed roof is oriented to the south-west, while its glazed internal walls have openable windows to the adjoining Academic Towers and teaching wings, automated in the former case, manually operated in the latter. Within the atrium, centrally placed bridges, connected together by an open stairway from the ground floor, link the two main wings at each level.

14.6 Level 1 Computing Laboratory

14.7 Basement Level Computing Laboratory

14.8 General view into the Atrium – Teaching Wing to the left, Academic Towers to the right

Active environmental control systems

Heating throughout the campus is provided via a coal-fired MTHW (115°C) district heating system. Cooling is obtained from a naturally occurring aquifer under the site from which water is extracted at 12.5°C and returned at 18°C. The MSCS Building makes use of both of these systems, together with local mechanical ventilation plant. However, the design of the building is such that the offices and the majority of the adjacent seminar rooms in the Academic Towers are naturally ventilated and heated by a conventional radiator system. With their deliberately northerly orientation and fixed overhangs (Figure 14.9), exposed thermally massive interior walls and ceilings, fixed and adjustable exterior and adjustable interior solar shading devices, and large number of window/natural ventilation opening options, the 90 or so office modules in the Academic Towers are equipped with a full range of passive thermal environmental control systems (Figures 14.8 and 14.10).

A 1.8m³/s air handling unit is located on the top of each tower. These supply fresh air to the double-height spaces and the ground floor seminar rooms and offices (Figure 14.4). For its ventilation, the Atrium is dependent on infiltration of outside air via the entranceways and on any spill air from the adjacent spaces, with extract via automatically opening windows at high level on the sloping glazed roof (Figure 14.11).

Nine separate AHUs (ranging from 0.6 to 1.4 m³/s) in the basement serve the air-conditioned computing laboratories. The teaching wing is served by two 5.4 m³/s AHUs, each one serving around half the plan area of each floor. These are housed in separate roof-top plant rooms (Figure 14.11), positioned centrally over the areas served and the corresponding vertical distribution shaft. Supply air is distributed via the vertical shaft to then pass through horizontal 'ducting' formed in the concrete structural floor slab before being supplied to the space above though circular floor diffusers. The aim here is to make maximum use of the thermal mass of the slab in maintaining an even temperature within the teaching wing. The exterior rooms on these levels have radiators under the glazing and windows opening directly to the exterior or to the Atrium as appropriate.

All the thermal environmental control plant and motorized window openers are under the control of the University's computer-based building management system. Design temperatures are 25°C for most

of the air-conditioned spaces in summer (outside design temperature 28°C) and 20°C for all spaces other than the Atrium (target 16°C) in winter (outside design temperature 1°C).

A *User's Guide* (MSCS Building Information, 2007) advises academic staff on how to optimise conditions in their offices under different climatic conditions using the various shading devices and ventilation openings at their disposal – this is available via the web pages of the two departments.

USERS' PERCEPTIONS OF THE BUILDING

Overall response

In this case, responses were sought from both staff (academic, research, and administrative) and undergraduate students, the former using the standard questionnaire, the latter a shorter version.

For all of the 57 or so staff respondents (19 per cent female, 81 per cent male), the building was their normal place of work, most

14.9 North façade of one of the Academic Towers – note the range of configurations of the external (wooden) and internal (Venetian blinds) shading devices

14.10 Interior close-up of staff office façade showing upper window actuator

14.11 Overview of the roof with Teaching Block on the left, Academic Towers on the right, and glazed roof of the Atrium in between with Service Towers at each end. Note the housings for the two large AHUs on the Teaching Block and the smaller ones on top of each of the Academic Towers

TABLE 14.1

Average staff scores for each factor and whether they were significantly better, similar to, or worse than the BUS benchmarks (student scores in brackets)

OPERATIONAL FACTORS

Factor	Score	Worse	Similar	Better		Factor	Score	Worse	Similar	Better
Image to visitors	6.26			●		Cleaning	5.68			●
Space in building	5.26			●		Availability of meeting rooms	5.57			●
Space at desk – too little/much⁴	4.37			●		Suitability of storage arrangements	5.29			●
Furniture	5.64			●		Facilities meet work requirements	na			

ENVIRONMENTAL FACTORS

Temp and Air in Winter

Factor	Score	Worse	Similar	Better		Temp and Air in Summer	Score	Worse	Similar	Better
Temp Overall (5.43)	5.25			●		Temp Overall (5.35)	5.14			●
Temp – too hot/too cold⁴	4.17			●		Temp – too hot/too cold⁴	3.49			●
Temp – stable/variable⁴	4.04			●		Temp – stable/variable⁴	4.08			●
Air – still/draughty⁴	3.02	●				Air – still/draughty⁴	3.27			●
Air – dry/humid⁴	2.91	●				Air – dry/humid⁴	3.22	●		
Air – fresh/stuffy¹	3.56			●		Air – fresh/stuffy¹	3.25			●
Air – odourless/smelly¹	2.87			●		Air – odourless/smelly¹	2.80			●
Air Overall (5.03)	5.07			●		Air Overall (5.03)	5.23			●

Lighting / Noise

Lighting	Score	Worse	Similar	Better		Noise	Score	Worse	Similar	Better
Lighting Overall (5.33)	5.17			●		Noise Overall (5.00)	5.39			●
Natural light – too little/much⁴	4.18		●			From colleagues – too little/much⁴	3.98			●
Sun & Sky Glare – none/too much¹	4.46	●				From other people – too little/much⁴	3.91			●
Artificial light – too little/much⁴	3.93		●			From inside – too little/much⁴	4.27			●
Art'l light glare – none/too much¹	2.95			●		From outside – too little/much⁴	4.07		●	
						Interruptions – none/frequent¹	5.39			●

CONTROL FACTORS [b] / SATISFACTION FACTORS

Control Factor	%	Score	Worse	Similar	Better		Satisfaction Factor	Score	Worse	Similar	Better
Heating	51%	4.14			●		Design (5.25)	5.61			●
Cooling	42%	3.44			●		Needs (5.56)	5.80			●
Ventilation	51%	5.23			●		Comfort Overall (5.44)	5.86			●
Lighting	46%	5.09			●		Productivity %	+9.80			●
Noise	40%	3.18			●		Health	4.52			●

NOTES: (a) unless otherwise noted, a score of 7 is 'best'; superscript ⁴ implies a score of 4 is best, superscript ¹ implies a score of 1 is best; (b) the per cent values listed here are the percentages of respondents who thought personal control of that aspect was important.

TABLE 14.2

Numbers of staff respondents offering positive, balanced, and negative comments
on nine aspects of performance (student responses to three aspects in brackets)

Aspect	Number of respondents			
	Positive	Balanced	Negative	Total
Design	13 (21)	3 (2)	6 (11)	22 (34)
Needs	2	1	3	6
Comfort Overall	2	0	7	9
Noise Overall	1 (0)	3 (0)	15 (29)	19 (29)
Lighting Overall	2	2	15	19
Productivity	3	7	1	11
Health	5	3	0	8
Work well	21	–	–	21
Hinder	–	–	29	29
General Environmental	(1)	(1)	(32)	(34)
(students only)	49	19	76	144
TOTALS (STAFF ONLY)	34	13	53	100
PER CENT	273	187	994	1454
PER CENT (Staff only)	18.8	12.9	68.3	100

(86 per cent) working 5 days per week or more, and averaging 7.7 hours per day. The majority (some 68 per cent) were over 30 and had worked in the building for more than a year, some 56 per cent at the same desk or work area. Hours per day spent at desk and computer averaged 5.8 and 4.8 respectively. Over 60 per cent worked alone while most of the rest shared with just one other colleague.

While the question was not asked directly, it was obvious that the vast majority of the 205 students who responded were under 30 – with 42 per cent female and 58 per cent male.

The average scores of the staff and students for each of the relevant survey questions are listed in Table 14.1. Table 14.1 also indicates those aspects of the building that the staff perceived as being significantly better, similar to, or worse than the benchmark and/or scale mid-point. Overall, some 37 aspects were significantly better, four were significantly worse, while the remaining four aspects had much the same score as the benchmark. Overall, these were exceptionally good results, causing even our analyst to query them given that this was the first such survey we had undertaken.

Significant factors

Given the good results overall, it mainly remains to highlight those factors that were particularly excellent, and those few exceptions.

All of the operational factors were significantly better than their respective benchmarks, with the score for building image the highest of this group, with an average value of 6.26.

Similarly, most of the environmental factors rated better than their corresponding benchmarks. Exceptions to this occurred in winter when, despite high overall comfort scores, staff perceived the air as slightly too still and dry; and their responses suggested there was too much glare from sun and sky (a score of 4.46 compared with an ideal of 4.00).

Scores for control factors averaged 4.21 (compared to a relatively low benchmark of around 2.60 at that time). All were better than their individual benchmarks, control of ventilation (5.23) and lighting (5.09) scoring particularly well. The proportion of respondents deeming personal control as important averaged a relatively high 46 per cent.

Average perception scores for the satisfaction factors were all well above their respective benchmarks and scale mid-points.

Student perceptions (responses to only eight overall variables were sought in the shorter student questionnaire) were mostly lower than those of the staff, but none dropped below 5.00.

Users' comments

Overall, some 144 responses were received from staff under the nine headings where they were able to add written comments – some 28 per cent of the 513 potential (57 respondents by nine headings). Table 14.2 indicates the numbers of positive, balanced, and negative comments – in this case around 34 per cent were positive, 13 per cent neutral, and 53 per cent negative.

While lighting overall rated highly, glare from the sun made up the majority of the negative comments on lighting (11 out of 15 received) and a significant number of the hinder comments (10 of the 29 received). This corresponds to the relatively poor rating of this aspect of lighting on the 7-point scale – low angle winter sun on computer screens in the middle of the day seemed to be the main issue. Negative comments on noise were mainly focused on internal noise – from nearby offices, meetings in the adjacent common space, and from colleagues on the phone (but with their office doors open) – though the scores for these factors were all better than their respective benchmarks. No other particular patterns emerged from the comments.

While the design of the building attracted a good number of positive comments from staff and students, comments on noise were almost entirely negative – the sounds from computers, other people, and the HVAC system being recurring themes. Asked to add any further comments on the environmental conditions, those received were predominantly negative, with a few mentioning the floor vents in that context.

Overall performance indices

The Comfort Index, based on the scores for comfort overall, noise, lighting, temperature, and air quality, works out at +2.43, while the Satisfaction Index, based on the design, needs, health, and perceived productivity scores, is +2.36, both significantly higher than the scale mid-point (noting these indices are scaled from -3 to +3).

The Summary Index, being the average of these, works out at 2.39, while the Forgiveness Factor, calculated to be 1.11 in this instance, indicates that staff as a whole are likely to be relatively more tolerant of minor shortcomings in individual aspects such as winter and summer temperatures, air quality, lighting, and noise (a factor of 1 being the mid-point on a scale that normally ranges from 0.8 to 1.2).

In terms of the Ten-Factor Rating Scale, the building was at the top of the 'Exceptional' band of the 7-point scale, thanks to a calculated percentage value of 100 per cent. When All-Factors were taken into account, the percentage value worked out at 90 per cent, still comfortably within the 'Exceptional' band.

OTHER REPORTED ASPECTS OF PERFORMANCE

Annual energy use

Heating via the central boiler system was separately (BTU) metered for the MSCS Building and amounted to some 780,700kWh for the year 2001, the system operating from February to October and from 6.00am to 9.00pm, Monday through Friday. Annual electricity use amounted to some 875,011kWh. Thus the overall AEUI worked out to be 143kWh/m^2.yr. This was estimated to consist of approximately 47 per cent heating, 28 per cent equipment (there were around 660 computers operating in the building), 15 per cent lighting (the lighting power density was just under 10W/m^2), 3 per cent fans and pumps, and 7 per cent miscellaneous.

Summer and winter inside temperatures

Inside (in the staff offices mainly) and outside temperatures were measured from December 2000 to February 2001, and during June and July 2001. During the summer period, the highest inside temperature recorded was 26°C (mid-afternoon in one of the top floor offices), the lowest 13.3°C (overnight). During winter, with heating on during weekdays, the lowest temperature measured was 14°C (again overnight) and the highest 24.3°C. Overall, it was found that the level of control given to the occupants allowed a range of temperatures to be achieved, depending on the preferences of the occupants. See Baird and Kendall (2003) for further detail of this aspect.

ACKNOWLEDGEMENTS

My particular thanks go to Patrick Clifford of Architectus and Dave Fullbrook of Arups for speaking so openly about the design of the building. Many people at the University of Canterbury have been of great assistance – it is my pleasure to acknowledge the help of the following: Doug Lloyd and Robbie Lancaster, Assistant Engineer and Operations Supervisor respectively, and their colleagues at Works and Services; Tim Bell and Doug Bridges, Heads of Departments of Computer Science and of Mathematics and Statistics respectively, and their staff.

REFERENCES

Architectus (1998) 'Meeting in Light', *Architecture New Zealand*, July/August: 36–49.

ASHRAE (2001) *ASHRAE Handbook: Fundamentals, SI Edition*, Atlanta, GA: American Society of Heating Refrigerating and Air-Conditioning Engineers.

Baird, G. and Kendall, C. (2003) 'The MSCS Building, Christchurch – A Case Study of Integrated Passive Design, Low Energy Use, Comfortable Environment, and Outstanding User Satisfaction', in *Proceedings of IRHACE Annual Technical Conference*, Hamilton, April 2003, pp. 60–8.

Clifford, P. (2000) Transcript of interview held on 19 October 2000, Auckland.

De Kretser, A .H. (ed.) (2004) *Architectus*, Auckland: The New Zealand Architectural Publications Trust.

Fullbrook, D. (2000) Transcript of interview held on 28 September 2000, Wellington.

Johnston, L. (2002) 'Mathematical Formula', *Architectural Review Australia*, 080(Winter): 58–65.

MSCS Building Information (2007) available at: www.cosc.canterbury.ac.nz/open/dept/dept.shtml (user name and password required for access).

Spence, R. (1998) 'Seductive', *Architecture New Zealand*, September/October: 84–90.

South façades of St Mary's Credit Union

15
St Mary's Credit Union
Navan, Ireland

THE CONTEXT

Completed in August 2005, this five-storey building (Figure 15.1) has a floor area of around 1300m². It is located in the town centre of Navan (population around 25,000), a Primary Growth Centre some 50km north-east of Dublin in Ireland's County Meath, at the confluence of the Rivers Blackwater and Boyne.

15.1 The new five-storey building, with the original 1980s building in the foreground

The building houses the banking hall and offices of the St Mary's Navan Credit Union, a long-established financial services provider with a membership that includes most of the population of the area. The Credit Union's operation had outgrown its original two-storey 1980s building on the same site, built when the organisation had around 6000 members and six staff. In the intervening period, the membership had grown to over 20,000. The new building was designed to house some 20 staff and allow for increased membership and services commensurate with the predicted growth in population.

The latitude of the town is around 54°N and local 1 per cent winter and summer design temperatures (these are for nearby Dublin) are -0.4°C and +20.6°C respectively (ASHRAE 2001: 27.36–7).

The building has won the An Taisce Ellison Award. The design process and architectural outcome have been described elsewhere in some detail (Leech, 2005a, 2005b). What follows is the briefest of outlines.

THE DESIGN PROCESS

The design of the building was undertaken by the small specialist Dublin-based architectural practice Paul Leech: Gaia Ecotecture. The team was led by Paul Leech, a graduate of University College Dublin in both Engineering and Architecture, a founding member of Gaia International and an advocate of holistic design (Leech, 2006). Director Sally Starbuck was the job architect and detailed mechanical and electrical services design was provided by consulting engineers Derham McPhillips.

While one might expect that an owner-occupying client would take a long-term view concerning any proposals for a new building, nevertheless, major design decisions were subject to rigorous value engineering and the intense scrutiny of the Building Committee of the Credit Union's Board of Directors. Earlier in his career Leech had established a practice in Navan and during his period there (1979 to 1987) had designed the original Credit Union building. Now, some 20 years later, he was engaged to undertake the design of the new premises, and was determined that this would be an exemplar ecological office building (Leech, 2005a) – this was not going to be a conventional developer-conceived office block.

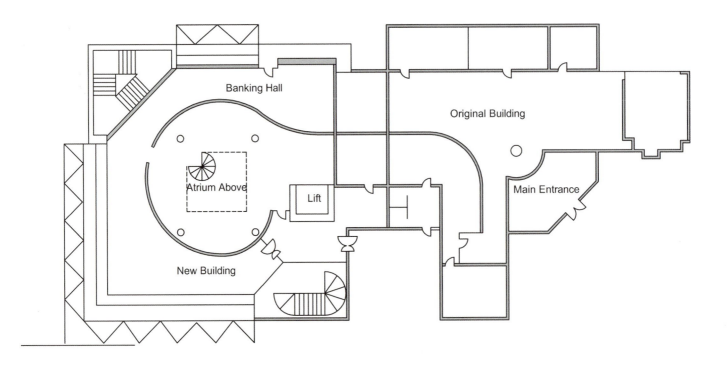

15.2 Ground floor plan – new building on the left, original on the right
Source: Adapted from Gaia Ecotecture

15.3 Cross-sectional view of new building – note the undercroft area, atrium, venturi device, and solar chimney, configured to enable natural ventilation
Source: Adapted from Gaia Ecotecture

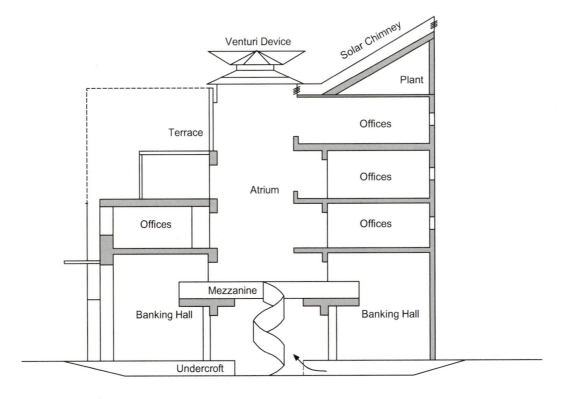

15.4 View looking down through the atrium from Level 5 to the Banking Hall

15.5 Inside the staff area of the banking hall – the spiral stair leads up to the mezzanine level, and down to the undercroft area

Achieving this aim was never going to be easy – from enduring the protracted process involved in obtaining planning permission for such a building and overcoming the resistance of the market to change, to meeting the challenges of coordinating a project which eschewed conventional construction materials, products, and methods. However, with a combination of determination on the part of the design team, the support of fellow members of Gaia

15.6 Level 4 with offices to the left and right of shot and outdoor area in the centre background on the other side of the atrium opening

15.7 Close-up of the south-west façade of the upper three levels – note the clay tile rain-screen, the double windows with air inlet grilles under, and the outdoor area on Level 4. The top of the venturi device is just visible at the top of the shot

15.8 Close-up of banking hall double façade – exterior screen of naturally shading wisteria plants at a very early stage

International during the design development phase, specialist input from researchers at Strathclyde and Brighton Universities, and the selection of main contractor P. J. Hegarty 'not on the basis of lowest initial price but on a total profile of quality and a preparedness to take on the challenges of innovation and adopt a partnership approach with the design team', the project was completed in 16 months by August 2005 (Leech, 2005a).

THE DESIGN OUTCOME

Building layout, construction, and passive environmental control systems

The basic plan of this five-storey building is a nine-square grid (Leech, 2005b), roughly 15m by 15m, oriented on the diagonal to the cardinal points of the compass (Figure 15.2). The central 'square' of the grid forms a full-height atrium space (Figure 15.3), designed to enable natural ventilation of the surrounding spaces and daylight penetration to the interior of the building – the atrium 'slopes' slightly to enhance the latter (Figure 15.4).

The ground floor banking hall is a double-height space with a mezzanine level (Figure 15.5), while the three floors above contain offices, meeting rooms, and other ancillary spaces (Figure 15.6). It is linked at ground level to the original building which houses the main boardroom.

With the design team's commitment to minimising embodied energy, its main structure and construction are predominantly dense pine, even to the extent of the lift shaft, but with other materials used where appropriate. The exterior rain-screen, for example (Figure 15.7), is comprised of 30mm-thick cavity clay tiles, while the heavy duty glazing bars of the venturi device at the top of the atrium are aluminium.

The building orientation means that south-east and south-west façades are 'available' to pick up solar heat gains. The glazing on these façades is designed to do just that, while the northerly façades have considerably less. In the long term, shading of the extensive glazing of the banking hall façades is to be provided by deciduous wisteria plants growing on an exterior screen (Figure 15.8) – with judicious deployment of the perforated security shutters serving that purpose in the interim.

15.9 Interior view of the double façade of the banking hall – note the automated window openers and trickle vents (see upper right) and the grilles for the heating/cooling terminal units built located at the bottom of the façade

15.10 Close-up of the lower part of the banking hall façade. The smaller lower set of grilles are the air inlets to the undercroft plenum, while the larger horizontal louvres just under the windows are the air inlets to the trickle ventilators in the double façade

Finally, in this brief outline, particular attention was given to getting the construction airtight – a prerequisite for effective control and operation of the natural ventilation systems. The architects had noted on return visits to the original 1980s building that the management, being conscious of security issues, rarely ventilated with windows, for fear of leaving them open overnight. There had been some minor problems of overheating and poor air quality as a result. The banking hall is extremely busy with many members calling in briefly daily, with wet coats, etc. Hence, the natural ventilation strategy was developed very early on to improve comfort for members and staff.

Leech (2005a) sees the whole building as 'a passively heated device'; with the double façade (Figures 15.8 and 15.9) of the banking hall and the double windows on the upper levels the main source of solar heat gain. These are also designed to enable trickle ventilation in winter, purging (of unwanted solar heat gains) in high summer, and ventilating appropriate to climatic conditions and user requirements the rest of the time.

In addition, openings around the perimeter (Figure 15.10) act as air intakes to a 1.4m high undercroft, via which air is ducted into the building at low level. At high level, atop the atrium, air is normally extracted via a specially designed venturi device with automated louvred openings responsive to the wind direction (Figures 15.11 and 15.12). A solar chimney has also been fitted at the top of the atrium to extract air during times when it is sunny but calm (Figure 15.13).

Active environmental control systems

Active heating is provided by means of three gas-fired modular condensing boilers located in the rooftop plant room and serving terminal units distributed throughout the building, while active cooling is via a gas-fired heat pump also located in the rooftop plant room.

Hot water for the building is provided by means of an evacuated tube solar panel on the roof, while alongside it a modest photovoltaic set up is used to power the building's pumps, fans, and natural ventilation control systems (Figure 15.13). The programmable control system itself, with input from the rooftop weather station and

15.11 External view of the rooftop venturi device located above the atrium. Designed to provide daylighting as well as the exhaust outlet for the natural ventilation of the building, the opening areas (see on left, for example) are dependent on wind direction

15.12 Underside of the venturi device with automated louvre arrangement visible

15.13 The sloping roof of the plant room housing the gas-fired modular condensing boiler set and heat pump. The solar chimney is in the centre of shot with the 'weather station' at its top; evacuated tube solar water heater to the left: photo-voltaic panels to the right

monitoring throughout the building, actuates the relevant louvres and double window devices to maximise the utilisation of ambient conditions and minimise the use of the active systems (the boilers and the heat pump). Considerable and sustained effort has been put into the commissioning and fine tuning of the control system to optimise its operation through the different seasons of the year and some effort made to quantify the contribution of the various passive and solar systems to the energy balance of the building during its first few months of operation (Leech, 2005c).

Rainwater is collected and stored in an underground tank for use in the irrigation of the extensive internal and external landscaping, and in the dual mode flush toilets.

USERS' PERCEPTIONS OF THE BUILDING

Overall response
The building was surveyed in September 2006. For all of the 14 or so respondents (92 per cent female, 8 per cent male), the building was their normal place of business, working on average 4.6 days per week and 8.1 hours per day, of which around 6.5 were spent at their desk and at a computer. The ratio of under-30s to over-30s was 54:46 per cent and most (77 per cent) had worked in the building for more than a year at more or less the same desk or work area. Some 50 per cent worked together in the open banking hall area while the rest had single offices or shared with one other colleague.

Significant factors
Table 15.1 lists the scores for each of the survey questions and indicates those aspects of the building that the staff perceived as being significantly better, similar to, or worse than the benchmark and/or scale mid-point. In this case some 24 aspects were significantly better, only two were significantly worse, while the remaining 19 aspects had much the same score as the benchmark.

In terms of the eight operational aspects, this building scores better than the benchmark in six instances, and the same in the other two – and equal to or above the mid-point of the scale in every case. With scores of 6.77 and 6.17 respectively, cleaning and image were particularly high.

TABLE 15.1

Average scores for each factor and whether they were significantly better, similar to, or worse than the BUS benchmarks

	Score	Worse	Similar	Better		Score	Worse	Similar	Better
OPERATIONAL FACTORS									
Image to visitors	6.17			•	Cleaning	6.77			•
Space in building	5.15			•	Availability of meeting rooms	6.54			•
Space at desk – too little/much⁴	4.36		•		Suitability of storage arrangements	3.85		•	
Furniture	4.91		•		Facilities meet requirements	5.73			•
ENVIRONMENTAL FACTORS									
Temp and Air in Winter					Temp and Air in Summer				
Temp Overall	5.33			•	Temp Overall	4.83			•
Temp – too hot/too cold⁴	4.30		•		Temp – too hot/too cold⁴	3.90			•
Temp – stable/variable⁴	3.78		•		Temp – stable/variable⁴	4.90	•		
Air – still/draughty⁴	4.27		•		Air – still/draughty⁴	3.89			•
Air – dry/humid⁴	4.33		•		Air – dry/humid⁴	4.50		•	
Air – fresh/stuffy¹	4.00		•		Air – fresh/stuffy¹	4.25		•	
Air – odourless/smelly¹	3.40		•		Air – odourless/smelly¹	3.55		•	
Air Overall	4.92			•	Air Overall	5.00			•
Lighting					**Noise**				
Lighting Overall	4.92			•	Noise Overall	5.85			•
Natural light – too little/much⁴	4.08			•	From colleagues – too little/much⁴	4.00			•
Sun & Sky Glare – none/too much¹	4.42	•			From other people – too little/much⁴	4.23		•	
Artificial light – too little/much⁴	3.67		•		From inside – too little/much⁴	4.09			•
Art'l light glare – none/too much¹	3.25			•	From outside – too little/much⁴	3.58		•	
					Interruptions – none/frequent¹	3.18			•

	%	Score	Worse	Similar	Better		Score	Worse	Similar	Better
CONTROL FACTORS [b]						**SATISFACTION FACTORS**				
Heating	29%	4.17		•		Design	5.62			•
Cooling	29%	4.69			•	Needs	5.50			•
Ventilation	14%	4.00		•		Comfort Overall	5.67			•
Lighting	14%	4.05		•		Productivity %	+10.83			•
Noise	14%	3.46		•		Health	4.67			•

NOTES: (a) unless otherwise noted, a score of 7 is 'best'; superscript ⁴ implies a score of 4 is best, superscript ¹ implies a score of 1 is best; (b) the per cent values listed here are the percentages of respondents who thought personal control of that aspect was important.

TABLE 15.2

Numbers of respondents offering positive, balanced, and negative comments on 12 performance factors

Aspect	Number of respondents			
	Positive	Balanced	Negative	Total
Overall Design	4	0	1	5
Needs Overall	0	0	2	2
Meeting Rooms	0	1	1	2
Storage	0	0	7	7
Desk/Work Area	1	0	2	3
Comfort	0	0	0	0
Noise Sources	0	2	1	3
Lighting Conditions	0	3	3	6
Productivity	1	0	1	2
Health	2	0	2	4
Work Well	7	–	–	7
Hinder	–	–	8	8
TOTALS (Staff only)	15	6	28	49
PER CENT (Staff only)	30.6	12.2	57.1	100.0

Overall scores for temperature and air in both summer and winter were all considerably higher than their corresponding benchmarks and the scale mid-point, while individual aspects mostly achieved scores around the benchmark or scale mid-point, though with summer temperatures on the variable side.

While lighting overall scored better than the benchmark and scale mid-point, staff indicated there was glare from sun and sky. Noise overall scored very high, at 5.85 – clearly a relatively quiet environment has been achieved, despite the open nature of the building and its banking hall function.

Only 29 per cent of staff rated personal control of heating and cooling as important, even fewer (14 per cent) in the case of the other aspects – the scores for these were all well above their respective benchmarks. Perceptions of the satisfaction variables (design, needs, overall comfort, productivity, and health) were all significantly better than their respective benchmarks, and all were higher than the scale mid-point.

Users' comments

Overall, some 49 responses were received from staff under the 12 headings where they were able to add written comments – some 29.2 per cent of the 168 potential (14 respondents by 12 headings). Table 15.2 indicates the numbers of positive, balanced and negative comments – in this case, around 30.6 per cent were positive, 12.2 per cent balanced, and 57.1 per cent negative.

Lack of storage was the most common complaint, echoing its relatively moderate score under operational aspects. The operation of the light sensors came in for some comment, but no other issues appeared to predominate.

Overall performance indices

The Comfort Index, based on the comfort overall, noise, lighting, temperature, and air quality scores, works out at +1.71; while the Satisfaction Index, based on the design, needs, health, and perceived productivity scores, is +1.75, noting that the scale mid-point in these instances is zero on a -3 to +3 scale.

The Summary Index, being the average of the Comfort and Satisfaction Indices, works out at +1.73, while the Forgiveness Factor, calculated to be 1.10 in this instance, indicates that staff are likely to be relatively more tolerant of minor shortcomings in individual aspects such as winter and summer temperatures, air quality, lighting, and noise (a factor of 1 being the mid-point on a scale that normally ranges from 0.80 to 1.20).

In terms of the Ten-Factor Rating Scale, the building was 'Exceptional' on the 7-point scale with a calculated percentage value of 100 per cent. When All-Factors were taken into account, the percentage value worked out at 78 per cent – in the middle of the 'Good Practice' band.

ACKNOWLEDGEMENTS

I must express my gratitude to Jim Watters, Chief Executive Officer, for granting permission for me to undertake this survey. Particular thanks go to Lorraine Fox, Michael Cahill, and Caoimhin O'Maollalaigh for their generous assistance with various aspects of the study during my visits to the building, to Kaethe Burt-O'Dea for helping with the distribution and collection of the questionnaires, and to Paul Leech for assisting my understanding of the building and its underlying design.

REFERENCES

ASHRAE (2001) *ASHRAE Handbook: Fundamentals, SI Edition*, Atlanta, GA: American Society of Heating Refrigerating and Air-Conditioning Engineers.

Leech, P. D. (2005a) 'Navan Credit Union: Redefining the Boundaries of Sustainable Building', *ConstructIreland*, 2: 11, see also www.constructireland. ie/Vol-2-Issue11/Articles/Design-Approaches/Redefining-Building-Boundaries.html (accessed 12 September 2008).

Leech, P. D. (2005b) 'Eco-office Building: Realised Project: Navan: Ireland', in *Proceedings of the 2005 World Renewable Energy Conference (SB05)*, Tokyo, September 2005, Paper 01-136, pp. 948–55.

Leech, P. D. (2005c) 'Primary Energy', available at: www.constructireland.ie/ articles/navanresults.php (accessed 9 September 2007).

Leech, P. D. (2006) Transcript of interview held on 28 August 2006, London.

Inner façades and partitions at Scottsdale Ecocentre

16

Scottsdale Forest Ecocentre
Tasmania, Australia

THE CONTEXT

Completed in 2002, this three-storey building (14m tall at its highest point) has a floor area of around 1100m². It is located at the western approach to the town of Scottsdale which is some 68km from Launceston in the north-east of Tasmania at a latitude of 41°S.

The building houses the offices of Forestry Tasmania, an outlet of the Tasmanian Visitor Information Network, a café, gift shop, and interpretative displays. The clients had originally envisaged 'two separate buildings – an office building and a visitor centre – side by side' (Norrie, 2003). The architect, however, with a strong background in the design of conservatories (Morris-Nunn, 2005), has combined these functions 'one inside the other' (Figure 16.1).

The clients were Forestry Tasmania and the local Dorset Council. The former is responsible for the offices, café, and gift shop (with over 40 staff, around half of whom may be working in the building at any one time); the latter for the Visitor Centre staffed mainly by volunteers (typically one or two on duty for one or two days per week).

The building has won several awards, taking no less than three major RAIA Tasmanian Architecture Awards in 2003 (for Commercial Architecture, Environmental Design, and Innovative Use of Steel, respectively) as well the Environmental Design Award category of the 2003 RAIA National Architecture Awards.

16.1 Truncated cone-shaped exterior envelope, with orthogonal office structure visible within

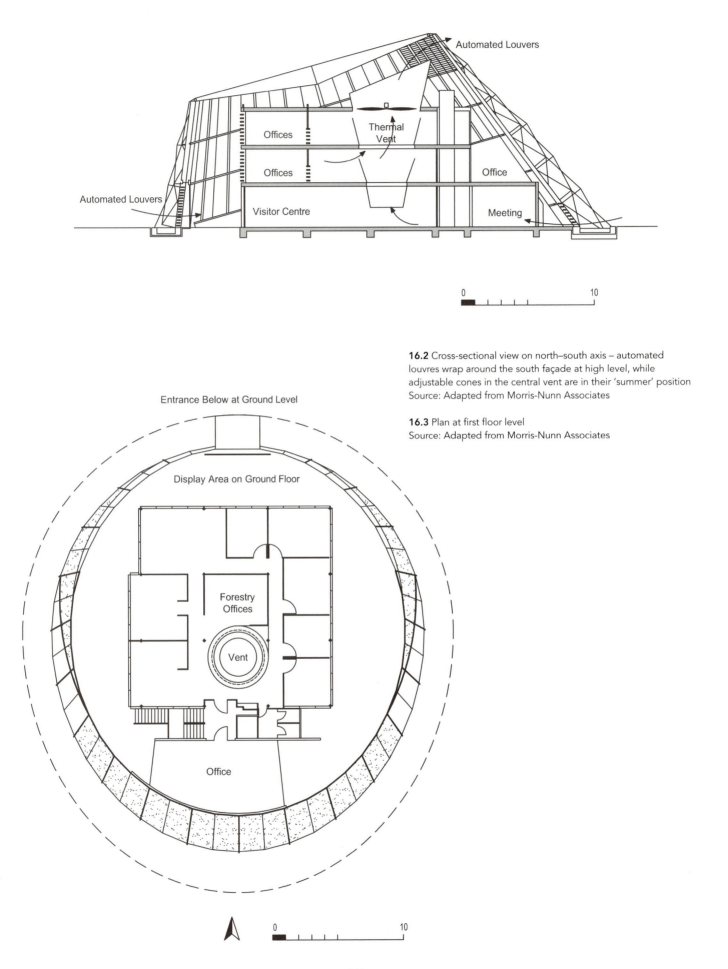

Automated Louvers

Offices

Thermal Vent

Office

Automated Louvers

Offices

Visitor Centre

Meeting

0   10

16.2 Cross-sectional view on north–south axis – automated louvres wrap around the south façade at high level, while adjustable cones in the central vent are in their 'summer' position
Source: Adapted from Morris-Nunn Associates

16.3 Plan at first floor level
Source: Adapted from Morris-Nunn Associates

Entrance Below at Ground Level

Display Area on Ground Floor

Forestry Offices

Vent

Office

0   10

164

16.4 Café area with exterior envelope to the left and office façade above right – note use of 'exterior' gas radiant heaters

16.5 View down through the circular vent from second floor office area to reception desk on the ground floor – note cord and pulley system used to adjust the position of the cones

THE DESIGN PROCESS

The design team for the building comprised local architect Robert Morris-Nunn of Hobart together with, *inter alia*, Sydney-based environmental design specialists Advanced Environmental Concepts.

Given his extensive experience in the design of large-scale conservatories, the architect was convinced of their environmental control potential as building enclosures. Interestingly, and unknown to him, at around the same time as the Scottsdale EcoCentre was being conceived, this potential was also being explored, albeit on a much larger scale, at the 13,000m² footprint Government Training Centre at Herne-Sodingen in Germany's Ruhr Valley (Kugel, 1999).

According to the architects, 'The building was conceived in its final shape from the outset; the external cone shape in order to reduce the overall surface area of the outer skin, and a three storey habitable building located within it' (Morris-Nunn and Associates, 2005) (Figure 16.1). Nevertheless, before submitting it to Forestry Tasmania in 1999, its environmental control potential was verified by Advanced Environmental Concepts – the subsequent model and report won the limited design competition (Morris-Nunn, 2005).

Realisation of the environmental control potential of the concept was then the subject of extensive computer modelling, resulting in the development of the circular internal vent as an air transfer device 'to encourage natural ventilation in summer and recirculate warm air in winter' (Spence, 2002: 2) (Figures 16.2 and 16.3).

The fact that there was very little in the budget for any research and development put very great pressure on the design team. However, subsequent to its construction, and thanks to the EcoCentre winning the 2002 Australasian Timber Design Award, the architect was able to visit and experience its rather larger cousin in the Ruhr.

16.6 External view of low-level automated louvres on west façade

16.7 Manually adjustable sliding windows on inner (Forestry Office) façade

16.8 Ground floor – Visitor Centre displays to the left and reception desk to the right – note that the red fabric cone above the reception area is fixed

THE DESIGN OUTCOME

Building layout and construction

As succinctly expressed by Spence (2002: 4), 'The building consists of an inner, orthogonal, steel and timber framed and glazed three storey office structure (approximately 15m square), enclosed by a truncated, largely translucent cone (of around 28m diameter) at its base' (Figure 16.3). The cone-shaped outer wall of timber, polycarbonate, and glass encloses the exhibition space and café in the form of a conservatory with indoor planting (Figure 16.4).

According to the architects (Morris-Nunn and Associates, 2005), 'Its external shape was determined by the desire to create the largest enclosed internal volume in relation to its external surface area.' In Spence's view (2002: 5), the design of the outer skin, in terms of the choice and disposition of materials, the tilt of the cone towards the north, and the location of adjustable louvres were 'an exercise in maximising solar gain and minimising heat loss in winter, while reducing excessive solar gain in summer'.

The roof material is a translucent double skin (with an air gap between the two skins) of a Teflon-coated fibreglass fabric. In addition, and essential to the realisation of the natural ventilation and thermal control concept, was the circular vent running the full height of the building in the centre of the offices (Figure 16.5).

Exposed concrete and stone paving on the ground floor and the concrete blockwork around the (as yet unused) lift shaft provide potentially useful thermal mass, while the lift shaft itself acts as a sort of cool air reservoir (Morris-Nunn, 2005).

Passive and active environmental control systems

As originally conceived and built, thermal environmental control of the building was to be achieved through a combination of high and low level automated louvred openings on the external envelope (Figure 16.6), manually adjustable sliding windows on the inner envelope (Figure 16.7), transfer grilles on the office doors (Figure 16.9), and cones in the vent running up the centre of the offices (Figure 16.8), with a reversible fan at the top (Figure 16.11), enabling air to be transferred as appropriate to the prevailing climatic conditions; together with small under-sill electric heaters in the offices.

16.9 Office floor internal corridor – note adjustable cone in 'winter' position (on left) and transfer grilles in the office doors (on right)

16.10 Second floor – typical four-person office layout – note ceiling-mounted air supply grill from retrofitted air-conditioning system

16.11 Second floor – reversible fan located at the top of the circular vent (switch located on adjacent wall) – adjustable cone in 'summer' position

In winter, for example, all the external louvred openings would be shut and the warm air generated in the 'conservatory' would rise to the top before being transferred back down the vent (with its fabric cones in the upper position – see Figure 16.9) and through the offices. The under-sill heaters provide early morning heat-up and the external louvres would operate to provide an appropriate fresh air quality, as determined by CO_2 levels in the café and office areas (Figure 16.10).

The external louvres are split between the east and west façades (Figure 16.6) at low level, while at high level they are on the southerly facing façade (Figure 16.3). Under summer conditions, all of these would be open, and through stack effect or appropriate operation of the fan, air would be drawn upwards through the central vent (this time with the fabric cones in their lower position – see Figure 16.11) to cool the building.

The system is computer-controlled – with the main display screen indicating, *inter alia*, temperatures and relative humidities outside, in the 'conservatory' space, and in all three office levels; carbon dioxode levels in the café and in the offices; and the degree of opening of each set of exterior vents. The fabric cones in the central vent are changed manually between their summer and winter positions using a system of cords and pulleys (Figure 16.5). In the event, some overestimation of the thermal properties of the teflon roof and the polycarbonate exterior wall cladding led to some overheating in the top floor offices and glare issues, leading to the installation of a small air-conditioning system in the top floor offices (Figure 16.10) and some shade-sails being hung in the 'conservatory' areas.

As an aside, lest the reader thinks that providing for natural ventilation out in the country has to be inherently easier than in town, in practice, the designer has to contend with the very real possibility that adjacent pastures may be subject to chemical spray and other treatments that can easily have an effect on the ambient outdoor air quality.

USERS' PERCEPTIONS OF THE BUILDING
Surveyed in July 2005, this building accommodated two distinct user groups: the Forestry Office staff and the Visitor Centre staff (mainly volunteers). Their responses will be discussed in parallel.

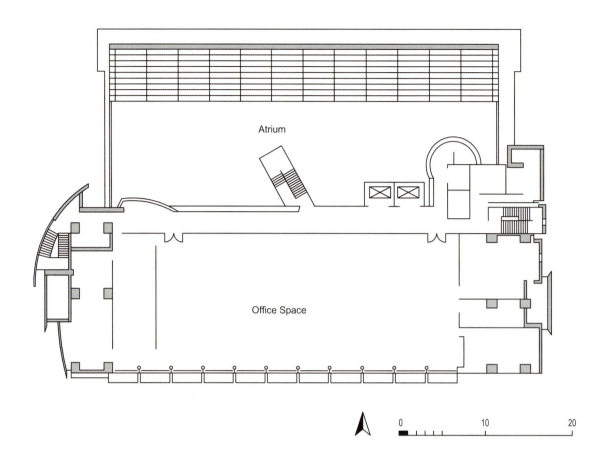

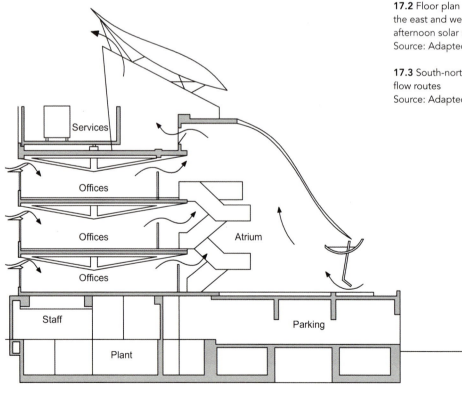

17.2 Floor plan at Level 4 – note service spaces 'protecting' the east and west office façades from low-angle morning and afternoon solar radiation
Source: Adapted from Nikken Sekkei

17.3 South-north cross-section indicating natural ventilation air flow routes
Source: Adapted from Nikken Sekkei

17.4 Internal view of the atrium, being used as a showroom/display space. Note the open staircase and mid-level meeting space, with glazed elevator shaft in background right

17.5 Exterior view from the south-west, with stair/ventilating tower on the left. Note the solar shading and light-shelf arrangement on the south façade

17.6 The western façade – atrium protected from direct solar penetration by fixed mini-louvres between the panes of the double glazing, offices by the stair tower and service areas

17.7 General view (looking north-west) of an open-plan office area. Atrium space visible to the right through ventilation openings above the partition

17.8 General view (looking south-west) of an open-plan office area – south glazing with its high level openable windows to the left. Note also the linear arrangement of the combined luminaire/air supply diffuser

The building has won many awards, including the 1996–1997 Good Design Award of the Ministry of International Trade and Industry/Japan Industrial Design Promotion Organisation, the 1998 Annual Architectural Design Commendation of the Architectural institute of Japan, and the 1998 Award of the Society of Heating, Air-Conditioning and Sanitary Engineers of Japan.

It has also achieved (though only just) the coveted 'S' or 'Excellent' rating on the Japanese CASBEE sustainability rating system, with a Building Environmental Efficiency of 3.00 in the Existing Building category (JSBC, 2004).

THE DESIGN PROCESS

The design of this building was carried out by a team from Nikken Sekkei Ltd., the largest firm of planners, architects, and engineers in Japan. Tokyo Gas already had an established relationship with Nikken Sekkei and worked with them directly to develop the concept. The Nikken Sekkei principals involved in the Earth Port project were architect Kiyoshi Sakurai and engineer/architect Fumio Nohara, both with a strong interest and track record in sustainable design.

The designers had the luxury of a comparatively long design development phase, around two years. This enabled the concept to be explored thoroughly through many design meetings involving Osamu Shibata of Tokyo Gas as well as Sakurai and Nohara, all the time refining and testing ideas. In the end, all three were involved in presenting their preferred solution to the Board of Tokyo Gas. There, their concept was given particularly close scrutiny by those members who were expert in energy efficiency matters and whose image of a low energy building was of a compact, heavily insulated box with lots of air recirculation via an HVAC system – rather different from what was being proposed (Sakurai *et al.*, 1999).

THE DESIGN OUTCOME

Building layout and construction

With its approximately 45m-long axis east–west, the main part of the building has three floors of offices on its south side and a full-height glazed atrium to the north (Figures 17.2 and 17.3). The office spaces

17.9 Exterior view along the north façade – note the row of automated natural ventilation openings running along below the vertical section of atrium glazing

17.10 View from the atrium showing the gap for natural air movement between it and an adjacent office space. Note also that air can move from the atrium corridor areas to the west stair/ventilation tower via a grillework door

17.11 Office lighting controls and thermal conditions indicator – 'Cool-biz' policy implemented

are around 14m deep and are daylit from both the north, via the glazed atrium, and from the south façade windows. The atrium is roughly triangular in section, around 40m long by 15m deep at its base, with its sloping glass facing north. As well as containing open stairs, elevators, and corridors for primary circulation, it is used for display and demonstration purposes.

The main building is located on top of a ground floor and basement containing parking and other service areas. Environmental control central plant such as the co-generator and chiller systems are located within an open equipment deck on top of the building (Figure 17.3).

The overall form of the building – relatively compact, slightly elongated on its east–west axis – is what one might expect of one designed with energy efficiency in mind. The north-facing glazing (see Figure 17.1) is angled to act as a 'light collector' ensuring an even light distribution in the wood-floored atrium space (Figure 17.4) and to the north side of the offices, while avoiding direct summer sun penetration, the slope of the double-glazed low emissivity façade being 75° to the horizontal compared to the maximum solar noon summer solstice elevation of around 77° (Figures 17.1 and 17.3).

On the vertical south façade, the continuous 2550mm-high bands of glazing at each of the three levels are shaded from the high altitude summer sun by a double set of fixed horizontal 'shelves' (Figure 17.5); the upper shallower one shading the top 1000mm of openable single-glazing, the lower deeper one shading the bottom 1550mm of fixed double-glazing, and acting as a light shelf reflecting light through the upper section of the glazing. To the west and east, the atrium elevation is designed (using double-glazing with fixed mini-louvres between the panes) to enable light penetration while obviating low angle morning and afternoon sun penetration; while the office elevations are taken up with service spaces of one kind or another, thus avoiding the issue of low angle sun penetration (Figures 17.1 and 17.6).

Passive and active environmental control systems

Designed from the outset to better the Japanese codes in terms of the energy consumed for ventilation, for air conditioning, and for lighting, the building's primary energy consumption has achieved its target of around 35 per cent less than the standard building

as well as operating the lighting and the 'active' thermal systems, actuates the natural ventilation openings when outside conditions are appropriate, turning off the office air conditioning when the windows are open.

Rainwater and waste water from the sinks is reclaimed for toilet flushing.

USERS' PERCEPTIONS OF THE BUILDING

Overall response

For all of the 17 or so respondents (44 per cent female, 56 per cent male), the building was their normal place of business, working on average 5.0 days per week and 8.5 hours per day, of which 7.3 were spent at their desk and 6.1 at a VDU. All were over 30 and over 70 per cent had worked in the building for more than a year at the same desk or work area. Most (88 per cent) worked in an open office area, the rest sharing with several colleagues.

Significant factors

Table 17.1 lists the scores for each of the survey questions and indicates those aspects of the building that the staff perceived as being significantly better, similar to, or worse than the benchmark and/or scale mid-point. In this case, some 14 aspects were significantly better, only eight were significantly worse, while the remaining 22 aspects had much the same score as the benchmark.

In terms of operational aspects, this building scores very well on all eight counts – very close to or above the mid-point of the scale in every case; significantly better than the benchmark in four instances, and close to it in three. Only in the case of Space in Building was the average score lower than the benchmark.

The users' responses to environmental factors were more variable. While the overall scores for temperature and air in winter were lower than both benchmark and scale mid-point, most of the detailed aspects rated the same or better. Summertime temperatures and air followed a similar pattern but with the former tending to the 'variable' end of the spectrum and the latter to the 'stuffy'.

The building rated very well with respect to noise control and quite well with respect to lighting, though there is a suggestion of there being slightly too much natural light and glare from the artificial lighting system. Interestingly, none of the respondents rated personal control as important, though their perceived level of control was the same as or better than the benchmark in every case.

Perceptions of the five satisfaction variables were all significantly higher than their scale mid-points, significantly better than their respective benchmarks for comfort overall, productivity and health, and the same in the case of design and needs. The score of 4.44 for health is particularly notable here – not only is it better than the benchmark, it is also higher than the mid-point of the scale, implying the staff felt healthier when in the building.

Users' comments

Overall, some 52 responses were received from staff under the 12 headings where they were able to add written comments – some 25.5 per cent of the 204 potential (17 respondents by 12 headings). Table 17.2 indicates the numbers of positive, neutral, and negative comments – in this case, around 26.9 per cent were positive, 9.6 per cent neutral, and 63.5 per cent negative. No particular or common issues emerged from these comments.

Overall performance indices

The Comfort Index, based on the comfort overall, noise, lighting, temperature, and air quality scores, works out at 0.00; while the Satisfaction Index, based on the design, needs, health, and perceived productivity scores, is +0.96, noting that the scale mid-point in these instances is zero on a -3 to +3 scale.

The Summary Index, being the average of the Comfort and Satisfaction Indices, works out at +0.48, while the Forgiveness Factor, calculated to be 1.20 in this instance, indicates that staff are likely to be relatively more tolerant of minor shortcomings in individual aspects such as winter and summer temperatures, air quality, lighting, and noise (a factor of 1 being the mid-point on a scale that normally ranges from 0.80 to 1.20).

In terms of the Ten-Factor Rating Scale, the building was well within the 'Good Practice' band on the 7-point scale with a calculated percentage value of 76 per cent. When All-Factors were taken into account, the percentage value worked out at 65 per cent – towards the upper end of the 'Above Average' band.

ACKNOWLEDGEMENTS

It is a great pleasure to acknowledge the tremendous assistance of Professor Toshiharu Ikaga of the Department of Systems Design Engineering, Keio University, Yokohama, for arranging the itinerary for my visits to Japan in 1998 and 2005. I must also thank both him and Ms Junko Endo, Senior Consultant at the Center for Environmental and Energy Planning at the Nikken Sekkei Research Institute, Tokyo, for co-hosting my visits to the building.

It is also a pleasure to thank Kiyoshi Sakurai and Fumio Nohara, Deputy Principal and Senior Mechanical Engineer respectively of Nikken Sekkei Ltd, Tokyo, and Osamu Shibata, Manager, Energy Sales and Service Planning Department, Tokyo Gas Co Ltd, whom I interviewed at the Earth Port building in 1999, together with Junko Endo who acted as translator (from Japanese to English) on my behalf. I must also thank Sanae Namatame, Assistant Manager, Energy Solution Business Department, together with Takahiro Nagata and Ryota Kuzuki of Tokyo Gas, whom I interviewed during a subsequent visit to the building in September 2005, and who distributed the questionnaire on my behalf; and Yukiko Fleetwood for the translation of the questionnaire into Japanese and the comments into English.

REFERENCES

CADDET (1998) 'Life Cycle Energy Savings in Office Buildings', *CADDET Energy Efficiency – Result 308*, The Netherlands.

JSBC (2004) *CASBEE for New Construction – Technical Manual*, Institute for Building Environment and Energy Conservation, Tokyo (see Case H, p. 30).

Kato, S. and Chikamoto, T. (2002) *Pilot Study Report: Tokyo Gas Earth Port*, IEA ECBCS Annex 35: Hyb Vent, February 2002, available at: http://hybvent.civil.auc.dk/ (accessed 8 June 2007).

Namatame, S., Nohara, F., Tamura, F., Shibata, O., Sakakura, A. and Ichikawa, T. (2005) 'The Initiative in Promoting Ecologically Efficient Building Projects Toward More Sustainable Society and Some Studies on the Findings of their Effectiveness', in *Proceedings of the 2005 World Sustainable Building Conference*, Paper 01-116, Tokyo, 27–29 September.

Ray-Jones, A. (ed.) (2000) 'Tokyo Gas Earth Port', in *Sustainable Architecture in Japan: The Green Buildings of Nikken Sekkei*, Chichester: Wiley-Academy, pp. 98–109.

Sakurai, K., Nohara. F. and Shibata, O. (1999) Transcript of interview of 25 August 1999, Yokohama, with Kiyoshi Sakurai and Fumio Nohara of Nikken Sekkei, and with Osamu Shibata of Tokyo Gas. Ms Junko Endo of Nikken Sekkei in the role of translator.

Adjustable perimeter terminal units at the Nikken Sekkei Building

18
Nikken Sekkei Building
Tokyo, Japan

with Junko Endo and Toshiharu Ikaga

THE CONTEXT

Nikken Sekkei Ltd is the largest firm of planners, architects, and engineers in Japan, and possibly the world, with approaching 2000 staff in its major offices in five Japanese cities and subsidiaries throughout South-East Asia. While they themselves are an integrated multi-disciplinary company, capable of undertaking most projects in-house, they have also undertaken many notable projects in association with some of the best design offices in the world (Ray-Jones, 2000).

Given that experience, it was perhaps only to be expected that the leadership of the company were fully aware of the challenges surrounding the design and operation of office buildings. Managing Director Yoshiako Ogura, for example, writing in 1995, noted that 'there are a plethora of office environments in which workers may find it hard to work as he/she is surrounded by documents or made to sit in awkward posture on an obsolete chair when accessing OA machines'. He added,

Only a limited number of offices give consideration to the lighting environment and furniture layout for diverse desk works, the filing system with rational storage system, secluded spaces fit for thinking individual thoughts, and the place for change of mood.

Clearly, there were going to be high expectations of the company's new office headquarters building.

The site for the building is Chiyoda-ku in the Iidabashi district of Tokyo, at approximate 35°N latitude and with winter and summer design temperatures of around 0°C and 32°C respectively (ASHRAE, 2001: 27.38–9).

The building achieved an 'A' on the Japanese CASBEE sustainability rating system, with a Building Environmental Efficiency in the 1.5 to 3.0 range (JSBC, 2004).

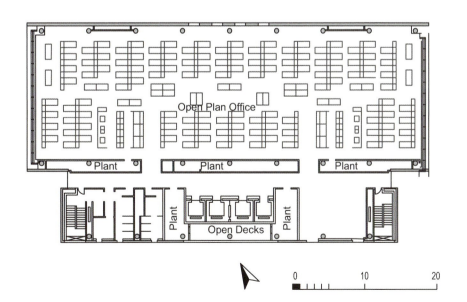

18.1 Floor plan of a typical office – note 'served' open-plan office space to the north and 'servant' space, containing elevators, stairs, WCs, etc., to the south
Source: Adapted from Nikken Sekkei

18.5 Demonstration of the louvre system used on the east and west façades – in fully deployed position

18.6 Louvre system in practice – fully deployed in an office space

18.7 Louvre system in practice – partially retracted in an office space

The fully glazed street façades (Figures 18.3 and 18.4) face in westerly and easterly (strictly speaking, WSW and ENE) directions, meaning that they will receive direct solar gain for all of the afternoon and most of the morning respectively on sunny days.

A specially designed motorised external louvre system was developed for the east and west façades – this can be deployed as required by the building occupants to suit their needs in accordance with the ambient sky conditions (Figures 18.5, 18.6, and 18.7).

Environmental control systems

The main central plant, comprising a gas engine heat pump and ice storage system, is located on the roof (Figure 18.8), while variable

18.8 Some of the rooftop services arrangement

18.9 South façade indicating semi-exposed structure and services, and limited glazing

air volume units at each level distribute warmed or cooled air to each floor (Figure 18.9).

USERS' PERCEPTIONS OF THE BUILDING

Overall response

The survey was carried out in August 2006 and was confined to the occupants of Level 5 of the building (Figures 18.10 and 18.11) – the Mechanical, Electrical and Environmental Engineering Department of Nikken Sekkei – normally with about 100 occupants all told.

18.10 Typical office floor, viewed along the line of the lighting and structural systems. Note the black painted ceiling and exposed services

18.11 Typical office floor, viewed perpendicular to the line of the lighting and structural systems

For all of the 48 or so respondents (19 per cent female, 81 per cent male), the building was their normal place of business, working on average 4.3 days per week in the building and 9.9 hours per day, of which 7.3 were spent at their desk and 6.3 at a computer. Some 71 per cent were over 30 and 79 per cent had worked in the building for more than a year at the same desk or work area. Most (82 per cent) worked in an open office area, 11 per cent had a single office, while the rest shared with a few colleagues.

Significant factors

Table 18.1 lists the scores for each of the survey questions and indicates those aspects of the building that the staff perceived as being significantly better, similar to, or worse than the benchmark and/or scale mid-point. In this case, some 21 aspects were significantly better, only five were significantly worse, while the remaining 19 aspects had much the same score as the benchmark.

In terms of operational aspects, this building scored very well for seven of the eight factors considered – significantly better than the benchmark and scale mid-point in four instances, and close to the benchmark or better than the scale mid-point in three. Only in the case of Space at Desk was the average score (3.29) significantly lower than the benchmark and scale mid-point.

The users' responses to the various environmental factors were consistently good. Only two of the 26 factors considered scored worse than their respective benchmarks and scale mid-points; the rest were almost equally divided between those that scored better than both benchmark and scale mid-point, and those with around the same score While the four overall scores for temperature and air in winter and summer were better than their benchmarks, there was a hint that temperatures were too cold in winter and too hot in summer (despite their being equal to or better than their respective benchmarks). However, respondents did rate the temperatures relatively stable and the air relatively still and odourless in both summer and winter.

The scores indicated satisfaction with the amount of artificial lighting and the relative lack of glare, but a perception of too little natural light, resulting in a lighting overall score lower than the benchmark, but still significantly higher (at 4.15) than the scale mid-point. Noise overall scored well (better than both the benchmark and the scale mid-point) – perhaps too much from colleagues, but on the 'too little' side of the spectrum for most of the other aspects. While perceived control scores were mostly in the 2–3 range, well short of the scale mid-point in all cases, very few respondents rated control of ventilation or noise as important – unlike heating, cooling, and lighting where around one-third did.

Perceptions of the five satisfaction variables were all significantly better than their respective benchmarks and the same as or higher than their scale mid-points. The score of +8.51 per cent for productivity is particularly notable here.

Users' comments

Overall, some 171 responses were received from staff under the 12 headings where they were able to add written comments – some 29.7 per cent of the 576 potential (48 respondents by 12 headings). Table 18.2 indicates the numbers of positive, balanced, and negative comments – in this case, around 30.4 per cent were positive, 7.6 per cent neutral, and 62.0 per cent negative.

In many cases, but not all, the comments received echoed the survey scores. In the case of storage and of space at desk, for example, the majority of the mostly negative comments reflected their relatively low scores (3.54 and 3.29 respectively). Similarly, the disturbance from other people's telephone conversations and meetings around adjacent desks echoed the moderate scores for some aspects of noise. Lack of storage and noise were also mentioned relatively frequently under hindrances.

By contrast, the relatively good rating for glare was not reflected in the comments where more than half the negative comments alluded to glare issues such as the contrast between the dark ceiling and the lights, and reflections from the white desks. Similarly, despite meeting rooms scoring well for availability, many respondents suggested there were not enough.

Finally, worth noting in the context of things that worked well, the computing systems and facilities received the most positive comments, as did the design of the building itself (the latter reflecting its good score of 5.31).

Overall performance indices

The Comfort Index, based on the comfort overall, noise, lighting, temperature, and air quality scores, works out at +0.59; while the

Part 3

Buildings in Warm–Temperate Climates

Chapters 19–27

The following nine case studies are all located in what could be classed broadly as warm–temperate climates, with wintertime design temperatures ranging from +3°C to +7°C. Six of these are located in the south-eastern quarter of Australia, two in the North Island of New Zealand, and the remaining one in Southern California. They will be described in the following order:

Four of these buildings have advanced natural ventilation systems and five have mixed-mode – four changeover and one (Landcare Research) zoned.

East façade detail of the Landcare Research Laboratory

19

The Landcare Research Laboratory
Auckland, New Zealand

THE CONTEXT

This three-storey 4400m² building is located in Auckland, New Zealand. It accommodates two organisations – Landcare Research and the Ministry of Agriculture and Forestry (MAF), with around 60 and 25 staff respectively. In addition to conventional office and administrative facilities, it also houses some specialist national facilities such as the 6.5 million specimen insect collection, a 600,000 fungal collection, research laboratories, containment facilities, and propagation glasshouses (Figures 19.1 and 19.2).

In keeping with its mission, Landcare Research wanted a sustainable design. The overall objective for the building was to 'manage our own environmental, social and economic performance in an

19.1 View of building from the north-east – Morrin Road in the foreground

19.2 South façade and staff car park. Collection spaces located behind the unglazed patterned upper façade; glasshouses and rainwater collection tank to rear of main building (on left of shot)

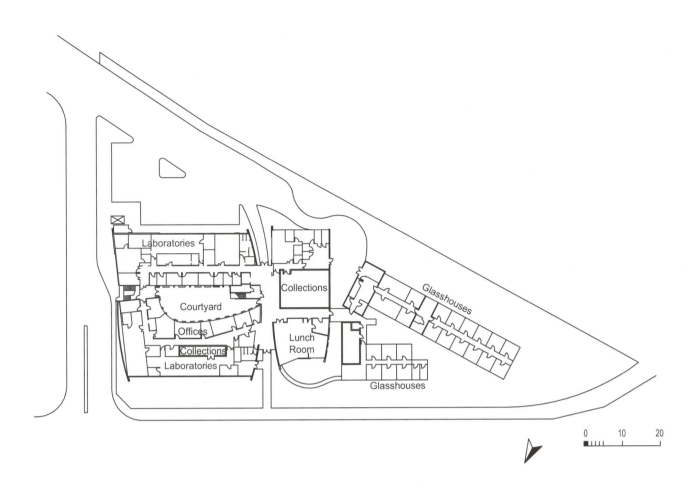

19.3 Ground floor plan and site
Source: Adapted from Connell Wagner

19.4 Plan of first and second floor
Source: Adapted from Connell Wagner

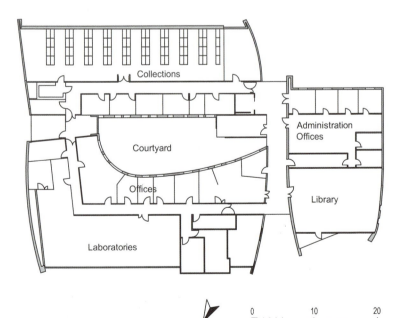

19.5 View showing roof-mounted ventilation equipment, upper part of courtyard area and office glazing/shading arrangement

integrated manner to demonstrate that this can be done' and to do so for the same construction costs as a conventional building (Landcare Research, 2006). Environmental objectives included the use of renewable, recyclable, and recycled materials as well as the minimisation of solid waste, wastewater, and stormwater going off site; social objectives included the provision of a healthy interior environment, incorporating natural light and ventilation together with shared and private spaces to encourage staff interactions; while economic objectives included low operational and maintenance expenditure and year-round energy efficiency, with an annual target for the latter of 100kWh/m^2 (Landcare Research, 2005).

The building is located on a narrow triangular site (Figure 19.3) on the edge of the University of Auckland's Tamaki Campus. The site itself has height and boundary constraints, rock and clay ground conditions, and a busy road on one side. The climate of Auckland (latitude 37°S), with winter and summer design temperatures of around 3°C and 24°C respectively (ASHRAE, 2001: 27.42–3) may be classed as warm–temperate.

In sustainability criteria terms, the building, which was completed in 2004, has been rated at 60 per cent on a preliminary version of the National Australian Built Environment Rating System for office

buildings (NABERS, 2008). This rating system covers land, materials, energy, water, interior, resources, transport, and waste, and to achieve 60 per cent or more requires a concerted holistic approach to all sustainability criteria, and is arguably rather more difficult to attain for a specialist building such as this one. The building also won the annual Energy-Wise Commercial Buildings Award in 2005.

THE DESIGN PROCESS

The design brief for this project emerged from a series of preliminary workshops involving experts in sustainability, ecology, and energy efficiency as well as Landcare Research and MAF staff. The resulting brief called for the building to be as sustainable as economically feasible, in keeping with the mission of the client – and this became a driving focus for the design team.

The winning design team, following a public tender process, was led by Maurice Keily and Stuart Mackie of Auckland-based design practice Chow:Hill in collaboration with specialist sustainable architect Peter Diprose and engineers Connell Mott MacDonald. Robert Vale was also involved as a specialist advisor, a role that has extended to his studying the building in operation. They, together with Landcare Research Operations Manager Maggie Lawton and her team, worked closely and collaboratively from the start to achieve the objectives of the brief.

According to Kiely, the Chow:Hill philosophy was to take an holistic approach to the design and development of the best possible working environment across a range of work settings, balanced against the achievement of sustainability outcomes and the challenges of a fixed budget (Kiely and Mackie, 2005). His colleague Stuart Mackie cited one example of this where, during three separate workshops in the course a week, the design team came up with over 20 conceptual ideas for how the site could be inhabited. Each of these was then evaluated in terms of the brief and the client's criteria, and narrowed down to five main options, from which the final design emerged. Environmental engineers Dave Fulbrook and Neil Purdie of Connell Mott MacDonald were involved from the start, the latter very much involved in monitoring the building's energy use and other services, and determined that it achieve its targets in operation (Adams, 2006).

Project programme demands mitigated against the investigation of some of the selected systems even more thoroughly, particularly newer systems where there is less experience of their effects on the building as a whole and their impact on overall life cycle costs are less apparent. The design team would also highly recommend longer-term commissioning and observation of building performance and a budget for tuning the building as a whole.

THE DESIGN OUTCOME

Building layout, construction and passive environmental control systems

According to the architect,

[T]he plan [was] predicated on a narrow footprint, organised around open courtyards or pedestrian spaces, allowing for maximum natural light and ventilation. Contained laboratories or areas requiring mechanical ventilation or air conditioning are nearest the road where they act as acoustic and solar

barriers to office spaces. Collection areas are in upper level concrete chambers with rigorously controlled temperature and humidity.

(Lawton et al., 2004)

There was some debate whether these too should be located on the road side, but it was successfully argued that this could be construed as the building turning its back on the street, and that it would be easier to expand the collection areas if they were on the other side. A further intention was that linking areas between various building blocks would function as social and display areas (see floor plans in Figures 19.3, 19.4(a) and 19.4(b)). According to the architect:

Significant research was carried out on building systems with respect to embodied energy, constructability and cost-in-use, rather than consideration of isolated elements or materials. As a result, materials are used in their least processed form. Concrete, timber and steel are left in exposed state, and fulfil other functions beyond structural or weathering roles. Much building services work follows a similar philosophy. The challenge was to reduce rather than add, and also to express solutions in an elegant manner.

(ibid.)

It almost goes without saying that the building is very well insulated (150–200mm thickness), has clear double-glazed windows, exposed thermal mass, and extensive use has been made of locally produced materials. 'Internal finishes include water-based paints, linoleum flooring (made from linseed oil and jute) and loose-laid carpets made of recycled plastics. Much of the existing furniture from the Mount Albert building [their previous premises] was re-used' (Vale et al., 2005).

Figure 19.3 indicates the ground floor plan of the main building, with the adjacent rows of glasshouses running out to the western apex of the triangular site. As can be seen from this and the first and second floor plans (Figures 19.4(a) and 19.4(b)), most offices face into the central atrium so that almost all the desks and workstations are near an opening window (see also Figures 19.5, 19.6, and 19.7)

19.6 Courtyard area at ground level looking east. Note reflections from north-facing inner façade

19.7 Interior of shared office. Note nature of room surfaces and re-use of existing furniture

19.8 General view of a laboratory space

Active environmental control systems

The wide range of facilities and processes housed (offices, laboratories, controlled environments for the different collection vaults, and coolrooms of various kinds – see Figures 19.8 to 19.10) necessitated the installation of a wide range of environmental control systems. While none of these involved new or innovative technology, their integration was notable.

The skirting convectors serving the naturally ventilated offices around the atrium, for example, are heated by hot water recovered from the refrigeration systems serving the various coolrooms (some 15kW in this case). Temperatures in these offices are designed to range from 20°C to 25.5°C, while the five coolroom/freezer areas require to be maintained around 4°C/–20°C respectively.

Two rooftop package units serve the north-facing laboratories, the south zone laboratories and NZ Arthropod Collection offices, operating in conjunction with the 11 fume cupboards they house. Not only is the air supply volume controlled to balance the variations in extract volume due to differing levels of fume cupboard utilisation, a heat exchanger recovers energy from some of these exhaust streams (Figure 19.11). With internal conditions allowed to range from 18 to 25°C, the air supply does not require heating or cooling while the outside air is between 12 and 22°C.

The central refrigeration system serves the collection vault air handling unit using refrigerant R404a. The vaults require to be maintained at around 17°C and 50%rh necessitating cooling of their supply air to 6 °C followed by reheat – in this case, utilising the heat rejected from the refrigeration system.

Specific areas are provided with individually controlled air conditioning systems – reverse cycle heat pumps on a VRV system – designed to maintain 21–23°C. One solar water heater serves the cafeteria. A second solar water heater serves the laboratory hot water use in conjunction with a gas-fired hot water unit. According to Sutherland (2004), the brief's requirement for rainwater harvesting

produced some of the building's more groundbreaking features: composting toilets on the first and second floors [the first commercial building in the country to do so]; and syphonic rain water collection off the roof for diversion into three 25,000 litre on-site tanks prior to use as grey water.

19.9 Typical laboratory fume cupboard

19.10 Fungal collection space

19.11 Upper-level corridor with exposed services

These are used for the conventional ground floor toilets and urinals, and for irrigation of the gardens and glasshouses (Lawton et al., 2004).

Having conventional toilets on the ground floor served to minimise the unpredictable effects of public use and obviated the need for what would have been expensive excavation of the hard rock of the site. A 400kW wind turbine powers the pump used to bring the grey water to a rooftop header tank. Elsewhere on the site, car park groundwater is diverted to a large rain-garden before any surplus reaches the public stormwater system.

USERS' PERCEPTIONS OF THE BUILDING

Overall response

For all of the 59 or so staff respondents (53 per cent female, 47 per cent male), the building was their normal place of work, most (81 per cent) working five days per week or more, and averaging 7.7 hours per day. The majority (some 86 per cent) were over-30 and had worked in the building for more than a year, some 81 per cent at the same desk or work area. Hours per day spent at desk and computer averaged 5.9 and 4.9 respectively. Around two-thirds sat next to a window, while roughly equal numbers had either single offices, or shared with one other, or shared with two or more colleagues.

The average scores of the staff for each of the relevant survey questions are listed in Table 19.1. Table 19.1 also indicates those aspects of the building that the staff perceived as being significantly better, similar to, or worse than the benchmark and/or scale mid-point. Overall, some 12 aspects were significantly better, 12 were significantly worse, while the remaining 20 aspects had much the same score as the benchmark.

Significant factors

In terms of operational aspects, this building scores well in terms of its cleaning, furniture, space at desk, and availability of meeting rooms, with no other factors significantly different from their benchmarks.

The users' responses to environmental factors were more variable. While overall scores for temperature and air in both summer and winter were close to their benchmarks, temperatures were assessed as too hot and variable in summer and too cold in winter, while the air was perceived as too still in winter and too dry in summer – however, the temperature was perceived as stable and the air fresh in winter, and odourless both summer and winter.

Overall perception of noise scored less than the benchmarks, the main issues being noise from colleagues, other internal noises, and to a lesser extent outside noises. On the other hand, lighting overall scored better than the benchmark, rating well for natural light and lack of glare.

Of the one-third or so of respondents who rated control important, that for heating and cooling rated worse than the benchmark, that for lighting better.

In terms of the satisfaction factors, users' perceptions varied somewhat, but most were either close to their respective benchmarks or scale mid-points. In the case of health, a score of 3.66 was above the benchmark, but somewhat less than the scale mid-point.

Users' comments

Overall, some 320 responses were received under the 12 headings where respondents could add written comments – some 45 per cent of the 708 (59 respondents by 12 headings) potential number of comments. Table 19.2 indicates the numbers of positive, neutral, and negative comments under each of the 12 headings – in this case, around 19.7 per cent were positive, 15 per cent neutral, and 65.3 per cent negative.

Echoing the trends evident in the scores for the corresponding sets of factors, noise issues attracted solely negative comments – external sounds from traffic and a nearby quarry, and internal sounds from adjacent rooms, corridors, the floor above, and internal equipment were mentioned most frequently; with external equipment and people noise in the same space also identified as common sources of disturbance.

By the same token, lighting attracted both the most positive and the least negative comment, in keeping with its relatively good score.

Of the rest, a perceived lack of on-site storage gave rise to negative comment – this despite it scoring no different from the (admittedly relatively low) benchmark; and while meeting rooms scored well for availability, the joint use of the larger venue (it also served as part of the cafeteria area) received adverse comment.

Some 34 respondents noted a wide range of things that worked well for them, while 37 noted things that were a hindrance – the latter mostly noise- or temperature-related issues.

Overall performance indices

The Comfort Index, based on the scores for comfort overall, noise, lighting, temperature, and air quality, works out at +0.14, while the Satisfaction Index, based on the design, needs, health, and perceived productivity scores, is +0.04, both higher than the scale mid-point (noting these indices are scaled from -3 to +3).

The Summary Index, being the average of these, works out at 0.09, while the Forgiveness Factor, calculated to be 0.95 in this

REFERENCES

Adams, G. (2006) 'Leading by Example', *e.nz magazine*, 7(1): 9–13.

ASHRAE (2001) *ASHRAE Handbook: Fundamentals, SI Edition*, Atlanta, GA: American Society of Heating Refrigerating and Air-Conditioning Engineers.

Baird, G. and Purdie, N. (2006) 'Environmental Design and Performance of the Landcare Research Headquarters Building, Auckland, New Zealand', paper presented at Ninth World Renewable Energy Congress, Florence, August.

Keily, M. and Mackie, S. (2005) Transcript of interview held on 9 May 2005, Auckland.

Landcare Research (2005) 'Energy Efficiency', available at: www.landcareresearch.co.nz/about/tamaki/energy_efficiency.asp (accessed 14 March 2005).

Landcare Research (2006) 'Design Objectives for this Building', available at: www.landcareresearch.co.nz/about/tamaki/design_objectives.asp (accessed 23 March 2006).

Lawton, M., Kiely, M., Sutherland, J. and Turner, D. (2004) 'Green, but Not Wacky', *Architecture New Zealand*, September/October: 78–85.

NABERS (2008) 'Environmental Rating – Tamaki Building', available at: www.landcareresearch.co.nz/about/tamaki/environmental_rating.asp (accessed 5 October 2008).

Sutherland, J. (2004) Transcript of interview held on 20 April 2004, London.

Vale, R., Lawton, M. and Kelsang, W. (2005) 'Walking the Talk – Landcare Research/Manaaki Whenua Tamaki Building', in *Sustainable Buildings in the Auckland Region*, Auckland: Waitakere City Council.

20

The Campus Reception and Administration Building, Auckland University of Technology (AUT Akoranga)
Auckland, New Zealand

THE CONTEXT

Completed in June 2001, this 992m² building marks the main entrance to the Akoranga Campus of the Auckland University of Technology in the suburb of Northcote – the main campus being located in the city centre.

The building was intended to meet the demands associated with increasing student numbers and to centralise the operation of the Faculty of Health Studies. According to the architects, a key driver was to enhance the identity of the campus and provide a focal point by the provision of a prominent 'front door' to the site (see Figures 20.1 and 21.2), while at the same time creating a healthy, environmentally friendly building with strong links to its surroundings (den Breems, 2003).

20.1 Main entrance to the building, viewed from the south

20.2 View from the west towards offices with motorised awnings deployed. Note too (in centre of photograph) the higher roof level of the corridor with its fixed external louvres and upper-level opening windows

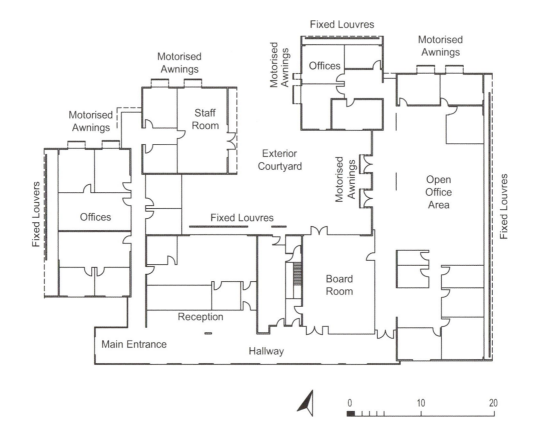

Fixed Louvres

Motorised Awnings

Motorised Awnings

Offices

Motorised Awnings

Motorised Awnings

Staff Room

Exterior Courtyard

Fixed Louvers

Offices

Fixed Louvres

Motorised Awnings

Open Office Area

Fixed Louvres

Board Room

Reception

Main Entrance

Hallway

0   10   20

20.3 Overall floor plan
Source: Adapted from JASMAX

20.4 Open-plan office –
note the open structure and provision of ceiling fans

20.5 Cross-section illustrating the principles of the passive environmental control systems
Source: Adapted from JASMAX

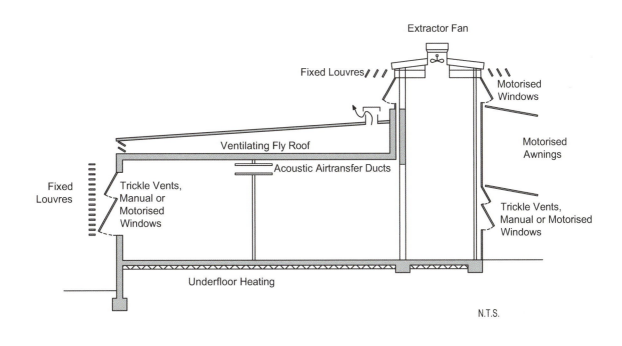

Extractor Fan

Fixed Louvres

Motorised Windows

Motorised Awnings

Ventilating Fly Roof

Acoustic Airtransfer Ducts

Fixed Louvres

Trickle Vents, Manual or Motorised Windows

Trickle Vents, Manual or Motorised Windows

Underfloor Heating

N.T.S.

While the brief asked that environmental issues be considered, it did not specify a cutting-edge energy-efficient building. However, as one of the first of the new buildings on this greenfield campus, following the development of a masterplan, the opportunity was taken, with the full support of the client and a design team 'passionate about environmentally sensitive design' (E-W N, 2002: 23) to pursue a 'low energy architecture' approach. While it might be thought that the warm–temperate climate of Auckland (latitude 37°S), with winter and summer design temperatures of around 3°C and 24°C respectively (ASHRAE, 2001: 27.42–3) might make this readily feasible, it is by no means conventional practice. Even for an owner–occupier client with what one would expect to be a relatively long-term view of these matters, air conditioning tends to be accepted without question and anything else seen as somewhat of a 'risk'.

The following year, the building entered and won the 2002 annual Energy-Wise Commercial Buildings Award. As this award is for recently completed projects, only limited energy use data is ever available – judging is therefore based mainly on an assessment of energy efficiency potential. The building also achieved a 'Good' rating after a trial assessment using the BRANZ Green Office Scheme (then in its pilot stage), reflecting the design's concentration on energy, health, well-being, and management issues (Jaques, 2003).

THE DESIGN PROCESS

Selection of the architects (JASMAX Ltd) for this project stemmed from their involvement in the 1998 masterplan for the Akoranga Campus, and from their involvement in the design of buildings for AUT's main campus. Their approach was a collaborative one from the start, involving the client, the environmental/services engineer, and the structural engineer. While the fundamental principles of low energy architecture are relatively straightforward, their application is almost a forgotten art. During this period of 'rediscovery' close collaboration between the various members of the design team, and between them and the eventual building users, was of the utmost importance.

According to architect Marko den Breems (2003), the design team had many meetings, 'just talking about ideas and just sketching without having a finished building'. Two environmental engineers were involved – Julian Sutherland (2004) during the conceptual design stage and Stephen Hogg (2003) during detail design development – both of Norman Disney Young. Consultations with the users were extensive, ranging from occupant group presentations on the implications of the alternative design strategies, to review meetings with facilities managers on operating systems, and even to discussion of the thermal comfort 'consequences' of different building options. In the event,

20.6 View of the entrance corridor with Reception area on the left and south-east façade to the right of shot. Note the high-level openable glazing (for daylight and ventilation) and the blockwork internal construction (providing thermal mass)

20.7 Rooftop view showing a row of vents for a section of the flyroof; shaded motorised high-level windows above a corridor; and, in the background, a couple of extract fan housings on top

20.8 North-east façade with its fixed louvres and openable windows behind

four main options were explored – a single-storey and a two-storey building, both with air conditioning or natural ventilation.

THE DESIGN OUTCOME

Building layout and construction

The eventual outcome was the single-storey naturally ventilated option, roughly U-shaped in plan (Figure 20.3), and enclosing a courtyard oriented to the north-west. The building is configured to house five separate administrative functions or areas, all linked by the circulation corridor/hallway.

These functions include the main reception, the academic registry, the health faculty offices, plus a staff room and a boardroom, many of which open directly onto the courtyard. While these spaces are all single storey, they gain maximum height advantage from the open structural system used (Figure 20.4). The circulation corridor/hallway, on the other hand, is taken up higher than the surrounding accommodation, enabling it to perform both ventilating and daylighting functions (Figures 20.5 and 20.6).

Aspects of the building construction and materials, such as the concrete floor slab and the exposed concrete brick veneer cladding on the inside of the building provide useful thermal mass (Figure 20.6).

Passive and active environmental control systems

A range of mechanical (active) and architectural (passive) systems of environmental control have been used in this mixed-mode building. The active systems comprise a zoned underfloor hot water heating system powered by a 76kW gas-fired condensing boiler, a split system air conditioning unit for the boardroom, and a set of rooftop extract fans along the length of the corridor.

Several passive elements contribute to the control of heat losses and gains via the building envelope – in particular, the use of 100mm thickness insulation throughout, the installation of a ventilated fly-roof plus the use of light colours externally (Figure 20.7) and thermal mass internally. In addition, window areas on the sunny façades are fitted with either fixed external louvres (Figure 20.8) or with motorised retractable awnings (Figure 20.9). Control of the underfloor

20.9 Motorised awnings deployed on the south-westerly façade of the open plan office area – high-level windows in open position

20.10 Typical single office window with a range of opening types – louvred on the left (three sets), manual casement (three different sizes), motorised casement (at high level, right), and a trickle vent

20.11 Showing acoustically treated transfer grilles above full height doors – sized to enable minimum ventilation rates when the door is shut

heating, the ventilation (natural and mechanical), the boardroom air conditioning, and the motorised awnings is via a computer-based building management system. Temperature and carbon dioxide sensors check conditions within the building, and a rooftop weather-station provides relevant data on local ambient conditions. Custom-drawn graphics screens allow the facilities manager to operate, monitor and adjust the building systems.

Natural ventilation is enabled through a range of perimeter window openings (manual, automatic, and trickle as shown in Figure 20.10), appropriately located acoustically treated transfer grilles (Figure 20.11), and automatic windows at high and low level along the corridors (Figures 20.2, 20.6, and 20.7). The perimeter and high-level glazing is also designed to provide daylight to most of the spaces, with glare control by means of the external louvres and awnings. For the artificial lighting system, 'the luminaires were designed specifically for the project and use T5 fluorescent lamps with electronic ballasts to provide 300lux. The occupants are provided with individual task lights to supplement this modest light level' (Cuttle, 2003).

USERS' PERCEPTIONS OF THE BUILDING

Overall response

For all of the 25 or so respondents (92 per cent female, 8 per cent male), the building was their normal place of business, working on average 4.8 days per week and 7.6 hours per day, of which 6.4 were spent at their desk and 5.8 at a computer. The majority (some 88 per cent) were over 30 and some 64 per cent had worked in the building for more than a year at the same desk or work area. Around two-thirds sat next to a window, nine had single offices, while the rest shared with one or more colleagues.

Significant factors

Table 20.1 lists the scores for each of the survey questions and indicates those aspects of the building that the staff perceived as being significantly better, similar to, or worse than the benchmark and/or scale mid-point. In this case, some 24 aspects were significantly better, only ten were significantly worse, while the remaining ten aspects had much the same score as the benchmark.

In keeping with the general tenor of its overall scores, the overall design of this building prompted a good number of positive comments and a reasonable list of things that worked well.

By the same token, and corresponding to the relatively low scores for these aspects, internal noise sources (from students and other colleagues mainly) attracted mainly negative responses (ten out of the 12 respondents) and were also noted as adversely affecting productivity. Lack of storage was an issue for all ten of those who commented on this aspect. Under needs, the majority of negative comments related to the provision of unisex toilet facilities shared with students. No other particular patterns emerged from the comments.

Overall performance indices

The Comfort Index, based on the scores for comfort overall, noise, lighting, temperature, and air quality, works out at +1.12, while the Satisfaction Index, based on the design, needs, health, and perceived productivity scores, is +1.23, both higher than the scale mid-point (noting these indices are scaled from -3 to +3).

The Summary Index, being the average of these, works out at 1.18, while the Forgiveness Factor, calculated to be 1.14 in this instance, indicates that staff as a whole are likely to be relatively more tolerant of minor shortcomings in individual aspects such as winter and summer temperatures, air quality, lighting, and noise (a factor of 1 being the mid-point on a scale that normally ranges from 0.8 to 1.2).

In terms of the Ten-Factor Rating Scale, the building was 'Exceptional' on the 7-point scale, with a calculated percentage value of 100 per cent. When All-Factors were taken into account, the percentage value worked out at 73 per cent, comfortably inside the 'Above Average' band.

OTHER REPORTED ASPECTS OF PERFORMANCE

The annual energy use index (AEUI) for this building was 180 kWh/m².year in 2002 (Jackson, 2004) compared to a benchmark for office buildings with natural ventilation of 210 kWh/m².year (Property Council of New Zealand, 2000). Gas consumption accounted for some 62 per cent of the energy use, the balance being electricity (downward trending over the previous two years) with lighting at 14 per cent, computers at 9 per cent, and photocopiers at 6 per cent the major items.

As far as temperatures in the offices were concerned, in summer, for example, with outside conditions ranging from 15°C at night to 27°C in mid-afternoon, the corresponding inside temperature range was from 17 to 28°C. In wintertime conditions, when outside temperatures dropped to 10°C overnight, the inside temperature never fell below 17°C, and warmed up quickly in the morning.

ACKNOWLEDGEMENTS

I must express my gratitude to AUT management, in particular, Jeffrey Ashkettle and Kurt Warn for their generous assistance with various aspects of the study; and thank designers Marko den Breems of JASMAX, together with Stephen Hogg and Julian Sutherland of Norman Disney Young for assisting my understanding of the building, and the underlying design processes.

REFERENCES

Cuttle, K. (2003) 'Architecture of Air and Light', *Cross Section*, October: 11–13.

den Breems, M. (2003) Transcript of interview held on 2 April 2003, Auckland.

E-W N (Energy Efficiency and Conservation Authority) (2002) 'An Educated Risk', *Energy-Wise News*, 76(April/May): 22–8.

Hogg, S. (2003) Transcript of interview held on 28 August 2003, Auckland.

Jackson, Q. (2004) *Energy Efficiency Audit – Te Mana O Akoranga, Campus Reception and Administration Building, Auckland University of Technology*, Centre for Building Performance Research, School of Architecture, Victoria University of Wellington.

Jaques, R. (2003) 'Pilots for Green Office Scheme', *Build*, February/March: 34–5.

Property Council of New Zealand (2000) *Office Building Energy Consumption*, Auckland: Property Council of New Zealand Incorporated.

Sutherland, J. (2004) Transcript of interview held on 20 April 2004, London.

21
60 Leicester Street
Melbourne, Victoria, Australia

THE CONTEXT

First occupied in late 2002, this four-storey building has a net lettable area of around 3400m². Located on the northern edge of the Melbourne CBD, the shell of the building is partly new and partly refurbished (Figures 21.1 and 21.2).

At the time of survey it housed some 15 separate tenants. These were mainly organisations with a strong interest in environmental issues, such as the offices of the Australian Conservation Foundation (the largest tenant, occupying the whole of the first floor), Environment Victoria, and the Australian Business Council for Sustainable Energy, together with the ground floor retail premises of 'Going Solar' (Figures 21.3 and 21.4).

Developed, owned, and managed by The Green Building Partnership (a collaboration of two ethical investment companies) 'the project was set up to demonstrate the viability and practicality of environmentally sustainable office design and construction in the *commercial* context' (GBP, 2003: 3).

21.1 Leicester Street (west) façade – note addition of new third floor above the top of existing façade

21.2 Refurbished Lansdowne Place (east) façade with service entry at Ground Floor level

21.3 Typical office – note room unit of reverse-cycle heating/cooling system at high level, ceiling-mounted fresh air supply diffuser, and exposed brickwork providing thermal mass

21.4 Ground floor retail premises – note high-level room unit and fresh air supply diffuser, exposed concrete, fixed double glazing and automated windows to light-well

21.5 Plan view at second floor level – note the central atrium running along two-thirds of the length of the building, together with the ventilation light-wells 'cut' into the north- and south-facing façades
Source: Adapted from Spowers

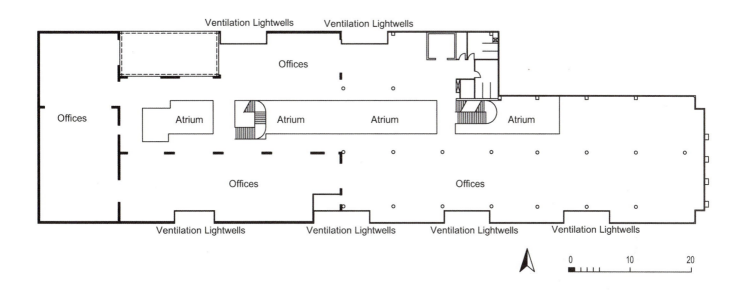

Four principles of sustainable development underpinned the project: 'materials sourcing efficiency; energy efficiency and greenhouse gas efficiency; water and waste water efficiency; and involvement of people' (ibid.: 4). While none of these will come as a surprise to readers, the partnership took the unique step of developing a 'green' lease in which the green building principles and rules are listed, while the tenant's obligations and the landlord's covenants are clearly spelled out in the context of an environmental management plan for the building. A tenancy fit-out manual and a tenant's guide to selection of materials, furniture, and fittings are also included (Hovenden, 2004). The claim was also made that '60L's healthy workplace will reduce "sick building syndrome" and increase productivity' (60L Brochure, 2003).

The building has won several awards, including the (Victorian) Premier's Award for Sustainability, the Category 10 (Leadership in Sustainable Building) Banksia Award, and the Australian Property Institute – Annual Excellence in Property (Environmental Development) Award, all in 2003.

THE DESIGN PROCESS

The design team commissioned by The Green Building Partnership, in conjunction with the Australian Conservation Foundation, comprised Spowers Architects of Melbourne together with Lincolne Scott Australia (building services consultants) and their associate Sydney-based environmental design specialists Advanced Environmental Concepts. The project was two years in the planning and 'all consultants were involved in the design charettes to evolve an integrated solution' (GBP, 2003: Attachment B, 9).

According to the Design Development Report (Design Consortium, 2000: 3), the overall design approach was 'to optimise passive [ventilation] systems as far as possible, within budgetary constraints [the building had to be commercially viable] and only once the building performance with passive systems had been optimised, consider the integration of complementary active [ventilation and air conditioning] services'.

In the event, a mixed-mode thermal environmental control strategy was proposed and adopted by which the building is naturally ventilated when the outside air temperature is between 19°C and 26°C, and mechanically ventilated (heated or cooled as appropriate) when it is outside these values – the winter and summer outside design temperatures being 3.5°C and 34.5°C respectively.

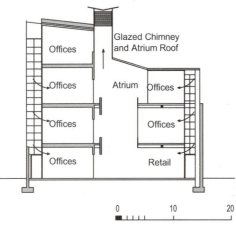

Thermal Chimney

Glazed Chimney
and Atrium Roof

Offices

Offices

Atrium

Offices

Offices

Offices

Offices

Offices

Retail

0   10   20

21.6 View down into one of the north façade light-wells – note the extensive glazing on the façade of 60L and the close proximity of the adjacent commercial building

21.7 View out and up from the light-well of a south-facing ground floor office space – note the automated windows on the vertical glazing. The nearby balconies are on the north façade of the adjacent residential development

21.8 Cross-section illustrating the passive ventilation system with air entering via the perimeter light-wells and exiting via the thermal chimneys
Source: Adapted from Advanced Environmental Concepts

Worth noting too in this connection (as it is sometimes overlooked) was that particular consideration was given to the thermal environmental design of the uppermost (third) floor, the climatic exposure of which is inherently different from the lower floors, particularly in this case with other buildings adjoining or closely adjacent on two sides.

An energy performance of 41kWh/m².year (based on a net lettable area of 3578m²) was predicted, less than 30 per cent of the suggested typical figure (Design Consortium, 2000: 4).

THE DESIGN OUTCOME

Building layout, construction, and passive environmental control systems

Rectangular in plan (Figure 21.5), on an approximately 20m by 72m site sandwiched between adjacent commercial and residential developments, and with its long axis aligned east–west, the building has retained its original (west-facing) façade to Leicester Street (Figure 21.1). It is occupied by a multiplicity of tenants (five on the ground floor, six on the second floor, three on the top floor, and one occupying the whole of the first floor) ranging from two to 40 staff.

Despite these constraints, the building has been planned to enable natural ventilation and natural lighting to be available whenever outside conditions permit. To this end, light-wells have been cut into the north and south façades (two in the former case, four in the latter – Figure 21.5). The light-wells are glazed and have openable windows at each level to enable air and light entry to the offices and shops (Figures 21.6 and 21.7). These occupied spaces are grouped around a central glazed atrium which enables daylight to penetrate down into the centre of the building. Air exits most of these spaces via louvered openings on their inner partitions (Figures 21.8 and 21.9) and other than on the third floor, exits the building via four thermal chimneys located at roof level (Figures 21.10 and 21.11).

The exposed brickwork and concrete provide usable thermal mass (Figures 21.3 and 21.4), while the roof and walls have R-values of 3.5 and 1.5m².°C/W respectively. Double glazing is used throughout except for the louvres and thermal chimneys. The roof of the atrium is a laminated low-E glass, equipped externally with retractable blinds.

21.9 A mid-level internal view into the atrium showing air transfer louvres and light-shelves

21.10 Roof-top view (looking west) of the glazed atrium showing the connection to the thermal chimneys (as it is a day with the outside temperature above 26°C, the louvres are all in the closed position)

21.11 Roof-top view (looking east) – thermal chimneys to the right, roof-mounted fresh air ventilation plant in the upper centre, top of lift shaft and access to roof area on the left

Active environmental control systems

As already noted, the building has a mixed-mode system of thermal environmental control combining natural ventilation, mechanical ventilation, and reverse-cycle heating/cooling.

Operation of the natural ventilation system involves the use of computer-controlled motorised louvres in many of the tenancy windows (see Figures 21.4 and 21.7, for example) and the thermal chimneys (Figures 21.10 and 21.11). These are only opened when the outside air temperature is between 19°C and 26°C, modulating from fully closed to fully open as appropriate. Under these conditions, the mechanical fresh air supply and the tenancy reverse-cycle heating/cooling systems are both off. Above or below that range the motorised louvres are shut and a mechanical ventilation system, incorporating return air heat recovery, provides the minimum regulatory volume of fresh air to the tenancies (Figure 21.11). The tenancy reverse-cycle systems may then be operated if required – each tenancy has its own system enabling occupant control of their particular zone, with set points of (not greater than) 19°C for heating and (not less than) 26°C for cooling, needless to say. Manual windows and louvres may be operated at any time, but only if the heating or cooling systems are switched off.

The tenancy units of the reverse-cycle systems are mainly located at high level in the occupied spaces (Figures 21.3 and 21.4), while the external condenser units are mounted on the roof.

The natural ventilation system may also be used to provide night purging to cool the building automatically under appropriate summertime conditions.

The building was designed to use less than 10 per cent of the mains water normally associated with a building of this nature. Water consumption has been reduced primarily by using water-efficient fixtures and fittings, including waterless urinals. Facilities installed include rainwater collection and storage for use, following treatment and sterilisation, in sinks and showers; wastewater treatment and recycling for use in toilets and for irrigation (GBP, 2003: Attachment B, 8); together with 64 grid-connected photoelectric panels on the rooftop. These panels generate less than 10 per cent of the building's power requirement, the balance being purchased as 100 per cent 'green' power.

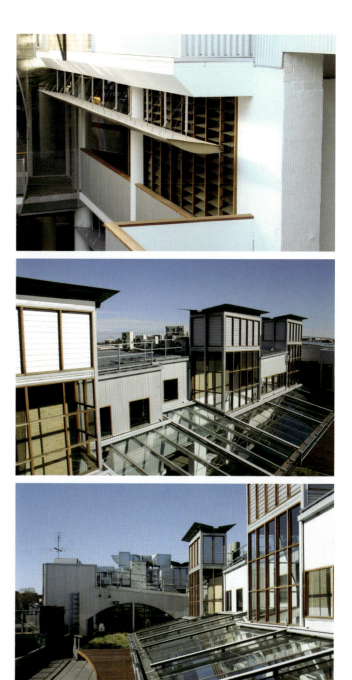

TABLE 21.1

Average scores for each factor and whether they were significantly better, similar to, or worse than the BUS benchmarks

OPERATIONAL FACTORS

Factor	Score	Worse	Similar	Better
Image to visitors	6.18			●
Space in building	5.59			●
Space at desk – too little/much⁴	4.52		●	
Furniture	5.31			●
Cleaning	4.99		●	
Availability of meeting rooms	5.41			●
Suitability of storage arrangements	4.44			●
Facilities meet work requirements	5.56			●

ENVIRONMENTAL FACTORS

Temp and Air in Winter

Factor	Score	Worse	Similar	Better
Temp Overall	4.56			●
Temp – too hot/too cold⁴	4.89		●	
Temp – stable/variable⁴	4.01			●
Air – still/draughty⁴	3.44	●		
Air – dry/humid⁴	3.33		●	
Air – fresh/stuffy¹	2.94			●
Air – odourless/smelly¹	2.70			●
Air Overall	4.64			●

Temp and Air in Summer

Factor	Score	Worse	Similar	Better
Temp Overall	5.50			●
Temp – too hot/too cold⁴	3.74			●
Temp – stable/variable⁴	3.72	●		
Air – still/draughty⁴	3.24		●	
Air – dry/humid⁴	3.46	●		
Air – fresh/stuffy¹	3.03			●
Air – odourless/smelly¹	2.86			●
Air Overall	5.33			●

Lighting

Factor	Score	Worse	Similar	Better
Lighting Overall	5.75			●
Natural light – too little/much⁴	3.96			●
Sun & Sky Glare – none/too much¹	3.30			●
Artificial light – too little/much⁴	4.02			●
Art'l light glare – none/too much¹	2.92			●

Noise

Factor	Score	Worse	Similar	Better
Noise Overall	4.22	●		
From colleagues – too little/much⁴	4.42	●		
From other people – too little/much⁴	4.39	●		
From inside – too little/much⁴	4.25	●		
From outside – too little/much⁴	4.04			●
Interruptions – none/frequent¹	4.12	●		

CONTROL FACTORS ᵇ

Factor		Score	Worse	Similar	Better
Heating	36%	4.39			●
Cooling	24%	4.37			●
Ventilation	24%	3.40		●	
Lighting	25%	4.66			●
Noise	28%	2.63	●		

SATISFACTION FACTORS

Factor	Score	Worse	Similar	Better
Design	5.61			●
Needs	5.87			●
Comfort Overall	5.62			●
Productivity %	+11.39			●
Health	5.25			●

NOTES: (a) unless otherwise noted, a score of 7 is 'best'; superscript ⁴ implies a score of 4 is best, superscript ¹ implies a score of 1 is best; (b) the per cent values listed here are the percentages of respondents who thought personal control of that aspect was important.

TABLE 21.2

Numbers of respondents offering positive, balanced, and negative comments on 12 performance factors

Aspect	Number of respondents			
	Positive	Balanced	Negative	Total
Overall Design	30	10	14	54
Needs Overall	11	7	20	38
Meeting Rooms	4	6	12	22
Storage	0	3	23	26
Desk/Work Area	7	5	19	31
Comfort	14	2	8	24
Noise Sources	4	6	32	42
Lighting Conditions	13	10	12	35
Productivity	21	13	5	39
Health	27	8	3	38
Work Well	58	–	–	58
Hinder	–	–	73	73
TOTALS	189	70	221	480
PER CENT	39.4	14.6	46.0	100.0

USERS' PERCEPTIONS OF THE BUILDING

Overall response

For all of the 100 or so respondents (56 per cent female, 44 per cent male), the building was their normal place of business, working on average 4.1 days per week and 8.0 hours per day, of which 6.8 were spent at their desk and 6.2 at a computer. The majority (some 77 per cent) were over-30 and around 70 per cent had worked in the building for more than a year at the same desk or work area; 55 per cent had single offices or work areas, while the rest shared with one other colleague.

Significant factors

Table 21.1 indicates those aspects of the building that the users perceived as being significantly better, similar to, or worse than the benchmark and/or scale mid-point. In this instance, some 30 aspects were significantly better, only three were significantly worse, while the remaining 12 or so aspects had much the same score as the benchmark.

In terms of operational aspects, this building scores very well on all eight counts – above the mid-point of the scale in every case, and better than the benchmark in all but two. The latter were space at desk where most respondents thought there was too much and cleaning, the score for which (4.99) was close to the benchmark. At 6.18, the score for image was particularly notable.

The users' responses to environmental factors were more variable. The overall scores for temperature and air in both summer and winter were all better than or close to their respective benchmarks, as were most of the 12 more detailed aspects of these factors. The only three exceptions were for the air, which was assessed as on the still side in winter, and a little too dry and stable in summer. All aspects of lighting scored significantly better than

Screening on the east façade of 40 Albert Street

22

40 Albert Road
South Melbourne, Victoria, Australia

Monica Vandenberg and Leena Thomas

THE CONTEXT

Szencorp's refurbishment of 40 Albert Road, which is located on an infill site in South Melbourne, was completed in 2005. Before the refurbishment, the building, consisting of five floors of office accommodation and a basement which ran along the full 55m length of the site, was typical of much of the mediocre 1970/1980s office accommodation in the area.

A number of key challenges were faced in greening the building, not least its orientation. The building is surrounded by medium- to large-scale office buildings and has a narrow 10m frontage to Albert Road and is bounded by buildings to its north and south (Figure 22.1). The service core, comprising male and female toilets, two isolated escape stairs, and a lift, is on the northern boundary (Figure 22.2).

The climate of Melbourne is characterised as warm–temperate with warm to hot summers and cool to cold winters. While the mean maximum temperature in summer is 25.5°C, the city experiences temperatures in excess of 32–35°C for at least 10 per cent of summer days. The mean maximum temperature in winter is 14.5°C and the mean minimum is 8°C.

Key environmental objectives were developed through consultation between the client and design team (SJB, 2006). They included: the minimisation of indoor climate problems, energy consumption and environmental impact; the production of imaginative and optimised daylight use, making the most of external views; the creation of desirable internal and external aesthetics, complying with building regulations and fire protection, smoke

22.1 The building in context with its narrow east-facing façade onto Albert Road and buildings on its north and south sides

22.5 The rear (west) façade with its tinted glazing, openable windows, and internal blinds. Note the photo-voltaic array arranged to provide some shading to the windows on the top floor

22.6 Level 4 – looking eastwards along the central corridor of the top floor, open areas in the far distance and immediately behind, meeting room to the right, and stairwell and toilets to the left

22.7 West-facing open-plan office on Level 4. Note the external shading (by a photo-voltaic array), the internal blinds, and the automated openable section of window (the actuator is visible just under the openable section)

as the façade remained shaded by adjoining buildings for much of the year (Figure 22.5). Where possible, suspended ceilings were removed to expose the thermal mass potential of the underside of the concrete slab and its permanent steel formwork.

The interior concept in the building follows directly from the architectural interventions to ensure the full realisation of the environmental concepts. The building is designed to accommodate 54 staff. The simple move of introducing two circulation spines (Figure 22.6), coupled with the location of open-plan offices at the two ends of the building (Figure 22.7) and placement of cellular offices needing acoustic isolation and privacy in the middle, ensures the maximum access to natural light and views. External amenity spaces for staff are provided both at roof level on the eastern end and over the enclosed car park at Level 2 (Figure 22.5).

In addition to the re-use of the existing structure, the building includes a fully integrated fit-out with materials and finishes carefully chosen to minimise environmental impact and improve indoor air quality.

Passive and active environmental control systems
The office spaces are designed to operate within a temperature range of 19 to 25°C during occupied hours. A mixed-mode of operation combines natural ventilation when ambient conditions permit and a HVAC system for periods where heating or cooling is required. All aspects of operation are controlled by a Building Management System (BMS).

Natural ventilation is achieved by admitting air in through openable windows (Figure 22.7) located at both façades of the building and using the stack effect in the open-tread stairwell (Figure 22.4) to draw the air across the office and exit through louvres at roof level. The system is also employed at night in summer and mid-season to provide night cooling. Cold night air (10–12°C cooler than the daytime maximum) is used to purge the interior and cool the concrete in the ceiling. This serves to stabilise internal temperatures during the day.

The external air conditioning units (Figure 22.8) are powered by natural gas engines. These were selected for their capacity to deliver lower carbon dioxide emissions and to reduce the peak electrical demand of the building. In the air conditioning mode,

22.8 Photo-voltaic array in the foreground, solar water heater and air handling unit in the background, gas-fired fuel cell and cooling unit in the housing immediately behind

22.9 Open-plan area at the west end of Level 3. Note the linear air supply diffuser, the casing around the structural beam, and the exposed formwork

22.10 The water treatment plant in the basement area car park with one of the storage tanks visible background right (just above the soft-top vehicle)

fresh air is admitted via an external air handling unit that filters and dehumidifies the air. The fan coil units serving the open-plan office areas are housed in casings integrated with the structural beams, and conditioned air is delivered to the space via linear diffusers (Figure 22.9).

Single linear T5 fluorescent fittings with specular low brightness louvres are installed with high frequency dimmable DSI electronic ballasts designed to minimise glare and power density. These are controlled via an innovative Managed Lighting System (MLS) consisting of motion sensors positioned around the building to detect occupancy. The MLS is used to provide switching and dimming controls to the lighting system, as well as interface with the BMS which can switch fan coil units off when an area becomes vacant.

In addition to purchasing 'green' power, attempts have been made to reduce dependence on the electricity grid by utilising on-site sources with lower carbon dioxide emissions than that of brown coal-generated electricity (the conventional source in that region) and by trialling a number of innovative technologies. The aim was to reduce the demand on the electricity grid, both overall and during peak periods, and this was done in several ways. The critical foundation was to integrate climate-responsive, energy-efficient, environmental control strategies into the building fabric and management system; while in terms of renewable energy, the hot water system was designed to use the combined input of a gas-boosted solar hot water system and waste heat recovery from a fuel cell, and a number of photo-voltaic arrays were located on the roof (Figure 22.8).

Australia's recent drought situation has meant that water use and re-use have become a significant issue within the built environment. Here, rain and grey water are used for toilet flushing, and water-saving devices have been used throughout the building (Figure 22.10).

USERS' PERCEPTIONS OF THE BUILDING

Overall response

A Building Use Studies (BUS) *pre*-occupancy evaluation was undertaken by Szencorp staff in their previous tenancy located about 1km away from 40 Albert Road. Twelve months after the new office refurbishment

TABLE 22.1

Average scores for each factor and whether they were significantly better, similar to, or worse than the BUS benchmarks

	Score	Worse	Similar	Better		Score	Worse	Similar	Better
OPERATIONAL FACTORS									
Image to visitors	6.73			●	Cleaning	5.54			●
Space in building	5.38			●	Availability of meeting rooms	5.96			●
Space at desk – too little/much^4	4.38		●		Suitability of storage arrangements	4.92			●
Furniture	5.50			●	Facilities meet work requirements	5.88			●
ENVIRONMENTAL FACTORS									
Temp and Air in Winter					Temp and Air in Summer				
Temp Overall	4.42			●	Temp Overall	5.35			●
Temp – too hot/too cold^4	5.08	●			Temp – too hot/too cold^4	3.65		●	
Temp – stable/variable^4	4.28		●		Temp – stable/variable^4	4.05			●
Air – still/draughty^4	2.44	●			Air – still/draughty^4	2.32	●		
Air – dry/humid^4	3.04	●			Air – dry/humid^4	3.45	●		
Air – fresh/stuffy^1	2.20			●	Air – fresh/stuffy^1	2.42			●
Air – odourless/smelly^1	1.64			●	Air – odourless/smelly^1	1.73			●
Air Overall	4.36		●		Air Overall	5.56			●
Lighting					**Noise**				
Lighting Overall	6.04			●	Noise Overall	5.12			●
Natural light – too little/much^4	3.88			●	From colleagues – too little/much^4	4.42		●	
Sun & Sky Glare – none/too much^1	3.38		●		From other people – too little/much^4	3.96			●
Artificial light – too little/much^4	4.20		●		From inside – too little/much^4	3.58	●		
Art'l light glare – none/too much^1	2.58			●	From outside – too little/much^4	3.36	●		
					Interruptions – none/frequent^1	3.77			●
CONTROL FACTORS [b]					**SATISFACTION FACTORS**				
Heating	19% 2.38		●		Design	6.27			●
Cooling	23% 2.38		●		Needs	6.00			●
Ventilation	15% 1.96	●			Comfort Overall	5.65			●
Lighting	15% 3.96		●		Productivity %	+10.0			●
Noise	31% 2.58		●		Health	4.73			●

NOTES: (a) unless otherwise noted, a score of 7 is 'best'; superscript ^{4} implies a score of 4 is best, superscript ^{1} implies a score of 1 is best; (b) the per cent values listed here are the percentages of respondents who thought personal control of that aspect was important.

TABLE 22.2

Numbers of respondents offering positive, balanced, and negative comments on 12 performance factors

Aspect	Number of respondents			
	Positive	Balanced	Negative	Total
Overall Design	4	1	4	9
Needs Overall	2	1	3	6
Meeting Rooms	1	1	1	3
Storage	1	0	6	7
Desk/Work Area plus Furniture	3	6	8	17
Comfort	4	1	3	8
Noise Sources	2	0	3	5
Lighting Conditions	3	1	5	9
Productivity	3	3	0	6
Health	1	2	1	4
Work Well	16	–	–	16
Hinder	–	–	14	14
TOTALS	40	16	48	104
PER CENT	38.5	15.4	46.1	100

a post-occupancy evaluation (POE) using a combination of BUS questionnaire and focus group study was undertaken.

The pre- and post-BUS analysis enabled a direct comparison between the two buildings, and the focus groups facilitated a deeper exploration of issues across the different floor levels. The following section will concentrate on the results from the new building.

Noting that during the first year only three-quarters of the building was occupied, for most of the 26 respondents (35 per cent female, 65 per cent male), the building was their normal place of business. They worked 4.4 days per week on average and 8.2 hours per day, of which around 6.8 were spent at their desk or present work space and 6.6 at a computer. The ratio of under-30s to over-30s was 31:69 per cent and some 35 per cent had worked in the building for more than a year, and at the same desk or work area. Around half the staff had a single office while the other half shared with from one to up to eight colleagues (there are only five cellular offices across three

floors). While half the respondents noted they had a window seat, the design intent was for the majority to have 'access' to natural light – 'Equity to natural light was an important component in the design process' (Mathieson 2007).

Significant factors

Table 22.1 lists the average scores for each of the survey questions and indicates those aspects of the building that the staff perceived as being significantly better, similar to, or worse than the benchmark and/or scale mid-point. In this case some 26 aspects were significantly better, eight were significantly worse, while the remaining 11 aspects had much the same score as the benchmark.

In terms of the eight operational aspects, this building scores significantly better than the benchmark on all counts but space at desk. The analysis indicated that 35 percent believed they had too much space and 25 per cent too little. In the latter situation, the team in one area had grown in a way that was not envisaged in the design and planning phase and staff were sharing desk space.

The users' responses to environmental factors were more variable. Although the overall scores for temperature and air in both summer and winter were better than their benchmarks, individual factor scores indicated it was very cold in winter and too hot in summer and this was echoed in some of the comments (see later). Staff scored the air as too still and too dry in both summer and winter. Fluctuations in temperature in winter were initially caused by incorrect set points, and the night purge system was operating regardless of the outside air temperature. These systems are now closely monitored and staff feedback is encouraged. Areas for improvement identified by staff included the glare and heat coming through the west-facing windows, and the temperature variation in winter. The building's owners are currently experimenting with solar shading – a set of photo-voltaic panels has been installed which partially shade the top floor windows of the west façade (Figure 22.5).

There was a positive response towards the quality of the air, with excellent scores for freshness and odour in both winter and summer.

Lighting scores exceptionally well overall (at 6.04) and in terms of the amount of daylight and relative lack of glare from artificial lighting sources. Noise too scored well overall (at 5.12) though with a suggestion of there being too little noise from inside and outside the building – possibly a result of the relatively low occupancy at the time.

Although users perceived a low level of personal control over their environment, this had little impact on overall comfort and perceived productivity. This would corroborate findings in other buildings (Leaman and Bordass, 2005; Thomas and Baird, 2006) that the strength of the relationship between perceived control and productivity declines as the buildings perform better.

In the case of the satisfaction variables, all five scored significantly higher than their respective benchmarks and their scale mid-points. Needs and design scored 6.00 or over and an average productivity increase of 10 per cent was perceived. In the latter case, 54 per cent of staff said their productivity had improved, 38 per cent indicating that there was no change and 8 per cent (two respondents) perceived a decrease. None of these differences could be attributed to a particular floor

Users' comments

Overall, some 104 responses were received from staff under the 12 headings where they were able to add written comments – some 33.3 per cent of the 312 potential (26 respondents by 12 headings). Table 22.2 indicates the numbers of positive, balanced, and negative comments – in this case, around 38.5 per cent were positive, 15.4 per cent balanced, and 46.1 per cent negative.

Of the specific categories, desk/work area plus furniture attracted the most comments, followed by design, comfort, and lighting.

Most aspects had a fairly even spread of positive and negative comments. However, storage attracted predominantly negative comments even though its score (4.92) was relatively good (there never seems to be enough for many people). Productivity, on the other hand, had entirely positive or balanced comments, reflecting its high score.

While comfort overall had a good balance of positive and negative comments, in keeping with the high score for that aspect, several comments under the hindrances heading noted issues with the temperature, again in keeping with the less than ideal scores for these factors.

Overall performance indices

The Comfort Index, based on the comfort overall, noise, lighting, temperature, and air quality scores, works out at +1.11; while the Satisfaction Index, based on the design, needs, health, and perceived productivity scores, is +1.73, noting that the scale mid-point in these instances is zero on a -3 to +3 scale.

The Summary Index, being the average of the Comfort and Satisfaction Indices, works out at +1.42, while the Forgiveness Factor, calculated to be 1.10 in this instance, indicates that staff are likely to be relatively tolerant of minor shortcomings in individual aspects such as winter and summer temperatures, air quality, lighting, and noise (a factor of 1 being the mid-point on a scale that normally ranges from 0.80 to 1.20).

In terms of the Ten-Factor Rating Scale, the building was 'Exceptional' on the 7-point scale with a calculated percentage value of 100 per cent. When All-Factors were taken into account, the percentage value worked out at 76 per cent – comfortably within the 'Good Practice' band.

OTHER REPORTED ASPECTS OF PERFORMANCE

A detailed analysis of the building performance to date was commissioned by Szencorp. The report (ECS, 2006) detailed the results of performance measurement in the three key areas of energy, water, and transport. Other building evaluations undertaken by external parties included waste, indoor environment quality assessment and an occupant study. Real-time monitoring of building water and energy performance is publicly available on a dedicated website for the building (see www.ourgreenoffice.com/monitoring).

These assessments have highlighted, *inter alia*, that: the air handling systems in the building have reduced air pollutants and dust by over 90 per cent compared to the outside air; sewer volumes have been reduced by 70 per cent through the harvesting of rainwater, water conservation and grey water treatment; a normalised carbon dioxide emission of 168 kg CO_2/m^2 per annum for the period April 2006 to April 2007 was achieved.

In summary, it can be seen that 40 Albert Road has achieved excellent environmental outcomes for energy, water and waste which are matched by positive user satisfaction feedback. Both sets of outcomes endorse the value of client commitment, clear environmental goals, as well as the user-responsive and integrated approach to building design, commissioning and management that was adopted, and continues. According to the Szencorp Manager of Sustainability, 'there is an ongoing commitment to being transparent about the building's performance' (Madden, 2007).

ACKNOWLEDGEMENTS

We must express our gratitude to Szencorp, in particular Rina Madden and Peter Szental for their generous assistance with various aspects of the study; and a special thanks to designers Michael Bialek and Paolo Pennacchia from SJB Architects, together with mechanical engineering consultant Peter Mathieson from Connell Wagner for enabling us to glean insights into the building's design and functionality.

REFERENCES

Bialek, M (2007) Transcript of interview with SJB architect held on 18 April 2007, Melbourne.

ECS (2006) *Szencorp Building – Performance Verification Report – 1st Year Full Report*, Melbourne: Energy Conservation Systems, available at: www.ourgreenoffice.com (accessed 19 September 2008).

Leaman, A. and Bordass, B. (2005) 'Productivity in Buildings – the Killer Variables', *Ecolibrium*, April: 16–20.

Madden, R. (2007) Transcript of meeting with Szencorp Group Manager (Sustainable Buildings) on 18 April 2007, Melbourne.

Mathieson, P. (2007) Transcript of interview with Connell Wagner engineer held on 18 April 2007, Melbourne.

SJB (2006) *RAIA EED+ESD Awards Information Submission: 40 Albert Road*, Melbourne: SJB Architects.

Szental, P. (2007) Transcript of interview with building owner held on 18 April 2007, Melbourne.

Thomas, L. and Baird, G. (2006) 'Post Occupancy Evaluation of Passive Downdraft Evaporative Cooling and Air Conditioned Buildings at Torrent Research Centre, Ahmedabad, India', in *Proceedings of the 40th annual conference of the Architectural Science Association (ANZAScA)*, Adelaide, November.

Thomas, L. and Vandenberg, M. (2007) '40 Albert Road, South Melbourne: Designing for Sustainable Outcomes: A Review of Design Strategies, Building Performance and Users' Perspectives', *BEDP Environment Design Guide*, May 2007, Case Study 45, The Royal Australian Institute of Architects.

Ventilation chimneys and louvres at the Red Centre

23

The Red Centre Building, University of New South Wales
Sydney, NSW, Australia

THE CONTEXT

The Red Centre Building was the first phase of the University of New South Wales' Science Precinct Development, and was the largest project undertaken by the University for a number of years. The site runs east–west alongside the University's Central Mall (Figures 23.1 and 23.2), and the central section was already occupied by a 1960s building housing the School of Architecture (Figure 23.3).

The new building was to occupy the whole site, integrate the existing building, and provide offices, classrooms, and studios for three major academic units – the School of Mathematics, the International Students Centre, and the Faculty of the Built Environment. The 150m-long, six-/eight-storey, 17,500m^2 gross floor area building was first occupied in 1996. University policy was for air conditioning

23.1 Looking westwards along the Central Mall – glazed and louvred east façade; terracotta-panelled north façade

23.2 Looking eastwards along the Central Mall – glazed and louvred west façade; terracotta-panelled north façade

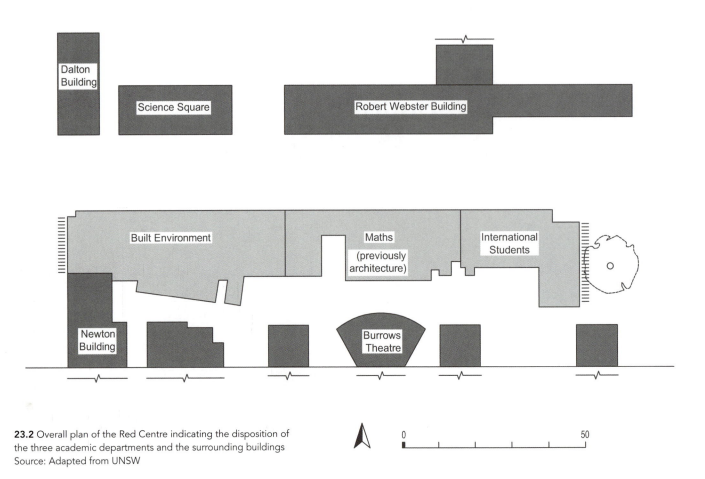

23.2 Overall plan of the Red Centre indicating the disposition of the three academic departments and the surrounding buildings
Source: Adapted from UNSW

0   50

not to be installed in other than specialist areas with high internal heat gains – a definite challenge to the designers, given the latitude and climate of Sydney. Situated at 34°S and with 1 per cent design temperatures of 6.8 and 29.5°C respectively, winter and summer (ASHRAE, 2001: 27.26–7), the cooling of the building by natural ventilation was never going to be easy.

THE DESIGN PROCESS

Following a limited architectural competition, the firm of Mitchell/Giurgola and Thorp (MGT) Architects, with offices in Canberra and Sydney, was chosen to design the building. The team was led by Richard Francis-Jones, an architect with the very clear view that 'A move away from a reliance on artificial servicing towards passive systems is very significant for architecture as an integrated cultural activity' (Francis-Jones, 1997). The engineering consultant in this instance was Ove Arup and Partners, following a successful presentation to the University by Paul A. Stevenson of their Sydney office.

The budget constraints of a typical university-funded development, the necessity to employ natural ventilation for relatively densely occupied spaces in the climate of Sydney, and the lack of thoroughly documented precedents at the time, threw up some major challenges for the design team, but ones which they were well motivated to resolve.

The architect and engineer undertook a series of meetings with the many academic units that were prospective users of the building – Mathematics, International Students, and the several groups that were eventually to be incorporated into a single Faculty of the Built Environment. One of the aims of these meetings was to develop the detailed brief for the project, no easy task given the number and variety of clients and the architectural expertise of one of the main groups of users.

However, with a university Vice-Chancellor who was 'very supportive of passive systems and green building issues' (Francis-Jones, 1999), and design team principals whose philosophies were disposed to a more sustainable view of the built environment, it was almost inevitable that the brief would call for the maximum use of natural ventilation and daylighting.

Various methods of achieving the former were explored – single-sided ventilation and cross-ventilation were both tried before the stack or chimney ventilation concept emerged.

23.4 Close-up of western end of north façade with studios on upper floors and staff offices on middle floors – note double horizontal band of windows in the latter case, with the lower band openable; and the array of ventilation chimneys

23.5 Looking westwards along the service roadway at the rear of the building – south façade on the right

THE DESIGN OUTCOME

The design process and architectural outcome have been described elsewhere in some detail (Cantrill, 1997; Baird, 2001); what follows is the briefest of outlines, together with more detail of the environmental control systems.

Building layout and construction

The overall form of the building approximates a 150m-long, variable width (15.7m to 19.3m), and six- to eight-storey high block, with a gross floor area of 17,500m². The site slopes down gently from east to west. The main accommodation comprises offices, classrooms, studios, lecture theatres, and computer rooms, only the last of which are air conditioned.

The north façade is mainly screened by Italian terracotta panels to give it an appropriate relationship with the surrounding parts of the campus (Figures 23.1 and 23.2). The upper studio floors on this façade have fixed horizontal shades while the twin glazing 'slots' on the lower office floors are recessed into their deep reveals (Figure 23.4). The south façade has extensive glazing to enable daylighting of the classrooms (Figure 23.5).

The east (Figure 23.1) and west (Figure 23.2) façades are fully glazed, but protected on the outside by sets of vertical photo-sensor-actuated motorised louvres. The predominant feature of the roofscape is the multiplicity of rotating-cowl-topped ventilating chimneys (Figure 23.6).

Passive and active environmental control systems

According to Richard Francis-Jones (1997):

> The cooling, heating, and ventilation process has been achieved through an integrated design of thermal mass, air shafts, thermal flues, sun shading, vents and 'breathing' facades. These systems are controlled by the individual users and also by a central computer management system that adjusts air flow relative to outside temperature.

23.6 Roofscape above the School of Mathematics – ventilating chimneys galore

23.7 Cross-section showing the principles of the natural ventilation design
Source: Adapted from Cantrill

23.8 View of typical air path between floors and ventilating ducts connecting classrooms to vertical chimneys

Thermal mass is clearly manifest in the amount of concrete surface left exposed on the interior surfaces of the building, not only in the stairwells and corridors, but on the ceilings and on the blockwork partition walls of offices, classrooms, and studios. Air shafts are integrated into the vertical cross-section of the building (Figures 23.7 and 23.8) so that air can move easily between selected floors, thus providing a variety of potential air paths for both cross- and stack ventilation.

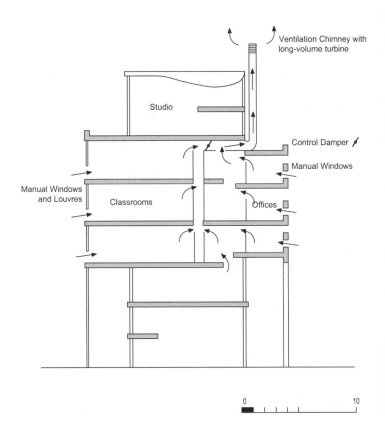

23.9 Sliding doors and partitions between studio and corridor with fixed cross-ventilation louvres top and bottom

23.10 Corridor adjacent to staff offices with openable glass louvres above each office door on the left, and a fixed transfer grille leading into an air shaft on the right

23.11 Staff office interior showing openable glazing below and ventilation slot above the window bookshelf, and a ceiling fan

The thermal flues or chimneys, the total cross-sectional area of which amounts to nearly 1 per cent of the total floor area, provide the method for exhausting air from the majority of the classrooms, studios, and office spaces in the lower two-thirds of the building (Figure 23.8). An automatic damper, designed to control the rate of air flow in response to inside temperature, is located in each flue. It is estimated this system can provide 10–20 air changes per hour as a result of the stack pressures generated (Stevenson, 1999).

In addition to conventional windows, substantial sections of the glazing on all four 'breathing' façades and some of the internal partitions are fitted with both fixed and manually operated ventilation

TABLE 23.1

Average staff scores for each factor and whether they were significantly better, similar to, or worse than the BUS benchmarks (student scores in brackets)

OPERATIONAL FACTORS

Factor	Score	Worse	Similar	Better
Image to visitors	5.10		●	
Space in building	3.88		●	
Space at desk – too little/much[4]	4.03			●
Furniture	4.92	●		

Factor	Score	Worse	Similar	Better
Cleaning	5.21			●
Availability of meeting rooms	4.37		●	
Suitability of storage arrangements	3.35		●	

ENVIRONMENTAL FACTORS

Temp and Air in Winter

Factor	Score	Worse	Similar	Better
Temp Overall (4.89)	3.54	●		
Temp – too hot/too cold[4]	5.39	●		
Temp – stable/variable[4]	4.50		●	
Air – still/draughty[4]	4.30	●		
Air – dry/humid[4]	3.32		●	
Air – fresh/stuffy[1]	3.41			●
Air – odourless/smelly[1]	3.00			●
Air Overall (5.09)	3.72	●		

Temp and Air in Summer

Factor	Score	Worse	Similar	Better
Temp Overall	3.22	●		
Temp – too hot/too cold[4]	2.68	●		
Temp – stable/variable[4]	4.38		●	
Air – still/draughty[4]	3.50		●	
Air – dry/humid[4]	4.41	●		
Air – fresh/stuffy[1]	4.00			●
Air – odourless/smelly[1]	3.34			●
Air Overall	3.35	●		

Lighting

Factor	Score	Worse	Similar	Better
Lighting Overall (5.01)	5.32			●
Natural light – too little/much[4]	4.22		●	
Sun & Sky Glare – none/too much[1]	4.60	●		
Artificial light – too little/much[4]	4.19		●	
Art'l light glare – none/too much[1]	3.33			●

Noise

Factor	Score	Worse	Similar	Better
Noise Overall (4.50)	3.29	●		
From colleagues – too little/much[4]	4.74	●		
From other people – too little/much[4]	4.85	●		
From inside – too little/much[4]	4.56	●		
From outside – too little/much[4]	4.66	●		
Interruptions – none/frequent[1]	4.71		●	

CONTROL FACTORS[b]

Factor	%	Score	Worse	Similar	Better
Heating	48%	4.09			●
Cooling	44%	2.68		●	
Ventilation	40%	4.62			●
Lighting	39%	5.34			●
Noise	45%	1.95	●		

SATISFACTION FACTORS

Factor	Score	Worse	Similar	Better
Design (5.01)	3.63	●		
Needs	4.11	●		
Comfort Overall (4.95)	3.75	●		
Productivity % (+8.54)	−5.00	●		
Health (4.35)	3.72		●	

NOTES: (a) unless otherwise noted, a score of 7 is 'best'; superscript 4 implies a score of 4 is best, superscript 1 implies a score of 1 is best; (b) the per cent values listed here are the percentages of respondents who thought personal control of that aspect was important; (c) student scores are in brackets – the temperature and air scores cover all seasons.

TABLE 23.2

Numbers of staff respondents offering positive, balanced, and negative comments on
12 performance factors. Student responses to general environmental issues in brackets

Aspect	Number of respondents			
	Positive	Balanced	Negative	Total
Overall Design	12	7	55	74
Needs Overall	5	8	46	59
Meeting Rooms	4	4	30	38
Storage	1	3	44	48
Desk/Work Area plus Furniture	13	5	36	54
Comfort	5	5	28	38
Noise Sources	0	8	46	54
Lighting Conditions	10	8	23	41
Productivity	3	13	24	40
Health	4	11	18	33
Work Well	58	–	–	58
Hinder	–	–	88	88
General Environmental (students only)	(9)	(5)	(75)	(89)
TOTALS (Staff only)	115	72	438	625
PER CENT (Staff only)	18.4	11.5	70.1	100

louvres as well as large sliding doors (Figure 23.9). These are designed to allow fresh air entry at the perimeter and at both high and low level in spaces such as classrooms, exhibition areas, and stairwells; and air transfer across the building in spaces such as the upper level studios and staff offices (Figures 23.10 and 23.11).

Manual control of the window openings, the ventilation louvres, the ceiling fans, the gas heaters, and the blackout roller blinds, is left in the hands of the academic and cleaning staff and the students, but guidance in the form of small wall plaques containing straightforward sets of operating instructions are provided at strategic points in each space.

While only around 10 per cent of the floor area (computer rooms mainly) is currently air conditioned, the building has been fitted throughout with a condenser water loop and condensate drain to enable it to cope with additional equipment heat gains or intensive summer use.

USERS' PERCEPTIONS OF THE BUILDING

Overall response

In this case, responses were sought from staff and students, the former using the standard questionnaire, the latter a shorter version. The survey was conducted during November 2002.

For all of the 122 or so staff respondents (43 per cent female, 57 per cent male), the building was their normal place of work, most (80 per cent) working five days per week or more, and averaging 7.9 hours per day. The majority (some 83 per cent) were over 30 and had worked in the building for more than a year, some 77 per cent at the same desk or work area. Around 67 per cent worked alone while most of the rest shared with one or more colleagues. Hours per day spent at desk and at computer averaged 6.2 and 5.1 respectively. Of the 122 respondents, approximately 42 per cent were from the Faculty of the Built Environment, 51 per cent from

Inter-floor opening at the Institute of Languages

24

Institute of Languages, University of New South Wales
Sydney, NSW, Australia

Leena Thomas

THE CONTEXT

The Institute of Languages building at UNSW was developed in 1999 as a key component to reinvigorate the University's Randwick campus as part of a masterplan. The immediate need was for an intensive languages school primarily for international students, for whom this building would be their first encounter with the University. In addition to the marketing and teaching perspective that required contemporary and comfortable accommodation for its international clientele, the University leadership and design team were keen to ensure the project was designed with a long-life loose-fit approach where future changes to larger lecture rooms or even open-plan offices were envisaged.

The building is located in Sydney, Australia (34° South), which has 1 per cent design temperatures of 6.8 and 29.5°C respectively, in winter and summer (ASHRAE, 2001: 27.26–7). The site selected was located at the entrance of the Randwick campus which allows the building to be oriented with its long axis running east–west. It faces onto busy King Street (Figure 24.1) and for the first seven years of its occupancy adjoined a major public bus depot.

The building has been cited in a number of articles and has received several awards, including the Royal Australian Institute of Architects (National) Sustainability Award in 2000 and the Architecture Show Magazine and the Francis Greenway Society Green Buildings Gold Medal in 2001.

24.1 South façade from King Street. Brick-clad elevator shaft, floor lobbies, and toilet areas to the left, classrooms to the right

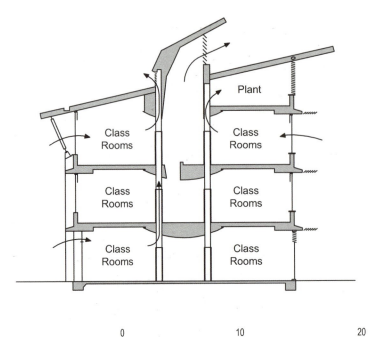

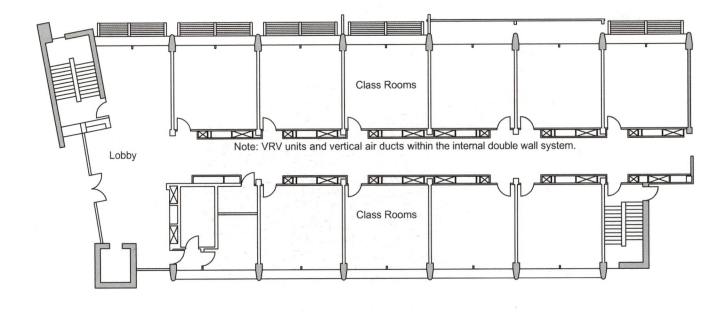

24.2 Cross-section of the building. Note the skylight and daylight penetration arrangement to the central corridors of the upper levels, and the air transfer paths for ventilation
Source: Adapted from Jackson Teece

24.3 Indicative floor plan showing classrooms on either side of a central corridor. Note the location of VRV units and vertical air ducts within the double wall system between classrooms and corridor
Source: Adapted from Jackson Teece

Note: VRV units and vertical air ducts within the internal double wall system.

24.4 Main entrance on the west side with fritted glass external shading to the glazed lobbies of the upper levels; stair tower on the left

24.5 Looking eastwards along the north façade. Shading provided by the trees, the overhang, and the fixed horizontal grillework

THE DESIGN PROCESS

The design team selected by the client was put together for their expertise in developing environmentally sustainable and contemporary educational buildings. Architects Jackson Teece Chesterman and Willis, who were also responsible for the University masterplan, were selected from a limited competition process and teamed up with University-appointed mechanical and environmental engineers Steensen Varming. The firms had completed a number of leading environmentally focused building projects both individually and in partnership with one another. When interviewed, architect Damian Barker (2003) and mechanical engineer Barry Tam (2003) were both very positive about the collaborative and integrated design approach which was instituted right from the inception of design concept.

The team developed a range of alternative design options that could satisfy the twin ambitions for flexibility and low energy. In addition, all design decisions were subject to stringent cost benefit analysis to ensure the project was completed with the tight University budget.

THE DESIGN OUTCOME

While the architectural outcome has been described elsewhere in some detail (Margalit, 2000), what follows is an outline of how the built form has been influenced in its layout and design by the programmatic and environmental considerations of the design.

A study (Thomas and Ballinger, 1997) which shows it is possible to achieve comfort in a free running office building (with comparable internal load levels to occupied classrooms) without air conditioning for approximately 80 per cent of the year in the Sydney climate has also argued that the success of such buildings hinged on the manner in which the residual period of discomfort was alleviated. Significantly, the approach adopted at the Institute of Languages was to design a building with a mixed-mode of operation relying on mechanical systems for heating and cooling under extreme conditions. This contrasts with the brief for no air conditioning that was adopted for an earlier UNSW project – the Red Centre (see Chapter 23). The building also aims to extend the principles of using the building

24.6 Detail of the south façade. Note the sets of louvres on either side of the sliding windows. Generally speaking, the set on the left have automated actuators fitted, while those on the right are operated manually (see also Figure 24.11)

24.7 External view of the corridor skylight arrangement on the roof. Note too the row of air outlet grilles from the natural ventilation system immediately below the glazing, and the air conditioning plant 'housing' in the foreground

24.8 Looking up into a typical skylight from the corridor of the top floor (Level 2)

fabric as an environmental modifier explored by this architectural practice at the Advanced Technology Centre at the University of Newcastle campus in 1993 (Prasad and Thomas, 1995).

The design concept evolved from an interrogation of a typical two–three storeyed teaching building with classrooms on either side of a central corridor that is often plagued with inadequate single-sided ventilation to classrooms, dark corridors, and high levels of ambient noise through internal louvres introduced above the head of the door to the central corridor for cross-ventilation. The final design was developed around a minimum module of 6m by 6m classrooms which could be independently climatically controlled and yet extended through removal of partition walls to develop larger lecture halls or open-plan offices.

Building layout, construction, and passive environmental control systems

Conceived as a gateway building, the final form of the Institute of Languages rises to three floors (Figure 24.2) and is essentially a simple, efficient arrangement of a series of 6m square classrooms to the north and south of a central corridor, with an entry foyer to its west (Figure 24.3). With short east and west façades (Figure 24.4), the building is characterised by extensive glazing to its north and south. The north (equator-facing) façade is protected from undue solar heat loads through the use of horizontal sunshades and a grove of trees (Figure 24.5). The basic treatment to the south remains more or less identical, with the façade reveal offering limited benefit in curtailing the early morning and late evening summer sun (Figures 24.1 and 24.6). Classrooms on the ground floor are able to open out onto sunny terraces. Intermediate walls between classrooms on each wing are not integral to the concrete load-bearing structure and can be removed should the space need to be expanded. In its present configuration, this format is evident in the top floor lecture theatre.

This departure from the traditional model involves the deployment of natural light to the internal corridors and an inventive attempt to provide acoustically isolated natural ventilation using the stack effect. A series of north-facing skylights over the top floor of the corridor (Figures 24.7 and 24.8) deliver daylight to the middle floor

24.9 Looking east along the corridor of the top floor (Level 2). Note the skylight openings in the ceiling, the balustraded voids allowing daylight penetration to the corridor below, and the light colour finishes

24.10 Internal view of a typical classroom, looking towards the corridor. Note the ventilation grille at low level and the glazed ventilation ducts at high level within the wall structure, one on each side of a central housing for the VRV unit. Narrow slot supply diffusers for the air conditioning system are just visible between the luminaires, and the controls for these are visible to the right of the doorway

24.11 South-facing classroom showing the typical louvre and blind manual actuator arrangement. The louvres on the other side of the windows have automated actuators

through voids in the upper level floor (Figure 24.9). A key innovation is the double wall system along the inner corridor which exploits the opportunity for natural ventilation using the stack effect and houses the variable refrigerant volume (VRV) air conditioning units. Rather than a separate housing of the VRV units in the ceiling of the classroom or corridor, the chosen configuration allows for seamless integration of the two environmental modes within the vertical duct, and simultaneously gains some acoustic benefit through the double wall (Figure 24.10).

In addition to the skylights and light wells, a further sense of openness and daylight in the corridors (Figure 24.9) is wrought

Natural ventilation through the windows is enhanced as air may be drawn through low-level louvres within the internal double wall system (Figure 24.10) and then vented through dedicated vertical exhaust vents to the roof (Figure 24.7). In the air-conditioned mode, each room is isolated by closing the external windows and its dedicated exhaust vent to the roof, and the space is heated or cooled via the VRV unit housed in the double wall system. Rather than reliance on a building management system to regulate the employment of air conditioning within predetermined temperature set points, the system is designed to be started on demand by occupants in each classroom and shut down by a timed switch.

The window system integrates a couple of louvered panels on either end of glazed sliding windows and manually operated internal blinds (Figure 24.11). For the most part, the rooms rely on daylighting, with artificial lighting provided through energy efficient fluorescent luminaires.

USERS' PERCEPTIONS OF THE BUILDING

Overall response

In this case, responses were sought from staff and students, the former using the standard questionnaire, the latter a shorter version. The surveys were conducted during 2004.

As most students typically attended the building for only one teaching semester, the survey was administered twice – once in August (winter students) and again in December (summer students) – to ensure that responses for the full range of seasonal variations were captured. The students comprised two further distinct groups: daytime students who spent an average of 18–20 hours per week, typically between 9am and 3pm; and evening college students who attended the building for an average of three hours a week typically between 6pm and 9pm. While the question was not asked directly, it was clear that the daytime students were overwhelmingly below the age of 30, whereas the evening college students were typically mature, aged and over 30 years.

All of the 26 or so staff respondents (80 per cent female, 20 per cent male) were over 30 and most (92 per cent) had worked in the building for more than a year. The Randwick campus was their normal place of work, with most having a shared office in an adjacent administration building. Time spent in the Institute building averaged 3.4 days per week and 4.3 hours per day (with a further 3.1 hours in the office).

Significant factors

The average scores of the staff and students for each of the relevant survey questions are listed in Table 24.1. Table 24.1 also indicates, for the staff only, those aspects of the building that they perceived as being significantly better, similar to, or worse than the benchmark and/or scale mid-point. Overall, some six aspects were significantly better, seven were significantly worse, while the remaining 32 aspects had much the same score as the benchmark.

A series of sub-analyses was undertaken to check for variations in user perceptions within the student sub-groups. Table 24.2 summarises these analyses.

Of all the operational aspects, staff scored the building highest on its image, while the low score for space at desk reflects conditions in the administrative building rather than the Institute.

In terms of the environmental factors, temperature and air conditions in winter and summer were scored reasonably well by staff, and even better by the students. However, staff expressed some concerns about the air being too dry and consequently this factor scored well below the benchmark overall.

The largely daylit design scored above the benchmark for lighting overall by staff, with its various components all similar to their respective benchmarks. The students, on the other hand, consistently rated lighting overall as being no different from the benchmarks, with too much wintertime artificial lighting.

Staff rated the building poorly with respect to noise from every source, with too much from colleagues, other people, and from both inside and outside the building. Comments and discussion with staff revealed that much of the noise emanated from mass movement and congregation of groups of students in the corridors before and after their lectures. With openable windows extending along the full external walls, it appears that there is also some flanking noise transmission from adjoining classrooms. The students scored the building better than the staff and the benchmark from this point of view.

TABLE 24.3

Numbers of staff respondents offering positive, balanced, and negative comments
on 12 performance factors. Student responses to general environmental issues in brackets

Aspect	Number of respondents			
	Positive	Balanced	Negative	Total
Design	0	2	12	14
Needs	2	2	7	11
Meeting Rooms	1	0	5	6
Storage	0	0	8	8
Desk/Work Area	3	2	4	9
Comfort Overall	0	0	5	5
Noise Overall	0	0	10	10
Lighting Overall	4	0	2	6
Productivity	1	3	2	6
Health	1	2	4	7
Work Well	13	–	–	12
Hinder	–	–	15	15
General Environmental (students only)	(3)	(12)	(75)	(90)
TOTALS (staff only)	25	11	74	110
PER CENT (staff only)	22.7	10.0	67.3	100

Perceived control scored low in several instances, but was similar to the (already relatively low) benchmarks for heating, ventilation, lighting, cooling, and noise. Depending on the aspect considered, 23 to 38 per cent of staff rated personal control as important. The low scores for perceived control of heating, cooling, and ventilation are somewhat surprising as it is possible to open windows, operate internal blinds, and initiate the air conditioning via wall mounted switches in the classrooms.

In the case of the satisfaction factors, staff registered moderately positive scores (all were above the mid-point of their respective scales) that were not significantly different to their benchmarks in most cases. On average, they attributed a marginally positive impact (+0.48 per cent) to their productivity from the environmental conditions within the building. Students averaged a +9.07 per cent increase in their perceived productivity and all the other scores in this category were greater than those of the staff. Day students who used the building for longer periods were less appreciative of the design and less satisfied with how the facilities met their needs compared to the evening college students.

Users' comments

Overall, some 110 responses were received from staff under the 12 headings where they were able to add written comments – some 35 per cent of the 300 potential (26 respondents by 12 headings). Table 24.3 indicates the numbers of positive, balanced, and negative comments overall – in this case 22.7 per cent were positive, 10 per cent balanced, and 67.3 per cent negative.

Generally speaking, the nature and type of comments reflected the scores, particularly in the case of lack of storage and noise. Staff noted noise and malfunctions with air conditioning (notably the inability to switch the air conditioning off) as the dominating issues that hinder ability to work. At the time of the survey the neighbouring bus depot was also noted to be a source of noise. It resulted in an inability to open windows on the south (street) side which exacerbated reliance on air conditioning instead of natural ventilation.

Staff commented on good lighting and the bright and airy classrooms as well as the audio-visual facilities. There were also some comments suggesting a variation in performance between the north (too hot in summer) and south (too cold in winter).

Around 20 per cent of the student respondents commented on the general environmental conditions in the building – these were predominantly negative and mirrored staff comments, covering issues such as internal noise from people and air conditioning, external noise from buses, unacceptable temperatures, and controls for air conditioning. They also made comments regarding facilities such as the lack of female toilets (only available on the first floor), break-out spaces, and drinking water.

Overall performance indices

The Comfort Index for the staff, based on the scores for comfort overall, noise, lighting, temperature, and air in winter and summer, works out at 0.04, while the Satisfaction Index, based on the design, needs, health, and perceived productivity scores, is 0.21, both above the scale mid-point (noting these indices are scaled from -3 to +3).

The Summary Index, being the average of these, works out at 0.12, while the Forgiveness Factor, calculated to be 1.11 in this instance, indicates that the staff as a whole are likely to be relatively forgiving as far as minor shortcomings in individual aspects such as winter and summer temperatures, air quality, lighting, and noise are concerned (a factor of 1 being the mid-point on a scale that normally ranges from 0.8 to 1.2).

In terms of the Ten-Factor Rating Scale, the building was at the top end of the 'Above Average' band of the 7-point scale, with a calculated percentage value of around 68 per cent. When All-Factors were taken into account, the percentage value reduced to around 59 per cent, towards the lower end of the 'Above Average' band.

Applying the same system to the ten overall factors assessed by the undergraduate students, a percentage value of 88 per cent would be obtained, at the bottom end of the 'Exceptional' band.

ACKNOWLEDGEMENTS

Completed with assistance from George Baird who undertook the summertime surveys, this case study draws on his interviews with Damien Barker of Jackson Teece Chesterman Willis and Barry Tam of Steensen Varming. We must also thank Alan Chow, Business Manager, Institute of Languages, UNSW, and Robert Grimmet, UNSW Energy Manager for their assistance to enable the survey to be undertaken.

REFERENCES

ASHRAE (2001) *ASHRAE Handbook: Fundamentals, SI Edition*, Atlanta, GA: American Society of Heating Refrigerating and Air-Conditioning Engineers.

Barker, D. (2003) Transcript of interview of 6 November 2003, Sydney.

Margalit, H. (2000) 'Logic and Language', *Architecture Australia*, July/August.

Prasad, D. and Thomas, L. (1995) 'Advanced Technology Centre, Newcastle', *RAIA Environment Design Guide*, (CAS1, February), Canberra: RAIA.

Tam, B. (2003) Transcript of interview of 6 November 2003, Sydney.

Thomas L. E. and Ballinger J. A. (1997) 'Climate Interactive Low-Rise Suburban Office Buildings for Sydney', in T. Lee (ed.) *Solar '97: Sustainable Energy, Proceedings of 35th ANZSES Conference*, Canberra, 69: 1–7.

General Purpose Building, University of Newcastle
NSW, Australia

Jodie Dixon

THE CONTEXT

Completed in 1995, the General Purpose Building was one of the first on the University of Newcastle campus to explore the limits of purpose-designed natural ventilation, at a time when such a move was not typical.

25.1 Atrium space, looking west from Level 3 – staff offices to the right, classrooms to the left, glazing and automated opening windows above. Note the louvred openings above the doors of offices and classrooms and the openings to the corridor below located behind and under the bench seats

On the east coast of New South Wales, Australia, the Newcastle conditions bring cool temperate winters with lows of 4°C and borderline temperate–sub-tropical summers reaching 40°C. At latitude 33°S and an elevation of 21m above sea level, buildings in this city commonly employ HVAC systems, particularly at times of high summer humidity.

Designed to a modest budget to accommodate classrooms and academic offices, the building utilises a cross-ventilated atrium. This ventilation design allows for personally controlled horizontal airflow through offices and classrooms in combination with vertical atrium airflows induced using automated opening clerestory windows just below roof level (Figure 25.1).

THE DESIGN PROCESS

A traditional consultant–client process was entered into, but the collaboration between architect and mechanical engineer ensured the feasibility of a passive design solution for this multi-level building. Suters Architects was chosen and a brief was developed between the university facilities management team and the architect.

Suters Architect's Dino Di Paolo (2007) acknowledges that early in the process the university client had some air-conditioning requirements. Thankfully they were 'not quite as focused on air-conditioning as a lot of clients are these days'. He describes it as one of his first passively designed buildings on a large scale:

> We had been … dabbling in this sort of passive approach for a short while prior to this on smaller projects … this was the first building that was … quite large in a sense, it was a commercial structure in a educational facility where we had an opportunity to put some of these things into place.

It is clear that the design team worked closely to implement a cultural change on the campus moving from the reliance on mechanical systems to low-energy initiatives.

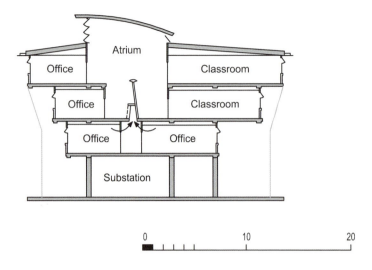

25.2 Generalised cross-section showing the disposition of staff offices and classrooms, and the provision for air movement and daylighting to the atrium space
Source: Adapted from Suters Snell Architects

25.3 Floor plan at Level 3 with offices to the north, classrooms to the south. Note the circulation walkways and bridge at Level 3, the large openings to Level 2, and the series of five smaller openings to the Level 1 corridor below that
Source: Adapted from Suters Snell Architects

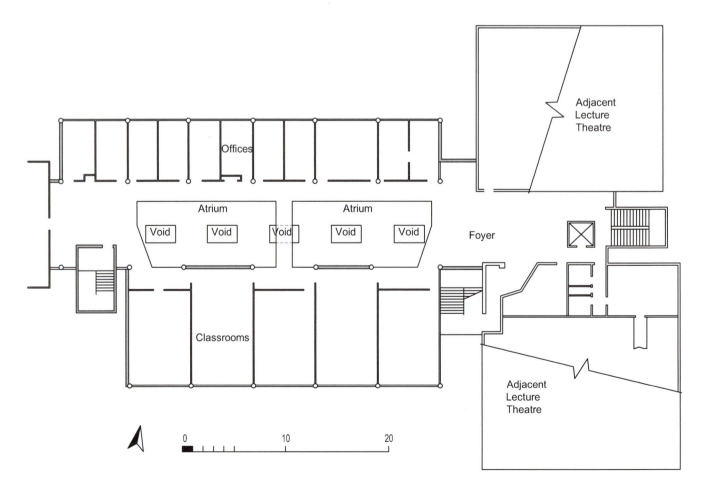

25.4 View of north façade. Note the overhanging floors, the skylight windows on top of the atrium at high level, and the circulation routes under the building at ground level on either side of the transformer housing. The brick cladding of one of the adjoining lecture theatres is just visible on the right

25.5 View of the south façade. Note the overhanging floors and the circulation route under the building

THE DESIGN OUTCOME

Building layout and construction

The design focused offices to the north on three levels, larger classrooms or staffrooms to the south, and a central north-facing atrium acting as the building circulation-airflow spine (Figures 25.2 and 25.3). The brief called for construction above an existing ground level substation and bridge over 'a very strong pedestrian circulation route'. Choosing to build perpendicular to the pedestrian route allowed Di Paolo (2007) to 'get the north–south orientation quite nicely' (Figures 25.4 and 25.5).

The building is four storeys high and consists of three floors above a public ground level. It is operated passively with the exception of air-conditioned lecture theatres located at the far east end of the building and a public clinic facility on the ground floor.

The upper floors of the building step out to shade the lower levels on the north (Figure 25.6) and provide weather protection on the south (Figures 25.4 and 25.5). Wider central thoroughfares on upper levels are vertically linked by open void spaces and walkways that access the large classroom spaces (Figures 25.1 and 25.7). Staff offices, staffrooms, and a small corridor occupy the floor below. The lower floor corridor is provided with ceiling openings to promote airflow up into the atrium levels above (Figures 25.2 and 25.8).

The building is framed by a concrete structure with light steel framed walls to the building perimeter, insulated and clad in metal sandwich panel. Masonry walls are internally exposed in the atrium (Figures 25.1 and 25.7) and a lightweight insulated metal sheet roof has set a dramatic curved ceiling profile (Figure 25.9). Clerestory glazed baffles on the north and south are automated to open and close just below the curved roof (Figures 25.9 and 25.10). Concrete slab floors are carpeted throughout and hidden by ceilings.

25.6 Western 'gable-end' view looking eastwards along the north façade with the overhanging structure clearly articulated. Note too the oversized gutter-sunshade arrangement and rainwater drainpipes

25.7 Atrium space, looking east from Level 2 – staff offices to the left, classrooms to the right, skylight above. Note the louvred openings above the doors of offices and classrooms and the openings under the bench seats to enable air transfer, as well as the thermally massive brick cladding and exposed concrete structure

25.8 Looking along the corridor of Level 1. Offices on either side and the series of five ceiling openings enabling air transfer to the atrium space above

Passive and active environmental control systems

Exposed masonry walls provide thermal mass running internally through the atrium of the upper two levels (Figures 25.1 and 25.7). In summer, the walls provide an internal heat sink due to sun block-out and are night-cooled to expel any stored daytime heat. The same walls are warmed in winter by sunlight entering north-facing clerestory windows.

The ventilation concept uses night venting and cross-ventilation and relies upon automated clerestory louvres (Figures 25.9 and 25.10) and the adjustment of louvres above internal office doors (Figures 25.1 and 25.7) and perimeter windows by occupants (Figure

25.9 Exterior view of the atrium skylight from the south-east. Note the baffled openings on the south side and the set of smoke extract vents visible on top

25.10 North-facing glazing of the atrium skylight. Note the baffles fitted outside the opening windows to prevent driving rain penetration

25.11 Typical staff office on Level 3. Note the range of window opening and shading options, the 1kW electric heater under the workbench and the desk top fan

25.11). The building section (Figure 25.2) shows how warmed air naturally rises up and expels through clerestory vents. University energy manager David Alexander (2007) notes that the automated clerestory system looks at 'the inside and outside temperature and wind direction and rain and decides whether to have them open or not'. Automated fire dampers are also fitted to the lower corridor voids to meet building code requirements for buildings over two storeys in height.

In addition, blinds moderate solar gains in winter or reduce heat losses through glass. North-facing windows are shaded in summer by the stepped building envelope and an upper level northern sunshade-oversized gutter (Figure 25.6). Personal heaters and fans are intended to meet personal heating and cooling needs (Figure 25.11).

Ample natural light floods the building via the atrium space. Changes in the daylight conditions are reflected throughout the whole building. Personal task lighting and fluorescent tube general lighting have been provided otherwise.

USERS' PERCEPTIONS OF THE BUILDING

Overall response

Of the 52 staff and postgraduates surveyed in the GP building, 23 responded, of which 19 (83 per cent) were 30 or older and 15 (65 per cent) were female. Private office arrangements account for 15 people working alone, the rest sharing with one or more others – 18 had access to windows. 18 (78 per cent) had worked in the same building for more than one year. Staff generally spent 4.5 days per week and 7.8 hours per day in the building, 5.6 hrs of which was spent at their desk or present work space and 5.2 at a computer.

As part of a six building campus study (Dixon, 2005), the General Purpose building produced the best overall responses from occupants in four purpose-designed, naturally ventilated buildings.

Significant factors

Table 25.1 lists the average scores for each of the survey questions and indicates those aspects of the building that the staff perceived as being significantly better, similar to, or worse than the benchmark

Mesh sunscreens on the east façade of the Student Services Centre

26

Student Services Centre, University of Newcastle
NSW, Australia

Jodie Dixon

THE CONTEXT

The Student Services Centre is a 2700m² building, completed in 2001 and located on the Callaghan Campus of the University of Newcastle, NSW, Australia. The building is a concrete and masonry, four-floor, split-level design. Originally constructed as a gymnasium, the building was refurbished in 2000 to operate as the centralised student services building for its student population and approximately 111 people who work daily within (Figure 26.1). It operates using a mixed-mode heating cooling and ventilation system.

The University of Newcastle campus is located centrally on the east coast of New South Wales, Australia, at latitude 33°S and at an elevation of 21m above sea level. The climate is borderline temperate–sub-tropical. The temperate conditions bring warm summers and cool winters, sub-tropical conditions are characteristically warm and humid in summer.

During the 1990s the university facility management group adopted a low-energy ventilation plan to rein in rising building energy costs. This was seen as an opportunity to develop low-energy, environmentally sustainable building practices on campus. The transformation of the original gymnasium building became representative of this philosophy, having been retained, refurbished, and reused to serve a new purpose.

26.1 View from the south-east. Note the brick masonry south façade (to the left) and the extensively screened east façade (to the right). The fresh air intakes to the HVAC system are just visible on the extreme left of shot, and the sawtooth shapes of the ventilated skylights are visible on the roof

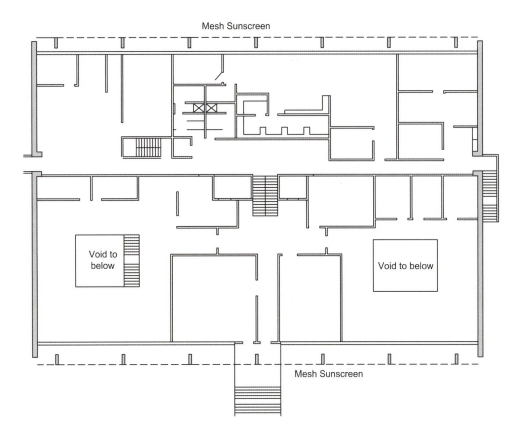

Mesh Sunscreen

Void to
below

Void to below

Mesh Sunscreen

26.2 Upper levels floor plan indicating the solid masonry walls to north and south, and the screened and glazed curtain walls to east and west. Note too the open areas or voids to the office spaces below and the mix of open-plan and cellular offices
Source: Adapted from Newcastle University Facilities Management

26.3 Upper floor (south-west corner) open office area. Note the void to the floor below, the timber wall cladding, the extensive skylit area of the ceiling, and the mechanical ventilation supply duct on upper right of shot

26.4 Looking down through the void between upper and lower office areas. Note the skylights above, the ventilation duct around the perimeter, and the windowless single offices on the right

26.5 Main entrance foyer area with enquiries desk on the left and computer 'commons' on the right

26.6 East–west section showing reconfigured arrangement of floor levels. Note the voids between the open plan offices and the ventilated skylights, designed to enable natural air exhaust under appropriate conditions Source: Adapted from Newcastle University Facilities Management

26.7 East façade showing the extent of the mesh screens used to shade the curtain wall glazing

26.8 Part of the west façade showing the extent of the mesh screens used to shade the curtain wall glazing. The entrance to the main foyer area is behind the external stairway. Note the skylights visible on the roof

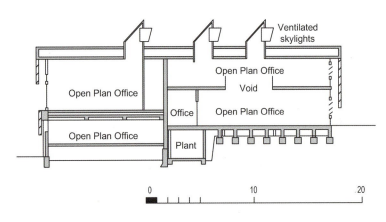

Outdoor temperature and humidity data reveal the challenges for passive thermal design concepts. While winter lows of 4°C and highs of 22°C indicate mild conditions with the potential to be easily tempered by solar gains or heating provisions, in summer, temperature highs of 37°C can occur in combination with high humidities, making it difficult to physiologically cool down in the absence of fan-assisted airflows or dehumidification.

THE DESIGN PROCESS

Driven by the university's concern for sustainable building practice, the design team chose to retain and redesign an existing gymnasium to meet the brief and budget for a new student services centre. The brief and schematic concepts were developed between the university architect Geoff Whitnall, mechanical engineer David Alexander, and the occupant clients. Further development by Shaddock Smith Architects, Bassets Consulting engineers, and environmental consultants Advanced Environmental Concepts (AEC) generated a roundtable design and documentation process.

This university client was pivotal in ensuring passive environmental opportunities were identified while acknowledging the need for intermittent mechanical heating ventilation and cooling. The provision of a new heating and cooling system was inevitable in this building since it did not provide an ideal winter solar or natural ventilation orientation and the user group had been previously acclimatised to an air-conditioned environment. The selected approach utilises a mixed-mode design, combining some passive design principles with the intermittent use of air conditioning. Whitnall (Alexander and Whitnall, 2007) notes that these systems were 'financially sound decisions'.

All parties were involved in the roundtable design process based on initial schematic sketches. This ensured the design developed with an optimal low-energy target using mixed-mode principles.

THE DESIGN OUTCOME

Building layout and construction

The completed building reused the existing masonry gymnasium to provide four tall, open-plan office spaces around a central

26.9 External view of two rows of ventilated skylights on the roof. Note the rainscreen baffles with louvred opening behind

26.10 View looking up into a typical west-facing skylight through the light-diffusing screen at ceiling level. The vertical glazing of the skylights is louvred to enable the air to exhaust under appropriate conditions

26.11 General view of some of the HVAC plant in the basement area. Note the heating and cooling water circuits feeding coils in the air supply ducts serving different zones of the building

foyer (Figures 26.2, 26.3, 26.4, and 26.5). All open-plan spaces are operated using a mix of natural ventilation and intermittently operated mechanical heating, cooling, and ventilation. Whitnall designed the mezzanine floors which split vertically the two original gymnasium spaces located on the west side (Figure 26.6). New glazed curtain walls were introduced to all open-plan spaces on the east and west and are fitted with metal grille sunscreens (Figures 26.7 and 26.8). Workstations on both the east and west sides abut the glazed curtain walls where occupants access plentiful daylight and can operate windows on all levels (see Figure 26.3, for example).

The original building fabric was retained where possible and aesthetically retains something of its gymnasium origins. Original sprung timber floors to the gym and dance studio were stabilised and polished. Plasterboard lined light framed walls surround the open-plan office spaces. However, all share one perimeter precast masonry concrete cavity wall on the north or south (Figure 26.2). These wall surfaces are typically faced with original internal timber lining boards that offer acoustic and thermal advantages (see Figure 26.3, for example).

Floors are tiled surfaces on concrete floor slabs. New walls are typically light framed timber and plasterboard with paint finishes or glazed internal windows between office and reception areas. The original concrete walls are exposed in some of the cellular offices.

Passive and active environmental control systems
In terms of building fabric, the internal timber wall linings were retained over otherwise masonry wall surfaces to temper the heat sink and acoustic disadvantages when exposing high mass surfaces indoors. Concrete floors are largely carpeted or timber-lined. New openable windows within curtain wall glazing assisted the natural ventilation design and these, together with ventilated skylights (Figures 26.9 and 26.10), provide natural daylight to the depths of the large open workspace (see Figures 26.3 and 26.4, for example). Steel mesh external sunshades are provided to screen the glazed curtain walls from summer solar heat gains from the west and east (see Figures 26.7 and 26.8, for example).

The building uses a sensor automated mixed-mode ventilation heating and cooling design. A thermostat system monitors internal and external air temperatures. The boiler and chiller serving the

Rooftop and south-west façade of the NRDC Building

27

Natural Resources Defense Council (NRDC)
Santa Monica, California, USA

THE CONTEXT

Named the Robert Redford Building, this 1400m² floor area office houses the Southern California headquarters of the Natural Resources Defense Council (NRDC), a non-profit organisation whose mission is to protect public health and the environment. The three-storey-tall building is located in Santa Monica, approximately 20km west of downtown Los Angeles and close to public transport facilities.

Given NRDC's goals, it was to be expected that the organisation would place a high priority on environmental principles when it came to renovating its offices around the country. When President John H. Adams decided in 1988 to relocate the NRDC's existing offices from mid-Wiltshire to the 'green oasis' of Santa Monica (Petersen, 2006), there was a determination to demonstrate sustainable design.

After selecting an existing building for adaptive reuse, stripping the building back to its original 1920s wooden structure, and completing a full renovation, the Robert Redford Building was opened in November 2003 (Figure 27.1). The brief for the building included offices, conference rooms, and support spaces for the NRDC's legal and administrative staff, as well as a street-front Environmental Action Center for public outreach and education.

The site itself is just one block back from the Pacific Coast (close to the western extremity of the historic Route 66 – now Santa Monica Boulevard) in the relatively benign climate of Southern California – latitude 34°N with summer and winter design temperature (for nearby Long Beach) of 30.9°C and 5.8°C respectively (ASHRAE, 2001: 27.8–9).

27.1 2nd Street frontage with entrance way to NRDC Offices via the lane on the left, and door to Environmental Learning Center to right of the tree trunk. Note also the fibre reinforced cladding on this and other façades

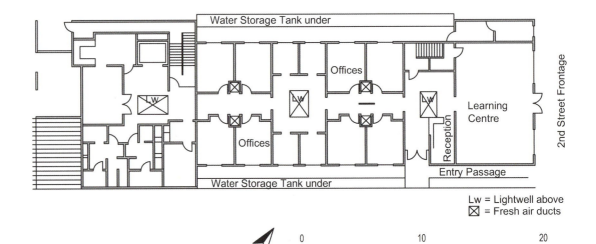

Water Storage Tank under

Offices

Water Storage Tank under

Offices

Learning Centre

Reception

Entry Passage

2nd Street Frontage

Lw = Lightwell above
⊠ = Fresh air ducts

0   10   20

27.2 Ground floor plan – note the location of the three light-wells and the layout of the vertical ducts for the supplementary air conditioning system
Source: Adapted from Moule and Polyzoides

27.3 View of rooftop and 2nd Street façade, with Pacific Ocean just visible at top of shot. Note the following: (1) Gaps between NRDC and adjacent buildings to enable daylight penetration. (2) Level 3 Conference Rooms and Staff Workroom clustered at the far end of the roof. (3) The horizontal photo-voltaic panels covering large sections of the rooftop. (4) Two of the light-wells in centre of shot, with attached extract fan housings visible, and photo-voltaic panels on top. (5) The regular arrangement of the six cowls which form the fresh air intakes to the supplementary air conditioning system. (6) The condenser units of the air conditioning system in their rooftop enclosures. (7) The heating system and other plant items on the roof of the Level 3 toilet block – see top left of shot

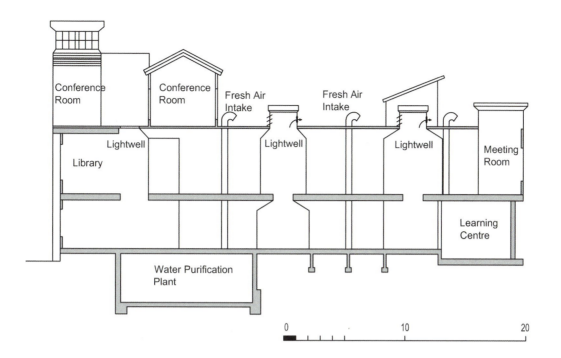

27.4 Long cross-section – note the position of the three light-wells and the vertical air distribution ducts
Source: Adapted from Moule and Polyzoides

27.5 Level 3 Patio Area with Staff Work area to the right and Conference Rooms centre and to left of shot. Note the glazed section of the patio floor which forms the top of a light-well

The building won the 2004 Congress for the New Urbanism's Charter Award (in the Block, Street, and Building Category) and was one of the first projects to attain Platinum in Version 2 of the US Green Building Council's LEED Certification process for New Construction (LEED, 2004), with the most points achieved of any building at that time.

The design process and architectural outcome have been described elsewhere in some detail (Griscom, 2003; NRDC, 2004; Scott, 2004). What follows is the briefest of outlines.

THE DESIGN PROCESS

Following an extensive interview process involving around 25 firms, Moule and Polyzoides, Architects and Urbanists of Pasadena were selected. The firm's partners included Stephanos Polyzoides and Elizabeth Moule, two of the founders of the Congress for the New Urbanism, 'an organisation dedicated to reconstructing the American metropolis with a focus on community and natural resource preservation' (Scott, 2004). Specialist mechanical, electrical, and plumbing design was undertaken by the Syska Hennessy Group.

According to lead architect Elizabeth Moule 'her team's first consideration was finding an existing, salvageable structure in a downtown location' (Griscom, 2003) with all the inherent resource efficiency potential that implies. Achieving low energy consumption was also a key consideration and this building was to maximise the use of daylight and natural ventilation.

The NRDC's mission as an environmental advocacy group, and NRDC senior scientist Rob Watson's close involvement with the LEED certification programme both contributed to the goal of achieving a high rating for this project. However, according to Moule:

27.6 Close-up view of the photo-voltaic arrays, some of the fresh air intakes, and the tops of the light-wells. The stairtower in the background gives easy access to the roof

27.7 View of the south-east façade looking along the gap between it and the adjacent building. One of the two main water storage tanks is located under the elongated planter. Note too the carefully articulated rainwater downpipes from the various sections of roof on the far façade

27.8 'Open' offices clustered round a light-well on Level 2. Note that an extract fan is located behind the grille alongside the upper glazing

The biggest challenge for the project had less to do with obtaining a LEED rating and more to do with grappling with a highly deficient existing building. Although the original structure dated from the 1920s, poorly executed 1970's renovations were not worth saving … The lesson from this is to be sure that you secure a building that has some structural and architectural integrity that can be salvaged.

In the end, only the exterior walls could be kept, with the rest of the demolition materials reused or recycled elsewhere. She also found that:

27.9 Typical office window with plinth heater located below. Sensors in the window frame are programmed to turn off the heater if the window is open. A simple roller blind is fitted to allow control of glare

27.10 Cooling equipment (one of six) located in a louvre-doored cupboard which forms part of the vertical duct fresh air distribution system. Temperature and relative humidity indicators and user controls conveniently located alongside

27.11 Temperature (°F) and carbon dioxide (ppm) indicators in a conference room. The red light comes on should the CO_2 level exceed a predetermined value – a reminder to the occupants to open the windows (an audible warning was fitted originally, but proved too distracting – the red light was installed subsequently)

Another challenge was working with the City. Santa Monica prides itself on being a progressive town with green guidelines of their own. But approvals from staff were not easily forthcoming on many of the technical issues being posed – both green and not green. A city that wants to produce green buildings must find ways to incentivize developers and owners through streamlined processes.

(Moule, 2004)

THE DESIGN OUTCOME

Building layout, construction, and passive environmental control systems

Rectangular in plan (Figure 27.2), the building abuts adjacent buildings on an approximately 37m by 14m urban site with its long axis running roughly north-east–south-west. It fills most of the site, except for a 2m gap between each of the long façades and the adjacent buildings (Figure 27.3).

Two main floors (Levels 1 and 2) run the entire length of the building (Figure 27.4). These floors accommodate the main NRDC offices and associated facilities. The building's main entrance is located on 2nd Street at the south-east side of the building. The NRDC's public face, including the Environmental Learning Center, presents a welcoming frontage on 2nd Street. There is a mix of enclosed and open offices, the latter clustered round a series of gathering spaces with light-wells above (Figure 27.2).

Level 3 has two main conference rooms, a staff work room and an outdoor patio, all grouped around the south-west end of the building (Figure 27.5). The remainder of that level, the roof, is the location of photo-voltaic panels, the solar water heater, condenser units, and other equipment (Figure 27.6). A compact basement space houses the water purification plant (Figure 27.4).

The 2m gap between the long façades and the adjacent buildings (Figures 27.7 and 27.3) enables daylight penetration to the perimeter of the building, while the three light-wells that punctuate the plan (Figure 27.2) enable daylight penetration to the building interior. The perimeter windows are all openable to allow natural ventilation, and the upper glazed section of two of the light-wells is fitted with a louvred opening and an extract fan (Figure 27.8). The top of the third light-well features a glass, walkable surface, and forms a portion of the patio above. Manually operated transom or fanlight windows above the doors of 'enclosed offices' enable air transfer.

The main cladding material, fibre reinforced cement which includes recycled content, is used on all the façades and the light-wells (Figures 27.1, 27.7, and 27.8). Windows have mostly low-emissivity double glazing, with interior roller blinds to allow control of any glare (Figure 27.9).

Active environmental control systems

While the high-ceilinged conference rooms on Level 3 are able to rely totally on natural ventilation, with air movement enhanced by ceiling fans when required, the deeper plan of the Levels 1 and 2 offices necessitated the installation of a supplementary mechanical ventilation system. Six small fresh air supply units are integrated into the structure to deliver heated or cooled air at peak times (Figure 27.10).

A gas-fired system distributes hot water to convectors or plinth diffusers in the offices. Thermostats in each office enable personal control of these systems – sensors are installed to determine when a window is open and programmed to turn the terminal unit off at that locality (Figure 27.9).

Considerable care has been taken to ensure the staff are aware of conditions in the building and can respond appropriately. Inside temperature and humidity readings on display at strategic points throughout the building (Figure 27.10), and CO_2 readings are also displayed. The carbon dioxide sensors include a warning light set to come on at around 750ppm as a way of reminding the occupants of a space to open the windows (Figure 27.11).

The artificial lighting installation includes energy-efficient luminaires such as the T8s that are used in the offices. In addition, both occupancy and daylight sensors have been installed, the former turning the lights off when a space is unoccupied, the latter dimming the lights when there is sufficient daylight. The manual switches for the lights in each office also have dimming controls.

A 7.5kW capacity grid-connected photovoltaic array (Figure 27.6), designed to provide around 20 per cent of the building's needs, has been installed on the flat roof of the building and on the flat tops of two of the light-wells.

Rainwater and grey water from sinks and showers are collected, treated, and stored in two large underground tanks. These are located under elongated planters running alongside the building (Figure 27.7, for example). The water is used for irrigation and toilet flushing. While the quality of the treated water exceeds that required for potable water, current city bylaws restrict reuse to non-potable purposes.

USERS' PERCEPTIONS OF THE BUILDING

Overall response

The building was surveyed in December 2005. For virtually all of the 20 or so respondents (83 per cent female, 17 per cent male), the building was their normal place of business, working on average 4.8 days per week and 8.9 hours per day, of which around 7.5 were spent at their desk and 6.9 at a computer. The ratio of under-30s to over-30s was 32:68 per cent and most (65 per cent) had worked in the building for more than a year at the same desk or work area. Most had single offices or work areas.

Significant factors

The average scores of the staff for each of the relevant survey questions are listed in Table 27.1. Table 27.1 also indicates those aspects of the building that the staff perceived as being significantly better, similar to, or worse than the benchmark and/or scale mid-point. Overall, some 30 aspects were significantly better, only four were significantly worse, while the remaining 11 aspects had much the same score as the benchmark.

In terms of the eight operational aspects, this building scores better than the benchmark in seven instances. The only exception was the score for desk space.

While the overall scores for temperature and air in both summer and winter were all considerably higher than their corresponding benchmarks, there was some variability in the individual aspects. The air itself was fresh and odourless in both seasons of the year, but was perceived to be on the dry and still side; and while the temperatures were stable in both seasons, they were perceived to be too cold in winter and too hot in summer.

While lighting overall scored better than the benchmark and scale mid-point, and there were no perceived issues with the artificial lighting, staff indicated there was an overabundance of natural light. Noise overall scored highly too, but there was a perception of too much colleague noise by comparison with the other potential sources.

Some 60–70 per cent of staff rated personal control of heating, cooling, ventilation, and lighting as important (among the highest proportion in the buildings surveyed) and scored these aspects better than their benchmarks. Noise, on the other hand, scored relatively low.

Perceptions of the satisfaction variables (design, needs, overall comfort, productivity, and health) were all significantly better than their respective benchmarks, and very much higher than the scale mid-point.

Users' comments

Overall, some 92 responses were received from staff under the 12 headings where they were able to add written comments – some 38.3 per cent of the 240 potential (20 respondents by 12 headings). Table 27.2 indicates the numbers of positive, balanced and negative comments – in this case, around 45.7 per cent were positive, 7.6 per cent balanced, and 46.7 per cent negative.

Lack of storage was an issue for some respondents, despite its good average score; while several had issues with noise and with sun and sky glare, echoing the moderate scores achieved for these aspects. In all three cases, comments were received under more than just the applicable heading. The comments on health were all positive, reflecting its very high score of 5.85.

Overall performance indices

The Comfort Index, based on the scores for comfort overall, noise, lighting, temperature, and air quality, works out at +2.27, while the Satisfaction Index, based on the design, needs, health, and perceived productivity scores, is +3.37, both higher than the scale mid-point (noting these indices are scaled from -3 to +3 normally).

The Summary Index, being the average of these, works out at 2.82, while the Forgiveness Factor, calculated to be 1.20 in this instance, indicates that staff as a whole are likely to be very tolerant of minor shortcomings in individual aspects such as winter and summer temperatures, air quality, lighting, and noise (a factor of 1 being the mid-point on a scale that normally ranges from 0.8 to 1.2).

In terms of the Ten-Factor Rating Scale, the building was 'Exceptional' on the 7-point scale, with a calculated percentage value of 100 per cent. When All-Factors were taken into account, the percentage value worked out at 82 per cent, towards the top of the 'Good Practice' band.

TABLE 27.1

Average scores for each factor and whether they were significantly better, similar to, or worse than the BUS benchmarks

	Score	Worse	Similar	Better		Score	Worse	Similar	Better
OPERATIONAL FACTORS									
Image to visitors	6.85			●	Cleaning	5.85			●
Space in building	6.20			●	Availability of meeting rooms	6.60			●
Space at desk – too little/much⁴	4.40		●		Suitability of storage arrangements	4.50			●
Furniture	6.05			●	Facilities meet requirements	6.40			●
ENVIRONMENTAL FACTORS									
Temp and Air in Winter					Temp and Air in Summer				
Temp Overall	4.84			●	Temp Overall	5.39			●
Temp – too hot/too cold⁴	4.67	●			Temp – too hot/too cold⁴	3.41		●	
Temp – stable/variable⁴	3.83		●		Temp – stable/variable⁴	3.53		●	
Air – still/draughty⁴	2.94	●			Air – still/draughty⁴	3.31		●	
Air – dry/humid⁴	3.22		●		Air – dry/humid⁴	3.59		●	
Air – fresh/stuffy¹	2.21			●	Air – fresh/stuffy¹	1.83			●
Air – odourless/smelly¹	1.47			●	Air – odourless/smelly¹	1.56			●
Air Overall	5.32			●	Air Overall	5.61			●
Lighting					**Noise**				
Lighting Overall	6.30			●	Noise Overall	5.05			●
Natural light – too little/much⁴	4.50	●			From colleagues – too little/much⁴	4.95	●		
Sun & Sky Glare – none/too much¹	3.85		●		From other people – too little/much⁴	4.47		●	
Artificial light – too little/much⁴	3.95			●	From inside – too little/much⁴	3.90			●
Art'l light glare – none/too much¹	2.53			●	From outside – too little/much⁴	4.60		●	
					Interruptions – none/frequent¹	3.53			●
CONTROL FACTORS[b]					**SATISFACTION FACTORS**				
Heating	70% 5.15			●	Design	6.65			●
Cooling	65% 5.20			●	Needs	6.20			●
Ventilation	70% 6.50			●	Comfort Overall	6.50			●
Lighting	60% 6.05			●	Productivity %	+23.00			●
Noise	50% 3.40		●		Health	5.85			●

NOTES: (a) unless otherwise noted, a score of 7 is 'best'; superscript ⁴ implies a score of 4 is best, superscript ¹ implies a score of 1 is best; (b) the per cent values listed here are the percentages of respondents who thought personal control of that aspect was important.

TABLE 27.2

Numbers of respondents offering positive, balanced, and negative comments on 12 performance factors

Aspect	Number of respondents			
	Positive	Balanced	Negative	Total
Overall Design	6	–	4	10
Needs Overall	1	–	5	6
Meeting Rooms	3	–	–	3
Storage	1	2	7	10
Desk/Work Area	2	1	3	6
Comfort	2	–	1	3
Noise Sources	1	3	5	9
Lighting Conditions	4	–	5	9
Productivity	5	1	–	6
Health	6	–	–	6
Work Well	11	–	–	11
Hinder	–	–	13	13
TOTALS	42	7	43	92
PER CENT	45.7	7.6	46.7	100

ACKNOWLEDGEMENTS

I must express my gratitude to Evelyne Slavin, Environmental Action Center Associate, for granting permission for me to undertake this survey. Particular thanks go to Office Administrator Gayle Petersen for assisting my understanding of the building and its operation and to David Thurman of Moule and Polyzoides for reviewing the draft of this chapter.

REFERENCES

ASHRAE (2001) *ASHRAE Handbook: Fundamentals, SI Edition*, Atlanta, GA: American Society of Heating Refrigerating and Air-Conditioning Engineers.

Griscom (2003) 'Who's the Greenest of Them All?' available at: www.grist.org/news/powers/2003/11/25/of/ (accessed 27 September 2005).

LEED (2004) 'Ratings and Awards', available at: http://leedcasestudies.usgbc.org/ratings.cfm?ProjectID=236 (accessed 15 September 2007).

Moule, E. (2004) 'Lessons Learned', available at: http://leedcasestudies.usgbc.org/lessons.cfm?ProjectID=236 (accessed 14 September 2007).

NRDC (2004) 'Greener by Design: NRDC's Santa Monica Office', available at: www.nrdc.org/cities/building/smoffice/into.asp (accessed September 2007).

Petersen, G. (2006) Transcript of interview held on 16 December, 2005, Santa Monica.

Scott, Z. D. (2004) *From Solar Power to Eco-Friendly Desk Chairs – A Resource Guide for the Greenest Building in the United States – the Robert Redford Building*. Santa Monica, CA: Natural Resources Defense Council.

Part 4

Buildings in Hot–Humid Climates

Chapters 28–31

The following case studies are all located in what could be classed broadly as hot–humid climates. Two of these are located in Malaysia, one in Singapore, and the remaining two on the same site in the state of Gujarat in the north-west of India. They will be described in the following order:

Of the five cases, one has advanced natural ventilation, two are fully air conditioned and two are mixed-mode (one changeover, the other zoned).

Kitchen extract ducts on the south façade of the hall at ITE Bishan

28

Institute of Technical Education
Bishan, Singapore

THE CONTEXT

The 20,300m² Institute of Technical Education at Bishan is one of the 11 or so institutes which make up Singapore's Institute of Technical Education. With around 100 staff, it caters for some 1600 students, 85 per cent of whom are female, providing mainly business studies and nursing courses. Its two parallel blocks of teaching accommodation are laid out on a curved plan, with an 18m-wide separation between. Administrative areas and library are located at the northern end, the multi-purpose hall and dining area at the south (Figure 28.1).

The design resulted from a 1989 competition held in Singapore for a new facility to re-house the National Institute of Commerce (NIC), predecessor of the yet to be established (in 1992) Institute of

Technical Education (ITE). The competition was won by Akitek Tenggara II and the building was officially opened on 28 July 1994.

The 4.6-hectare site, for what was to become one of two ITE institutes providing post-secondary business studies, is located at the new town of Bishan, close to the geographical centre of Singapore Island. Lying approximately 1.5° north of the equator, the 1 per cent design temperatures range from around 23°C to 32°C (ASHRAE, 2001: 27.48–9).

The design process and architectural outcome have been described elsewhere in some detail (Baird, 2001). What follows is the briefest of outlines.

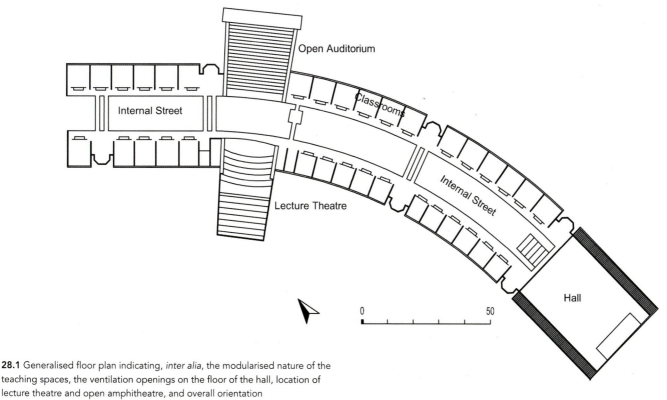

28.1 Generalised floor plan indicating, *inter alia*, the modularised nature of the teaching spaces, the ventilation openings on the floor of the hall, location of lecture theatre and open amphitheatre, and overall orientation
Source: Adapted from Powell (1994: 71)

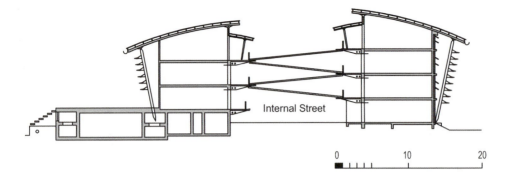

Internal Street

0   10   20

28.2 Typical east–west section through the teaching blocks –
note the solar shading and ventilation openings, and the bridges
between the two blocks
Source: Adapted from Powell (1997: 125)

28.3 A typical air-conditioned teaching space with the ceiling-
mounted cassette unit of the split system air conditioner
providing cold air to the space

28.4 Naturally ventilated classroom – looking towards the openable windows of the exterior façade

28.5 Naturally ventilated classroom – looking towards the inner façade – note the fixed louvred ventilation opening at high level and the grilled one below the lockers, as well as the open doorways and provision of both wall- and floor-mounted fans

THE DESIGN PROCESS

The designers' aims for the Institute were 'both to project an image of technical progress and to respond to the tropical climate with the least use of artificially produced energy by exploiting the geometries of site and section' (Powell, 1994: 68). They wanted '[to] encapsulate a microcosm of the city in a tropical climate' (Powell and Akitek Tenggara, 1997).

Tay Kheng Soon of Akitek Tenggara sees the practice as multidisciplinary in its thinking, and firmly eschews some of the fashionable, but frequently superficial, approaches being taken to sustainability issues, seeing much of it as 'eco-aesthetics or eco-styling'. With a clear concept of how to achieve climatic control by architectural means appropriate to the climate of their site, coupled with a well-justified scepticism of the energy-efficiency claims made for some systems of air conditioning, the practice assumed full responsibility for all aspects of the design (Tay, 1999).

Detailed design of the building services was carried out by Loh Kay Weng and Alice Goh of the Singapore office of Beca Carter Hollings and Ferner (S E Asia) Pte Ltd (BECA for short). While they have cooperated on several projects since, ITE Bishan was the first project on which the two firms had worked together. As far as the design process itself was concerned, Loh Kay Weng of BECAs recalls it as being fairly typical of conventional practice in Singapore, with regular technical and client consultation meetings once they had been appointed (Loh, 1999).

According to the architects, 'Climatically, the design emphasizes transparency and permeability in the spatial structure. The sheltering effect of the overhangs over the passageways creates an architecture of shade rather than an architecture of mass' (Powell and Akitek Tenggara, 1997).

28.6 Looking southwards along the landscaped internal street – note the louvred extensions from the walkways, the cross-bridges between the two blocks, and (upper background) the open roof over the amphitheatre

28.7 View looking in from the open north end of the building

28.8 Looking along the inner façade of the eastern block from the south (from the steps to the main hall)

THE DESIGN OUTCOME

Building layout, construction, and passive environmental control systems

The site is a flat one and is open to the elements on all sides. Anchored at its south end by the dining area and large multi-purpose hall, the long axis of the building curves gently to the north-east with an inside radius of 170m (Figure 28.1). The twin parallel teaching blocks, one four-storeys high, the other three (Figure 28.2), house the facilities and classroom spaces one might expect of such a training institution – specialist computer rooms, simulated office, language laboratory, library, predominantly air conditioned (Figure 28.3) – together with more general purpose teaching spaces, many naturally ventilated (Figures 28.4 and 28.5), some air conditioned. A large air-conditioned lecture theatre and an open amphitheatre punctuate the plan (Figure 28.1).

The overall orientation – long axis roughly north–south – does not conform to conventional wisdom as far as minimising morning and afternoon solar heat gains is concerned, but instead places the building squarely into the path of the predominant winds. The twin block arrangement with a shaded internal street (Figure 28.6) does, however, serve to reduce the amount of solar radiation that would otherwise reach the east and west façades and the curved plan means that some part of the street will have shade even in the middle of the day (Figures 28.7 and 28.8).

Direct solar heat gain to the teaching areas is mitigated by means of the large overhangs on the east/north-east and west/south-west sides of the curved roof structures of the two blocks (Figure 28.2). In addition, the exterior façades are extensively louvred (Figures 28.9 and 28.10). The interior façades, facing the landscaped inner street, are shaded by the roof overhangs and by the external walkways with their louvred extensions at each level, while a high-level section of roof bridges the gap where the amphitheatre and lecture theatre are situated (Figure 28.6). The landscaping itself provides a low reflectivity to direct solar radiation.

Natural cross-ventilation of the non-air-conditioned teaching spaces is provided for by means of openable windows on the outer side (Figure 28.4) and fixed openings on the inner side, the latter taking the form of high-level louvred openings and low-level grilles

28.9 Shading arrangement on the western façade, looking south towards the open dining area on the ground floor

28.10 East façade with open sports ground in the foreground. Curved roof of main hall just visible on the upper left; roof structure over the open amphitheatre and lecture theatre on the right

28.11 View of one of the west façade modules – note the main horizontal solar louvres, the windows, and the mounting framework and louvred screens for the condenser units of the split-system air conditioning

(located above and below the whiteboard) (Figure 28.5). Wall, free standing, and ceiling fans are also provided. The dining area, located under the multi-purpose hall, is completely open on its east and west sides for cross-ventilation (Figure 28.9). The semi-circular cross-sectioned multi-purpose hall has large continuous openings running along both edges at floor level, around the curved edge of the gable ends, and along the crest of the roof, for natural ventilation. The teaching blocks themselves are punctuated at intervals along their lengths to enable the wind to pass through the structure, into and out of the landscaped street (see Figure 28.10). In the view of Powell (1994: 69–70), 'Every component has a structural reason or is an essential climatic controlling device.'

Active environmental control systems

A multiplicity of split system units is used for the air-conditioned teaching spaces. With a cooling capacity of 12kW typically, each unit would serve one architectural module of around 7.5m wide and 9.0m deep. The majority of the individual condensers are mounted on the outside wall, behind a louvred screen, adjacent to the teaching space being served (Figure 28.11). Some, regrettably, have been located under the overhang in close proximity to the opening windows of the naturally ventilated classrooms. A few, such as those serving the staff area, are at ground level. A packaged unit with a cooling capacity of 90kW supplies 3.2m³/s to the centrally located lecture theatre. The unit is located on top of the lecture theatre, but still under the shade of the main curved roof structure. The system is under the control of the lecturer, air supply and extract being at high level in the ceiling. The design conditions for the air-conditioned spaces are 23 ±1°C db and 17.5°C wb.

Two types of extract system are in use, one from the stacked sets of student toilets which are located at intervals along the plan, the other serving the several kitchen areas located in the dining area. These latter are collected into twin extract ducts discharging at roof level at the south end of the building.

Significant factors

The average scores of the staff and students for each of the relevant survey questions are listed in Table 28.1. Table 28.1 also indicates, for the staff only, those aspects of the building that they perceived as being significantly better, similar to, or worse than the benchmark and/or scale mid-point. Overall, two aspects were significantly better, 25 were significantly worse, while the remaining 16 aspects had much the same score as the benchmark.

In terms of the seven operational aspects considered, the staff scored this building below the benchmark and the scale mid-point in every instance.

A similar picture emerged as far as temperature and air in the naturally ventilated spaces were concerned, with low overall scores of 2.70 and 2.85 respectively – temperatures were too hot and the air relatively humid, stuffy, and smelly. The situation with the air-conditioned spaces was somewhat better, with overall scores of 3.88 and 3.55 respectively for temperature and air – however, conditions were still scored a little on the hot and humid side, and equally stuffy and smelly.

The staff scored the building above the scale mid-point for lighting overall, but below the benchmark. While the score for glare from sun and sky was better than the benchmark, the score for the amount of natural light suggested there was not enough (one could speculate on a certain tension between these two aspects).

There appeared to be too much noise from every source – from colleagues, other people, inside and outside the building, resulting in an overall score (3.29) well under the benchmark and the scale mid-point.

Some 32, 38, and 41 per cent respectively of staff rated personal control of noise, ventilation, and cooling as important, but the scores for control of these and other factors considered were within the 2.2 to 2.8 range.

The Satisfaction variables (design, needs, overall comfort, productivity and health) were well under their respective benchmarks and scale mid-points, mostly around 3.

Student perceptions (responses to a smaller number of overall variables were sought in the shorter student questionnaire) followed a similar pattern, but with the exception of lighting, the student scores were higher than those of the staff. Average scores for the naturally ventilated spaces were consistently lower than those for the air-conditioned spaces, the biggest differential occurring with temperature overall (2.84 cf 3.73). Arguably most notable were the student scores for productivity at +1.70 per cent and + 6.22 per cent for naturally ventilated and air-conditioned spaces respectively, both higher than the benchmark and considerably higher than the staff score of -10.61 per cent

Users' comments

Overall, some 166 responses were received from staff under the 12 headings where they were able to add written comments – some 37.4 per cent of the 444 potential (37 respondents by 12 headings). Table 28.2 indicates the numbers of positive, balanced, and negative comments overall – in the case of the staff, around 12.7 per cent were positive, 8.4 per cent neutral, and 78.9 per cent negative; corresponding figures for the students were zero, 9.2 and 90.8 per cent.

Generally speaking, the nature and type of comments reflected the scores. The lack of meeting rooms and storage generally attracted predominantly adverse comment, and half the negative comments about space at desk related to lack of storage. Under design and needs, the lack of shelter from the rain dominated the negative comments while inadequacies in the toilet arrangements and provision for handicapped people were highlighted by several respondents. Directly echoing its score, the main noise issues for both staff and students related to the activities and movement of other students outside the classrooms (the naturally ventilated ones in particular), plus the noise from renovations and the air conditioning system.

Overall performance indices

No Comfort, Satisfaction, or Summary Indices were estimated in this early survey, but the Forgiveness Factor, calculated to be 1.15 in this instance, indicates that staff as a whole are likely to be relatively tolerant as far as shortcomings in individual aspects such as temperatures, air quality, lighting, and noise are concerned (a factor of 1 being the mid-point on a scale that normally ranges from 0.8 to 1.2).

In terms of the Ten-Factor Rating Scale, the air-conditioned sections of the building were just within the 'Below Average' band of the 7-point scale, with a calculated percentage value of 29 per cent, while the naturally ventilated sections were just in the 'Poor' category at 24 per cent. When All-Factors were taken into account, the corresponding percentage values worked out at 41 and 36 per cent, both in the upper part of the 'Below Average' band.

Applying the same system to the eight factors assessed by the students, percentage values of 49 and 36 per cent were obtained – in the 'Average' band for the air-conditioned section and 'Below Average' for the naturally ventilated.

ACKNOWLEDGEMENTS

It is my pleasure to thank Tay Kheng Soon, Director of Akitek Tenggara II, and Loh Kay Weng, Associate Director, and Alice Goh, Mechanical Services Discipline Leader, of BECAs, whom I interviewed in connection with the design of ITE Bishan.

I must also thank Deputy Principal Mrs Angela Lim and Campus Manager Ms Michelle Low for their assistance during my visits and the various staff members, including Training Officer Chong Chai Yi, who gave freely of their time.

REFERENCES

ASHRAE (2001) *ASHRAE Handbook: Fundamentals, SI Edition*, Atlanta, GA; American Society of Heating Refrigerating and Air-Conditioning Engineers.

Baird, G. (2001) *The Architectural Expression of Environmental Control Systems*, London: Spon Press, Chapter 4.

Loh, K. W. (1999) Transcript of interview of 5 May, Kuala Lumpur.

Powell, R. (1994) 'The Great Unlearning', *Architectural Review*, 194(1171): 68–71.

Powell, R. and Akitek Tenggara (1997) *Line, Edge & Shade*, Singapore: Page One Publishing.

Tay, K. S. (1999) Transcript of interview of 4 May, Singapore.

The atrium space at the MEWC Building

29

Ministry of Energy, Water and Communications (MEWC) Building
Putrajaya, Malaysia

with Maisarah Ali and Shireen Jahnkassim

THE CONTEXT

Completed in September 2004 following a two-and-a-half-year construction period, this six-storey office building has an air-conditioned area of just over 19,200m², surmounting two levels of parking. Comprised of two linked blocks, it is located at the north-eastern corner of Government Complex Parcel E in Precinct 1 of the city of Putrajaya, the Administrative Capital of the Malaysian Federal Government.

The building houses the Ministry of Energy, Water and Communications. It was designed to be a showcase building for energy efficiency and low environmental impact and to exemplify the Malaysian Government's commitment to 'achieving sustainable development through energy efficiency and conservation' (MEWC, 2006). As well as leading by example, the Ministry wanted '[to] dispel the notion that it is not financially viable to employ energy efficiency in buildings', the hope being 'that it will inspire a greater

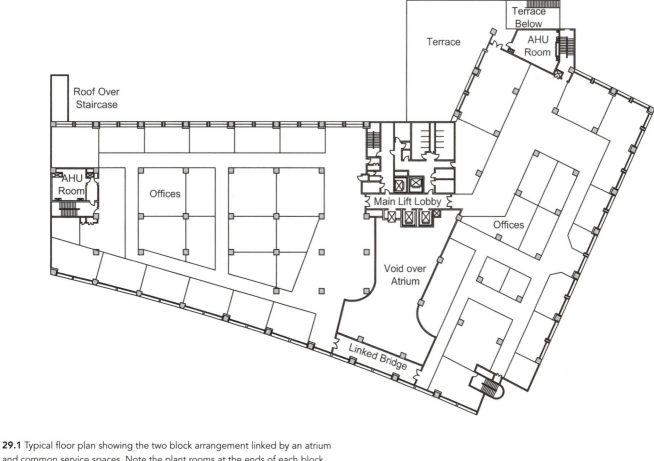

29.1 Typical floor plan showing the two block arrangement linked by an atrium and common service spaces. Note the plant rooms at the ends of each block housing the air handling units serving each floor
Source: Adapted from SNO Architects

0   10   20

29.2 View along the north façade. The lower three levels have the characteristic 'punched-hole' windows with light-shelves, while the two upper levels have a triple horizontal band of louvred shading devices. Note too the unglazed west façade to the right of the photograph

29.3 The view from the south-west, with the glazing and shading arrangement evident, and the canopy roofs just visible on the top of each block. The main entrance is to the left on the southern façade under the extended portico. The vertical strip of glazing punctuating the southern façade indicates the location of the atrium and the thermal flue can be seen above

number of similar buildings, both in the public and private sectors' (Danker, 2004: 24, 84).

The brief called for the building to demonstrate, without compromising the comfort of the occupants, energy savings of 50 per cent compared with the operation of a more conventional office building, at an additional capital cost of not more than 10 per cent. No easy task in a climate with year-round temperatures ranging from 22 to 34°C and high humidity levels at this virtually equatorial location of around 3°N latitude. Integral to this demonstration was a commitment, not only to comprehensively monitor and give extensive feedback on the performance of the building, but also to provide a study and research opportunity for professionals and academics (MEWC, 2004), and a demonstration of the feasibility of meeting

what at that time was the new 2001 Malaysian Standard for non-residential building energy efficiency.

The building was the overall winner of the 2006 ASEAN Energy Award, in the new and existing building category.

THE DESIGN PROCESS

A large team of designers was involved in this project, the developer for which was Putrajaya Holdings Sdn Bhd. The lead architect was Ar Saifuddin bin Ahmad of SNO Architects, Kuala Lumpur, who developed the concept of the two blocks linked by a common atrium space and services area (see Figure 29.1), located and oriented in keeping with the overall plan for Parcel E, but with a building envelope designed

29.4 Close-up exterior view of the two main types of fenestration with their different shading/light-shelf arrangements. The lower levels have 'punched-hole' windows with light-shelves, while the upper levels have a triple horizontal band of louvred shading devices

29.5 Interior view of the naturally ventilated atrium space. The glazing at the upper level provides daylight to the space, and beyond that, the thermal flue acts to provide air movement

to minimise heat gains and maximise the use of daylight (Saifuddin, 2006). The firm of Norman, Disney Young was responsible for the basic mechanical and electrical engineering systems design.

Design input in relation to the minimisation of the energy consumption of these systems (as well as their subsequent monitoring), was provided by a group of specialists led by Poul Kristesen (2006) under the auspices of the Danish International Development Assistance (DANIDA) programme (MEWC, 2004). Their computer modelling indicated that the 50 per cent savings target could be met, with a predicted energy use index of around 100kWh/m^2.year, less even than the 135kWh/m^2.year set by the new Malaysian Standard.

29.6 External view of the vertically glazed thermal flue with automated louvred openings at the top for air to exit the atrium. The sloping glazing at low level provides daylight to the atrium and is fitted with retractable sailcloth shades to control glare

29.7 Typical perimeter single-person office. Note the vertical louvres for glare control on the left, and the glazed partition on the right which enables some daylight penetration to the adjacent corridor

29.8 Typical open plan office adjacent to atrium space

THE DESIGN OUTCOME

Building layout, construction, and passive environmental control systems

The site for the building is in the north-east corner of Parcel E. Roughly L-shaped in plan (see Figure 29.1), the layout is designed to give the majority of the façades a northerly or southerly orientation in order to minimise direct solar heat gain (Figures 29.2 and 29.3). The walls are well insulated and light in colour (by comparison with some of the neighbouring buildings), while the top floor has 100mm of insulation and an additional canopy roof (Figure 29.3).

Single-glazed throughout and predominantly non-openable, the building fenestration (Figure 29.4) has been designed to minimise solar heat gain and optimise the penetration of daylight. The windows on the upper floors have a triple set of external louvres, one at high level functioning as a shading device, the others at intermediate levels acting as both shading device and partial light-shelf (they have an open structure to enable air to pass though). On the lower floors, what the designers term the 'punched-hole' windows (Suifuddin, 2006) are heavily recessed to provide an initial measure of shading and are fitted with a solid external light-shelf at around mid-height which provides additional shading as well as enabling daylight penetration up to 6m depth. There is no glazing on the western façade, other than some minor windows into an emergency stairwell, while the windows on the easterly (ESE) façade have been given a deeper light-shelf than those on the north and south to help cope with low-angle morning sun (Figures 29.2, 29.3, and 29.4).

While the two main blocks are fully air conditioned, their linking four-storey high atrium and entrance area is naturally ventilated (Figure 29.5), and acts as a transition space from a climatic as well as a functional point of view. Fully open at the lower level to allow entry of outside air, the atrium is surmounted by a two-storey, fully glazed, easterly-oriented, thermal flue, designed to draw air up through the space using natural convection, to exit via automated louvres at high level (Figure 29.6).

While the deep plan of the building makes it difficult to provide daylight to the entire floor plate, there has been an attempt to prioritise permanent work areas on the perimeter of the building (Figure 29.7), with secondary functions (storage areas, meeting

29.9 Open-plan office – note various environmental sensors at high level as well as typical ceiling layout

29.10 Typical plant room (see Figure 29.1 for locations) housing the air handling unit serving a floor of one of the blocks. Note the louvred fresh air inlet in the centre of the wall to the left of shot, the bank of eight electrostatic filters at intake to the AHU, the supply air duct issuing from the top of the AHU, and the chilled waterpipe connection from the district cooling plant

29.11 Central building control system – visible to staff and visitors through a window from the adjacent entrance area

rooms, etc.) in the interior (KTAK, 2006, Paper 3). In addition, the use of glazed interior partitions and the location of some offices adjacent to the atrium provide an additional link to the ambient daylight condition (Figures 29.8 and 29.9).

Active environmental control systems

As already noted, apart from the atrium area and a few emergency openings, the building has a sealed envelope and is fully air conditioned, with a chilled water supply from a nearby gas-fired district cooling plant. Each floor of each block has an air handling unit located at one end of its floor plate (Figures 29.1 and 29.10). These AHUs supply chilled air to their respective office floors via a zoned variable air volume system, designed to maintain an inside temperature of 24°C.

The fresh air supply rate is controlled via CO_2 sensors, and electrostatic air filters (Figure 29.10) are used to clean the mixture of fresh and return air before supplying it to the offices. Separate and independent electrically driven split system air conditioners are used where continuous 24/7 operation is required (for computing and telecommunications installations, for example).

In keeping with the care taken over daylighting, the artificial lighting has been kept down to an installed load of around 11W/m² while maintaining an average illuminance of 350 lux.

A comprehensive building energy management and control system monitors and controls the operation of these environmental control systems as well as reporting on the building's energy consumption in some detail (Figure 29.11). Arguably just as important, a highly qualified in-house energy manager oversees this aspect of the building's operation (MEWC, 2004) and provides guidance documentation for the building users.

Rainwater from the canopy roof is collected in rooftop tanks and used for plant irrigation, while a 3kWp grid-connected photo-voltaic array is used to power a water feature in the atrium.

TABLE 29.1

Average scores for each factor and whether they were significantly better, similar to, or worse than the BUS benchmarks

	Score	Worse	Similar	Better		Score	Worse	Similar	Better
OPERATIONAL FACTORS									
Image to visitors	5.52		•		Cleaning	4.99		•	
Space in building	5.10			•	Availability of meeting rooms	5.44			•
Space at desk – too little/much^4	4.86		•		Suitability of storage arrangements	4.87			•
Furniture	5.36			•	Facilities meet requirements	5.22	•		
ENVIRONMENTAL FACTORS									
Temp and Air in Winter					Temp and Air in Summer				
Temp Overall	5.16			•	Temp Overall				
Temp – too hot/too cold^4	4.51	•			Temp – too hot/too cold^4				
Temp – stable/variable^4	4.54		•		Temp – stable/variable^4				
Air – still/draughty^4	4.13			•	Air – still/draughty^4				
Air – dry/humid^4	4.21		•		Air – dry/humid^4				
Air – fresh/stuffy^1	3.95		•		Air – fresh/stuffy^1				
Air – odourless/smelly^1	3.55		•		Air – odourless/smelly^1				
Air Overall	4.96			•	Air Overall				
Lighting					**Noise**				
Lighting Overall	5.10			•	Noise Overall	4.99			•
Natural light – too little/much^4	4.32		•		From colleagues – too little/much^4	3.49		•	
Sun & Sky Glare – none/too much^1	3.68		•		From other people – too little/much^4	3.53		•	
Artificial light – too little/much^4	4.10			•	From inside – too little/much^4	3.17		•	
Art'l light glare – none/too much^1	3.91	•			From outside – too little/much^4	2.99	•		
					Interruptions – none/frequent^1	3.19			•
CONTROL FACTORS ^{b}					**SATISFACTION FACTORS**				
Heating	7% 2.90		•		Design	5.44			•
Cooling	22% 3.04		•		Needs	5.26			•
Ventilation	8% 3.17		•		Comfort Overall	5.20			•
Lighting	18% 3.95		•		Productivity %	+16.00			•
Noise	8% 3.46	•			Health	4.77			•

NOTES: (a) unless otherwise noted, a score of 7 is 'best'; superscript ^{4} implies a score of 4 is best, superscript ^{1} implies a score of 1 is best; (b) the per cent values listed here are the percentages of respondents who thought personal control of that aspect was important.

TABLE 29.2

Numbers of respondents offering positive, balanced, and negative comments on 12 performance factors

Aspect	Number of respondents			
	Positive	Balanced	Negative	Total
Overall Design	26	3	7	36
Needs Overall	19	–	7	26
Meeting Rooms	18	1	9	28
Storage	5	1	14	20
Desk/Work Area	19	3	10	32
Comfort	14	3	2	19
Noise Sources	12	1	8	21
Lighting Conditions	16	1	10	27
Productivity	7	6	3	16
Health	8	4	3	15
Work Well	36	–	–	36
Hinder	–	–	30	30
TOTALS	180	23	103	306
PER CENT	58.8	7.5	33.7	100.0

USERS' PERCEPTIONS OF THE BUILDING

Overall response

For most (84 per cent) of the 148 or so respondents (56 per cent female, 44 per cent male), the building was their normal place of business, virtually everyone working five days per week and averaging 8.6 hours per day, of which 7.1 were spent at their desk and 6.1 at a computer. Some 46 per cent were over 30, 56 per cent less, and around 71 per cent had worked in the building for more than a year, mostly at the same desk or work area. Around 33 per cent shared with five or more colleagues, with the remainder equally divided between single offices, sharing with one other, or sharing with two to four others.

Significant factors

Table 29.1 lists the scores for each of the survey questions and indicates those aspects of the building that the staff perceived as being significantly better, similar to, or worse than the benchmark and/or scale mid-point. In this case, some 16 aspects were significantly better, only two significantly worse, while the remaining 19 aspects had much the same score as the benchmark (note the absence of wintertime data for this location).

In terms of operational aspects, this building scores very well on all eight counts – above the mid-point of the scale, and the same as or better than the benchmark, in every case. The score for space at desk (4.86) implied respondents felt they had too much space at their desks!

The users' responses to environmental factors were more variable. The overall scores for temperature and air were better than their respective benchmarks and well above their scale mid-points. However, there were indications that the temperature was felt to be on the cold and variable side, and the air a little on the humid side. While lighting overall scored significantly better than the benchmark and scale mid-point and respondents did not perceive glare to be excessive,

Shading on the north-west façade of Menara UMNO

30

Menara UMNO
Penang, Malaysia

with Shireen Jahnkassim

THE CONTEXT

Menara UMNO is a 21-storey, 16,700m² floor area, commercial development in Georgetown, the capital of the state of Penang and the main city of Pulau Pinang which lies just off the west coast of Peninsular Malaysia. Situated on a 1920m² site in a predominantly shopping district, it is comprised of a podium containing a banking hall, an auditorium, and several levels of parking, surmounted by 14 levels of office space, occupied by a range of small to medium-sized organisations (Figures 30.1 and 31.2). Construction was completed in December 1997.

According to architect Ken Yeang (1999), the building was designed initially to be non-air-conditioned,

> Because in Penang at that time the rentals were so low, that if you put up an air conditioned building you would not get sufficient return. In Penang they were also competing with low rise buildings which were non-air-conditioned (though all the tenants would come in and install their own air conditioning systems later).

30.1 Looking towards north-western façade

30.2 View from the north – car parking below, office floors above, north-eastern wing wall on upper left

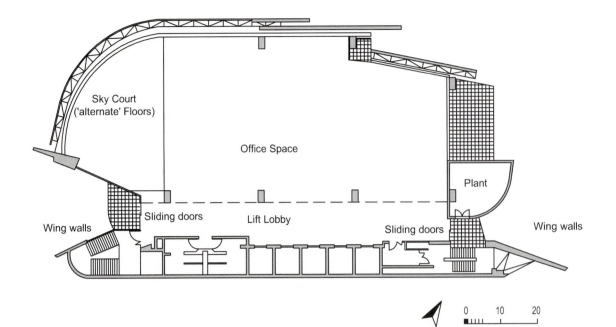

Sky Court
('alternate' Floors)

Office Space

Plant

Wing walls

Sliding doors

Lift Lobby

Sliding doors

Wing walls

0   10   20

30.3 Typical floor plan, indicating wing walls, balconies and openings, with line of skycourts indicated. Note the elongated service core on the south-east façade and plant room for the air handling units
Source: Adapted from Hamzah and Yeang

30.4 South-eastern façade

30.5 Typical air handling unit serving one floor

The near-equatorial latitude (around 5°N) and warm humid climate of this island location (the 1 per cent design temperatures being 22.9 and 32.2°C (ASHRAE, 2001: 27.40–1)) represented a real challenge to designers who wish to employ natural ventilation.

Yeang's response to the challenge was to say:

All right, I will design the building for you with a gantry on the outside, as a framework or a walkway. When the tenants put in their own air conditioning, they can locate the condensers on the gantry which is hidden by the sun shades. Then half way through construction, the developer felt confident of the market and said, 'Yes, I think we can put this building up with air conditioning', and so central air conditioning was added much later.

(Yeang, 1999)

Such are the uncertainties of the building industry. Despite these issues, the building won the Royal Australian Institute of Architects' International Award in 1998 (RAIA, 1998).

THE DESIGN PROCESS

Prompted by a brief which, at least initially, did not include for total dependence on a full air conditioning installation, and assisted by the knowledge that the main wind directions were from the north/ north-east and from the south-west, Yeang set out to design a building which offered the potential for natural ventilation to be used as a significant provider of thermal comfort, while still making provision for tenants to install their own air conditioning systems.

In many respects, the design process did not follow his preferred procedure, which was to bring in the other key consultants right at the beginning. However, given the nature of the changes that took place in the brief during the design and construction phases of this project, that proved not to be feasible on this occasion. The involvement of the specialist consultants was at the checking and modifying stage rather than the conceptual stage of the design process, and the detailed HVAC design, or redesign, was carried out during the construction stage after it was decided that market conditions had improved sufficiently to justify the installation of a centralised system. Interestingly enough, this did not cause any problems for the engineers (Kuala Lumpur-based Ranhill Bersekutu Sdn Bhd) – presumably adequate space had been allowed for individual tenants to install their own systems – but some minor architectural modifications were needed to accommodate the fresh air intakes to the AHU on each floor (Chow, 1999).

Advice was also received from Dr Phil Jones, Director of Architectural Science Research at the Welsh School of Architecture and Richard Aynsley (at that time Director of the Australian Institute of Tropical Architecture at James Cook University, Queensland) on the building's aerodynamics in general and the 'wing walls' in particular. These latter were the proposed projections from the building façade, located in the vicinity of openings, such that the prevailing winds are captured, and their natural ventilation potential enhanced. A fuller description of the design process and outcome may be found in Baird (2001, Chapter 18).

30.6 Reception area of an office floor

30.7 Internal layout of a typical office floor

30.8 North-east-facing wing wall – wing wall to the left, curved façades of plant rooms to the right

THE DESIGN OUTCOME

Building layout and construction

With its long axis approximately NE–SW, Menara UMNO's 14 floors of offices, atop its seven-storey podium, sit well clear of the surrounding shops, and are thus well exposed to both sun and wind (Figures 30.1 and 30.2). The typical office floor – with a gross floor area of 615m² and a 2:1 aspect ratio – has an elongated service core along the SE façade and a fairly open plan interior (Figure 30.3).

Three major features demonstrate Yeang's efforts to minimise solar heat gains, while still allowing reasonable views and daylighting potential. The first of these is the placement of the elongated services core and an opaque wall on the SE façade and a plant room on the NE, effectively eliminating low angle early morning solar heat gain (Figures 30.3 and 30.4). Second, heat gain from the north and westerly sun is partially controlled by the deep bands of louvred solar shades and the skycourts (on six of the 14 office levels) which articulate these façades of the building (Figure 30.1). Finally, the shading of the rooftop and the three cooling towers, which otherwise would receive most of the solar heat gain at this latitude, is achieved by the extension upwards of the elongated service core and the large curved canopy (Figure 30.1).

Passive and active environmental control systems

To enable natural ventilation, the 'experimental' (Hamzah and Yeang, 1998) wing walls project from each of the short façades to catch the predominant winds and funnel them towards glazed openings (Figure 30.3). Sets of sliding doors, two wing-wall-assisted at opposite ends of the floor plate and two more conventional facing the NE, together with the occasional skycourt and the provision of openable windows all round complete this provision for natural ventilation under suitable climatic conditions (or power cut emergencies for that matter).

Most of the office floors have been fitted out with packaged air handling units, one per floor, and with a cooling capacity of around 76kW or 100kW depending on the floor area of the particular office. These are connected via a common riser to three cooling towers on the roof. Located (Figure 30.5) in relatively generously sized plant rooms against the NE façade through which they draw their fresh air,

30.9 South-west-facing wing wall

30.10 Looking down into a skycourt – west-facing corner

30.11 Westerly elevation, indicating extent of vertical solar shading

the AHUs supply air to the adjacent office space (Figures 30.6 and 30.7) via ductwork and diffusers in the false ceiling. These systems are under the control of the floor tenant and operate independently of the natural ventilation system.

Passive environmental control is provided mainly by the wing walls in concert with the balcony and window openings on each office floor. The two main wing walls are orientated to the NE (Figure 30.8) and the SW (Figure 30.9), funnelling the air towards the corresponding windward balcony opening. Subsidiary balcony openings and openable windows are distributed around the NE, NW, and SW façades (Figure 30.3). Around half of the office floors

TABLE 30.1

Aspects of the building perceived as significantly better, similar to, or worse than the BUS Benchmarks, out of a total of 19 aspects considered

ENVIRONMENTAL FACTORS

	Score	Worse	Similar	Better		Score	Worse	Similar	Better
Temp and Air All Year Round					Additional Questions				
Temp Overall	4.36			●	Temp Morning –comf/uncomfortable¹	4.3		●	
Temp – too hot/too cold⁴	4.56	●			Temp Afternoon –comf/uncomfortable¹	4.6	●		
Air – still/draughty⁴	3.56		●		Temp Morning – too hot/cold⁴	4.3		●	
Air – dry/humid⁴	3.64		●		Temp Afternoon – too hot/cold⁴	4.2		●	
Air – fresh/stuffy¹	4.07		●						
Lighting									
Lighting Overall	3.71	●							
Natural Light – too little/much⁴	4.00			●					
Sun & Sky Glare – none/too much¹	4.33	●							
Artificial Light – too little/much⁴	3.92			●					
Art'l Light Glare – none/too much¹	3.69			●					

CONTROL FACTORS ᵇ	Score	Worse	Similar	Better	**SATISFACTION FACTORS**	Score	Worse	Similar	Better
Heating	2.88	●			Design	2.21	●		
Cooling	4.47		●		Comfort Overall	3.30			●
Ventilation	4.15		●						

NOTES: (a) unless otherwise noted, a score of 7 is 'best'; superscript ⁴ implies a score of 4 is best, superscript ¹ implies a score of 1 is best; (b) the per cent values listed here are the percentages of respondents who thought personal control of that aspect was important.

also have a skycourt (Figure 30.10) cut out at an angle on the west-facing corner, providing further natural ventilation options as well as shading on this difficult orientation.

More conventional solar shading is provided on the NW façade (Figure 30.11), comprising bands of external louvres held out from the glazing on the gantry framework, originally designed, *inter alia*, to provide a convenient but unobtrusive location for the ubiquitous condenser units, had retrofitting of split system air conditioning been left to the individual tenants.

USERS' PERCEPTIONS OF THE BUILDING

Overall response

In the case of Menara UMNO, the survey questionnaire was somewhat modified from that used in the other case study buildings. However, a significant number of the standard questions remain, some additional specific questions were added, and a thorough investigation of the building's design and its thermal and visual performance undertaken by a team from the Environmental Analysis Group of the Kulliyyah of Architecture and Environmental Design at the International Islamic University Malaysia (Jahnkassim *et al.*, 2004). In broad terms, questions related to temperature, air quality, lighting, personal control, and satisfaction were included, while operational and noise issues and some aspects of satisfaction were omitted, but additional questions were asked about conditions in specific areas of the building (e.g., the entrance, the lift lobbies, the skycourts) and for the offices at different times of day.

For most of the 52 or so respondents (50 per cent female, 50 per cent male), the building was their normal place of business, virtually everyone working 5.5 days per week on average. Some 37 per cent were over 35, 63 per cent less, and around 53 per cent had worked in the building for more than a year, mostly at the same desk or work area. Around 37 per cent shared with five to eight colleagues, 14 per cent were normally alone, with the remainder equally divided between sharing with one other, or sharing with two to four others.

Significant factors

Table 30.1 indicates those aspects of the building that the users perceived as being significantly better than, similar to, or worse than the benchmark and/or scale mid-point. Of the 15 'standard' questions about which responses were sought, in this instance, some seven aspects were significantly better, four were significantly worse, while the remaining four or so aspects had much the same score as the benchmark.

No questions were asked on operational aspects in this survey, while in the case of environmental factors the focus was mainly on aspects of temperature, air, lighting, and personal control of these.

While the overall score for temperature was better than its benchmark and well above the scale mid-point, there were indications that the temperature was felt to be on the cold side. This finding was reinforced by the responses to the additional questions on thermal comfort and temperature in the workplace during morning and afternoon. Thermal comfort scored 4.3 and 4.6 respectively (on a 7-point scale where 1 is comfortable and 7 is uncomfortable), while on a 7-point scale where 1 is too hot and 7 is too cold, the respective scores averaged 4.3 and 4.2.

Lighting overall scored significantly worse than the benchmark and scale mid-point. While the amount of both natural and artificial light was perceived to be fine on average and glare from the latter was not a major issue, it seemed that glare from sun and sky was the major contributor to the low overall score. Personal control of lighting, ventilation and cooling scored significantly higher than their respective benchmarks.

Perceptions of the satisfaction variables (only design and comfort overall in this case) gave mixed results. While design was not rated highly, overall comfort came out well, with a score of 3.6 (on a 7-point scale where 1 is comfortable and 7 uncomfortable).

Overall performance indices

The focused nature of the survey precluded the calculation of Comfort, Satisfaction, and Summary Indices in this case. However, in terms of their average perception scores for the overall study variables, the staff rated comfort overall and temperature overall highly (better than benchmarks and/or scale mid-points), with lighting overall under its corresponding values, probably on account of sun and sky glare.

OTHER REPORTED ASPECTS OF PERFORMANCE

The design and performance of this building have attracted the attention of several researchers, and the results of different investigations have formed part of at least two PhD theses (Kishnani, 2002; Jahnkassim, 2004). The building owners and designers are to be congratulated on their willingness to enable these independent studies.

Kishnani did not undertake detailed user studies as only one floor was occupied at the time of his study. However, he did take the opportunity to carry out comparative measurements of temperature, humidity, air movement, and lighting on that air-conditioned floor and on unoccupied, but naturally ventilated, floors. During the study period (19–25 January 2000) outside air temperatures and relative humidities ranged from 23.7 to 33.5°C and from 65 to 77%rh respectively. Inside air temperatures in the air-conditioned offices during that period ranged from 21.3 to 24.3°C, while in the naturally ventilated floor temperatures ranged from 28.0°C in the main part of the floor to 38.8°C close to the west-facing façade (this floor did not have a skycourt); humidities were within the 59 to 75 per cent range in both cases (Krishnani, 2002: 104). Simultaneous temperature logging of the two floors indicated overnight temperatures on the naturally ventilated floor only 1°C higher than the air-conditioned floor (27.5°C as against 26.5°C). During the day the air-conditioned floor was brought down to around 23°C, while the temperature naturally ventilated floor only rose by 1°C or so (Krishnani, 2002: 128).

He also carried out simultaneous temperature logging of two of the naturally ventilated unoccupied floors, one with and the other without a skycourt. It was found that the skycourt had a significant effect, keeping the air temperature anything from 1 to 3°C lower (the difference increasing as the day progressed) and some 7°C lower near the west-facing façade during the afternoon peak (ibid.: 117).

Air velocities in the air-conditioned space were found to be in the 0.0 to 0.1m/s range, while on an unoccupied naturally ventilated office floor, with all doors and windows fully open, velocities ranged from under 0.3 up to 5m/s, with corresponding outside wind speeds ranging from 0.7 to 4.4m/s (ibid.: 105).

ACKNOWLEDGEMENTS

Our thanks go to all the designers who were interviewed in connection with this project – Dr Ken Yeang of T. R. Hamzah & Yeang and Ir Choon Yan Chow of Ranhill Bersekutu, both based in Kuala Lumpur, plus Professor Phil Jones of the Welsh School of Architecture. We are particularly grateful to Shytul Shahryn Mohamad Shaari, Deputy Project Manager with Amanah Capital Property Management for conducting George Baird around Menara UMNO in 1999 and to Mohammed Zahry Shaik Abdul Rahman of the Department of Housing and Building, Universiti Sains Malaysia, for arranging a further visit in 2006.

REFERENCES

ASHRAE (2001) *ASHRAE Handbook: Fundamentals, SI Edition*, Atlanta, GA: American Society of Heating Refrigerating and Air-Conditioning Engineers.

Baird, G. (2001) *The Architectural Expression of Environmental Control Systems*, London: Spon Press, Chapter 18.

Chow, C. Y. (1999) Transcript of an interview held on 6 May, Kuala Lumpur.

Hamzah, T. R. & Yeang (1998) 'Umno Tower, Penang, Malaysia', *Domus*, 808: 22–5.

Jahnkassim, P. S. (2004) 'The Bioclimatic Skyscraper: A Critical Analysis of the Theories and Designs of Ken Yeang', unpublished PhD thesis, University of Brighton.

Jahnkassim, P. S., Ali, M., Abkr, Y., and Aripin, S. (2004) 'Environmental Performance Menara UMNO', Centre of Built Environment Report EAG 101-03, Kulliyyah of Architecture and Environmental Design, International Islamic University Malaysia.

Kashnani, N. (2002) 'Climate, Buildings and Occupant Expectations: A Comfort-Based Model for the Design and Operation of Office Buildings in Hot Humid Conditions', PhD thesis, School of Architecture, Construction and Planning, Curtin University of Technology, Perth, Australia, available at: http://adt.curtin.adu.au/theses/available/adt-WCU20030526.135244/.

RAIA (1998) 'International Award – Menara UMNO, Malaysia', *Architecture Australia*, 87(6): 58–9.

Yeang, K. (1999) Transcript of an interview held on 5 May, Kuala Lumpur.

31

Torrent Research Centre
Ahmedabad, Gujarat, India

with Leena Thomas

THE CONTEXT

The Torrent Research Centre building in Ahmedabad was completed and fully occupied in 1997 as the new research facilities for Torrent Pharmaceuticals Ltd (Figure 31.1). The building design has achieved national awards including the 2000 JIIA-ANCHOR Award for excellence in Public Architecture as well as the Indian Architect and Builder 'Designing for Corporate Culture' Award 2004 and has been widely reported for its energy-efficient and passive solar design (Baird, 2001;

Majumdar, 2001). Originally designed for 150 staff, the building now accommodates over 300, some working in shifts (Figure 31.2).

Ahmedabad has three distinct climatic seasons – hot and dry from March to June with temperatures reaching well over 40°C, warm and humid from July to September during the monsoon, and cool and dry from October to February, the 1 per cent values ranging from +12.8°C in the cool season to +41.0°C in the hot (ASHRAE, 2001: 27.36–7). The hot dry season in particular provided a challenging

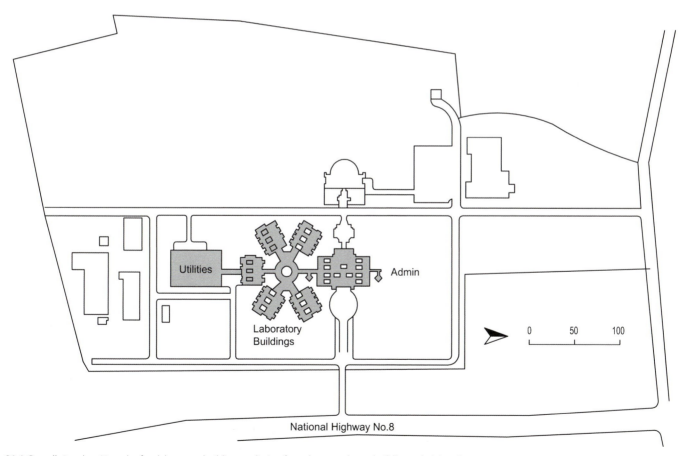

31.1 Overall site plan. Note the five laboratory buildings radiating from the central core building, administration building to the north, and utilities building to the south. The three PDEC laboratories and administration building have their tower penetrations unshaded, while the two AC laboratories are completely shaded
Source: Adapted from Abhikram

313

31.2 Viewed from the north-west – administration building to the left of shot, and one of the five laboratory buildings to the right

31.3 Typical cross-section of a laboratory building showing the ventilation principle and location of the PDEC microniser system, with central air inlet towers, air distribution and perimeter exhaust towers. The towers are used as distribution routes for the air ducts in the two air-conditioned (AC) laboratory buildings
Source: Adapted from Abhikram

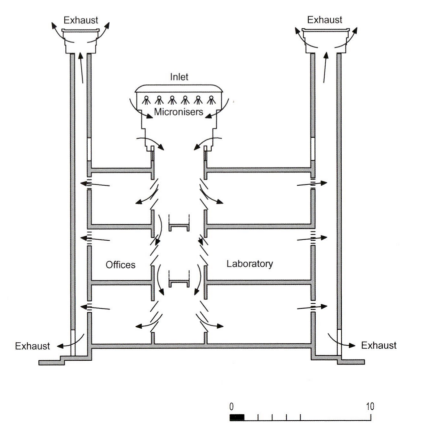

31.4 Exterior view of a typical PDEC laboratory building. Note the relatively squat structures housing the air intakes on the roof, and the taller, narrower air exhaust towers around the perimeter

31.5 Typical laboratory building floor plan with office spaces to the left and laboratory spaces to the right. Note too the disposition of the ventilating towers and the voids in the corridor to enable vertical air movement
Source: Adapted from Abhikram

climatic context for the environmental ambitions of the project – to maximise the use of natural light and ventilation, use locally available natural materials, and control the ingress of dust.

The design process and architectural outcome have been described elsewhere in some detail (Baird, 2001). What follows is the briefest of outlines.

DESIGN PROCESS

The design process was developed from a platform of client commitment for environmental design, clear goals for environmental performance, an integrated multidisciplinary team approach to design that is mindful of user needs, and responsive building management during commissioning and operation, that have been noted as hallmarks for successful environmental design (Thomas and Hall, 2004).

Principal architects for the project were the Nimish Patel and Parul Zaveri of Abhikram. Designing of the first laboratory block commenced in early 1992, and from the outset, the design team had resolved that all of their buildings would be able to work during daylight hours using the minimum of electrical energy. The London-based firm of Short Ford Associates provided the environmental design

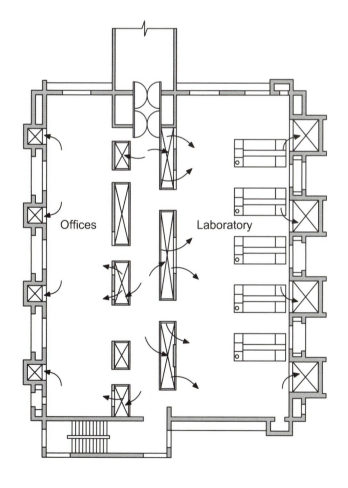

31.6 Close-up of a set of air inlet towers, showing the water-supply manifold for the PDEC micronisers

31.7 Looking up into the top of one of the air inlet towers. Note the array of microniser piping and nozzles supported on a rectangular frame at high level

31.8 Looking along the corridor of the middle floor of a typical laboratory building with openings above and below to enable air movement between. Note the arrangement of the hopper window openings to the spaces on either side, designed to capture descending cooler air and direct it into the offices and laboratories

consulting services for the typical laboratory block on this project. Their concept for the passive down-draft evaporative cooling system (Figure 31.3) served as a prototype for the remaining laboratory buildings and administrative buildings that were developed and detailed by Abhikram with assistance from Solar Agni International, Pondicherry. The design process also included Torrent's in-house engineering team headed by S. B. Namjoshi, as well as the services of air conditioning consultant M. Dastur from New Delhi.

The Passive Downdraft Evaporative Cooling (PDEC) technology had previously been used by Short Ford at a brewery in the relatively benign climate of Malta. However, its adoption as the exclusive mode of cooling for four of the six laboratory buildings and the administration building (Figure 31.1) in the climatic context of Ahmedabad, where temperatures routinely exceed 35 and 40°C, was not without calculated risk. In addition to the expertise and collaborative resolution within the design team, its implementation can be attributed to the willingness of the client to accept the approach of designing for a threshold temperature (28–28.5°C, based on a model of adaptive comfort) which could be exceeded for a certain number of hours, rather than the stringent comfort band of conventional air-conditioned buildings. In this connection, the designers were unstinting in their admiration for Dr C. Dutt, Torrent's Director of Research as both a critical but immensely supportive client (Chauhan, 1998), who was also quite prepared to take a 'wait and see' position on some issues – for example, on the questions of the potential for rain penetration via the ventilation towers, or for lack of air movement in some locations.

THE DESIGN OUTCOME

Building layout and construction

This study was focused on the main group of five three-storey laboratory buildings and one administrative block radiating from a circular-plan core building (Figure 31.1) amounting to some 12,000m² of floor space, all told. Two of the five laboratory buildings are air-conditioned, the other three equipped with the PDEC system. A concept for a central corridor flanked by working spaces, where air was supplied via the central corridor and exhausted at the perimeter

31.9 View inside a typical laboratory space. Note the louvred openings at high level on the left which lead directly to the exhaust towers, and the provision of ceiling fans

31.10 Close-up view of a laboratory façade. Note the combination of high and low level windows on each floor, and the extensive shading provided by the combination of horizontal overhangs and vertical towers

(Figures 31.3 and 31.4) was developed and then adopted for the final design in February 1994. All laboratory buildings are similar in plan – 22m by 17m, with a 4m-wide corridor flanked by 5m-deep office spaces and 8m-deep laboratory spaces (Figure 31.5). The larger main administrative building is located to the north of the laboratories, and a utilities building to the south, linked by a two-level corridor spine (Figure 31.1).

Passive and active environmental control systems

A reinforced concrete construction framed structure with plastered cavity brick infill walls and hollow concrete blocks filling the roof coffers plastered inside ensures a thermally massive structure. Vermiculite is used as an insulating material on both roof and walls. External surfaces are white – the walls painted, the roof using a china mosaic finish.

The critical climatic time of the year is the hot dry season when mid-afternoon outside temperatures regularly reach 40°C or more. These are the conditions under which the PDEC system is designed to operate. It does so by piping water through nozzles at a pressure of 50Pa to produce a fine mist (dubbed the 'microniser' system by Brian Ford) at the top of the three large air intake towers located above the central corridors of each laboratory building (Figures 31.6 and 31.7). Evaporation of the fine mist serves to cool the air which then descends slowly through the central corridor space via the openings on each side of the walkway (Figure 31.8). At each level, sets of hopper windows, designed to catch the descending flow, can be used to divert some of this cooled air into the adjacent space. Having passed through the space, the air may then exit via high-level glass-louvred openings (Figure 31.9) which connect directly to the perimeter exhaust air towers. Night-time ventilation is also an option during this season.

During the warm humid monsoon season when the use of the microniser would be inappropriate, the ceiling fans (introduced to ameliorate the muggy conditions experienced during the first monsoon season) can be put into operation to provide additional air movement in the offices and laboratories. In the cooler season the operating strategy is designed to control the ventilation, particularly at night, to minimise heat losses – this is done simply by the users adjusting the hopper widows and louvred openings in their individual

spaces to suit their requirements. The central plant for this research facility includes two oil-fired steam boilers with a capacity of 4T/hr each, two 175cfm air compressors, two 725KVA diesel generator sets, and some 350 tons of refrigeration capacity.

The building has a number of instances of integrated design where architectural elements serve more than one purpose. Solar control is achieved by recessing windows between the outlet towers along the perimeter, as well as limiting window area, and shading via horizontal overhangs (Figure 31.10). The clerestory opening in the air inlet towers also introduce diffused daylight to the central walkways adjoining them.

TABLE 31.1

Average staff scores for each factor and whether they were significantly
better, similar to, or worse than the BUS benchmarks – Buildings with PDEC only

OPERATIONAL FACTORS

Factor	Score	Worse	Similar	Better
Image to visitors	6.56			●
Space in building	5.03			●
Space at desk – too little/much[4]	4.19		●	
Furniture	4.91			●
Cleaning	5.92			●
Availability of meeting rooms	5.06			●
Suitability of storage arrangements	4.89			●
Facilities meet requirements	5.06	●		

ENVIRONMENTAL FACTORS

Temp and Air in:

Factor	Winter	W	S	B	Monsoon[c]	Summer	W	S	B
Temp Overall	5.84			●	4.97	4.61			●
Temp – too hot/too cold[4]	4.61	●			4.04	3.38		●	
Temp – stable/variable[4]	3.81		●		3.89	3.87		●	
Air – still/draughty[4]	3.66		●		4.05	3.70		●	
Air – dry/humid[4]	3.48		●		4.95	3.68		●	
Air – fresh/stuffy[1]	3.10			●	3.48	3.50			●
Air – odourless/smelly[1]	3.15			●	3.33	3.24			●
Air Overall	5.54			●	3.68	4.44			●

Lighting

Factor	Score	Worse	Similar	Better
Lighting Overall	5.86			●
Natural light – too little/much[4]	3.82			●
Sun & Sky Glare – none/too much[1]	2.93			●
Artificial light – too little/much[4]	4.86		●	
Art'l light glare – none/too much[1]	3.52			●

Noise

Factor	Score	Worse	Similar	Better
Noise Overall	5.09			●
From colleagues – too little/much[4]	3.45		●	
From other people – too little/much[4]	3.13		●	
From inside – too little/much[4]	2.91		●	
From outside – too little/much[4]	2.24	●		
Interruptions – none/frequent[1]	3.20			●

CONTROL FACTORS [b]

Factor	%	Score	Worse	Similar	Better
Heating	14%	3.85		●	
Cooling	16%	4.08		●	
Ventilation	17%	3.74		●	
Lighting	18%	4.97			●
Noise	16%	3.91		●	

SATISFACTION FACTORS

Factor	Score	Worse	Similar	Better
Design	5.86			●
Needs	5.44			●
Comfort Overall	5.03			●
Productivity %	+13.66			●
Health	4.74			●

NOTES: (a) unless otherwise noted, a score of 7 is 'best'; superscript [4] implies a score of 4 is best, superscript [1] implies a score of 1 is best; (b) the per cent values listed here are the percentages of respondents who thought personal control of that aspect was important; (c) there are no benchmarks for the monsoon season

TABLE 31.2

Average staff scores for each factor and whether they were significantly

better, similar to, or worse than the BUS benchmarks – Buildings with full air conditioning

OPERATIONAL FACTORS

Factor	Score	Worse	Similar	Better	Factor	Score	Worse	Similar	Better
Image to visitors	6.39			●	Cleaning	6.11			●
Space in building	5.29			●	Availability of meeting rooms	5.68			●
Space at desk – too little/much[4]	3.97			●	Suitability of storage arrangements	5.16			●
Furniture	4.75		●		Facilities meet requirements	5.26		●	

ENVIRONMENTAL FACTORS

Temp and Air in:

Factor	Winter	Worse	Similar	Better	Monsoon[c]	Summer	Worse	Similar	Better
Temp Overall	5.54			●	5.75	5.86			●
Temp – too hot/too cold[4]	5.29	●			4.66	4.35		●	
Temp – stable/variable[4]	3.06		●		3.12	3.32		●	
Air – still/draughty[4]	3.74		●		3.65	3.38		●	
Air – dry/humid[4]	3.53		●		4.35	3.32	●		
Air – fresh/stuffy[1]	2.38			●	2.41	2.43			●
Air – odourless/smelly[1]	2.14			●	2.72	2.59			●
Air Overall	5.62			●	5.47	5.73			●

Lighting

Factor	Score	Worse	Similar	Better
Lighting Overall	6.46			●
Natural light – too little/much[4]	3.96			●
Sun & Sky Glare – none/too much[1]	2.52			●
Artificial light – too little/much[4]	4.79	●		
Art'l light glare – none/too much[1]	3.36			●

Noise

Factor	Score	Worse	Similar	Better
Noise Overall	5.39			●
From colleagues – too little/much[4]	3.59		●	
From other people – too little/much[4]	2.79		●	
From inside – too little/much[4]	2.31		●	
From outside – too little/much[4]	1.95	●		
Interruptions – none/frequent[1]	2.87			●

CONTROL FACTORS [b]

Factor	%	Score	Worse	Similar	Better
Heating	19%	4.45			●
Cooling	25%	4.43			●
Ventilation	11%	4.35			●
Lighting	12%	4.94			●
Noise	17%	4.43			●

SATISFACTION FACTORS

Factor	Score	Worse	Similar	Better
Design	6.10			●
Needs	5.79			●
Comfort Overall	5.72			●
Productivity %	+20.88			●
Health	5.53			●

NOTES: (a) unless otherwise noted, a score of 7 is 'best'; superscript [4] implies a score of 4 is best, superscript [1] implies a score of 1 is best; (b) the per cent values listed here are the percentages of respondents who thought personal control of that aspect was important; (c) there are no benchmarks for the monsoon season

31.11 Average scores on a 7-point scale for the AC and PDEC buildings under winter, summer, and monsoon conditions, compared to an 'ideal' (in this instance) of 4.00. (a) Temperature (too hot/too cold scale); (b) Air (dry/ humid scale)

Each of the building blocks surveyed was originally designed for an occupancy of 25 scientists. With the expansion of activities, increase in staff and overlapping shifts in recent years, some of the buildings currently house as many as 70 to 80 people working at the same time.

USERS' PERCEPTIONS OF THE BUILDING

Overall response
The survey was administered to staff at the Torrent Research Centre in December 2004. In addition to the variables normally covered in the standard form, questions relating to comfort, temperature and air in the monsoon season were also included. A total of 292 surveys were distributed and 164 responses returned, 64 from the air-conditioned (AC) buildings, 100 from the buildings with passive downdraft evaporative cooling (PDEC). Respondents in both groups were predominantly male (92 per cent in AC, 89 per cent in PDEC) and the majority were under the age of 30 (80 per cent in AC, 70 per cent in PDEC). Most of the respondents had worked in the building longer than one year (54 per cent in AC, 53 per cent in PDEC), and roughly a quarter to a third of respondents reported that they were seated next to a window (23 per cent in AC, 30 per cent in PDEC). The offices were predominantly open plan with the exception of senior management. In the buildings with PDEC, 47 per cent of respondents shared their office with more than eight others, and another 24 per cent shared their office with five to eight others. Similarly, in the AC buildings, 43 per cent shared their office with more than eight others, and another 30 per cent shared their office with five to eight others.

The Torrent building was only the second building to be surveyed in India using this methodology. Although that limits the scope for comparisons regionally, the co-location of passive downdraft evaporative cooling (PDEC) and air-conditioned (AC) buildings at Torrent offers a unique opportunity to compare performance while overcoming any potential issues arising from contextual differences such as demographics, conditions of work, attitudes and expectations of employees likely to occur between respondents in different countries.

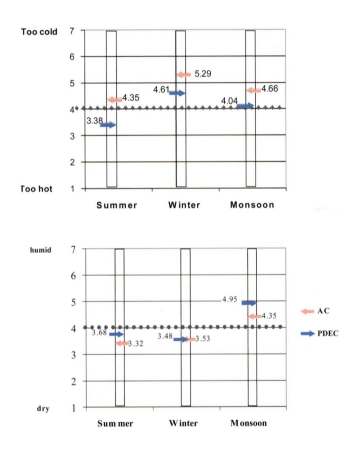

Significant factors
For the PDEC and AC buildings respectively, Tables 31.1 and 31.2 list the scores for each of the survey questions and indicates those aspects of the building that the staff perceived as being significantly better, similar to, or worse than the benchmark and/or scale mid-point. In the PDEC case (Table 31.1), some 26 aspects were significantly better, only two were significantly worse, while the remaining 17 aspects had much the same score as the benchmark. In the AC case (Table 31.2), some 30 aspects were significantly better, only four were significantly worse, while the remaining 11 aspects had much the same score as the benchmark.

As can be seen, the staff perceptions were exceptionally positive for all key variables in both types of buildings (PDEC and AC) at

Torrent. The PDEC buildings returned average scores for comfort overall of 5.03 and a perceived productivity increase of 13.66 per cent; the AC buildings 5.72 and 20.88 per cent.

While the average scores for the AC buildings are somewhat better than the PDEC buildings, it is important to note that the latter buildings were also consistently better than the corresponding benchmarks and scale mid-points.

The image of the building was given the highest average score by the staff in both buildings types, with most other operational variables also yielding better than benchmark scores.

In terms of environmental conditions, the highest rating was achieved for lighting overall for both building types. The scores for the more detailed factors indicate that the strategy of judiciously sized windows, coupled with the provision of diffused daylight to the central walkways and offices adjoining air inlet/outlet towers, has been successful; albeit with a suggestion of too much artificial lighting.

Both the PDEC and AC buildings scored above the benchmark for temperature overall and air overall in the winter, monsoon, and summer seasons. Further details of temperature and air are presented in Figure 31.11 (see also Thomas and Baird, 2006). As shown in Figure 31.11(a), the occupants of the air-conditioned buildings consistently rated temperatures on the colder side of neutral or 4.00 (the mid-point of the 'too-hot/too-cold' 7-point scale). In these buildings the temperatures ranged around 22–24°C all year in comparison to the more adaptable temperature range (approximately five degrees less than the outside mean temperatures) in the PDEC buildings. The corresponding scores for the PDEC buildings are close to neutral during the monsoon and on the colder and warmer sides of neutral in winter and summer respectively. The generally positive user feedback to overall temperature for all three seasons is particularly significant, given the indoor temperature ranges that are higher than those deemed acceptable in air-conditioned and western contexts.

Following the first year of occupancy, ceiling fans were installed as a consequence of the experience of 'muggy conditions' in the building as noted by the client (Dutt, cited in Majumdar, 2001). Figure 31.11(b) shows that although occupants experienced some concern about humidity during the monsoon, they rated the air conditions as close to satisfactory in summer in the PDEC buildings.

While there was consistent satisfaction with the noise conditions overall, the green-field setting of the Torrent buildings on the outskirts of the city has meant there is little or no noise from external sources.

While there was a low perception of control for heating, ventilation, lighting, cooling and noise, only 14–25 per cent of staff rated personal control as important. However, as seen above, these low scores had little impact on overall comfort and perceived productivity, which would corroborate Leaman and Bordass' findings (2005) that the strength of the relationship between perceived control and productivity declines as the buildings perform better.

The staff rated all of the satisfaction factors (design, needs, comfort overall, productivity, and health) significantly above their benchmarks in both cases.

Users' comments
Overall, some 497 responses were received under the 12 headings where respondents could add written comments – some 25 per cent of the 1968 (164 respondents by 12 headings) potential number of comments. Table 31.3 indicates the numbers of positive, balanced, and negative comments under each of the 12 headings – in this case, around 50.7 per cent were positive, 8.3 per cent neutral, and 41.0 per cent negative.

Generally speaking, the nature and type of comments reflected the scores. Interestingly, many staff expressed a sense of pride at working in a building seen to adopt a climate-responsive and low-energy approach. While comments relating to design, health, and comfort were predominantly positive, there were some concerns about discomfort in summer, odours and stuffiness for the PDEC buildings. Given the ongoing increase in internal heat gains and latent loads from increased occupancy, this aspect might require further investigation in the future. Despite positive scores for noise conditions overall, some staff commented on noise emanating from equipment and colleagues. Most comments relating to aspects that hindered ability to work centred on increasing crowding in the workplace and associated issues with space and storage, although a few complained about insufficient (natural) light.

TABLE 31.3

Numbers of respondents offering positive, balanced, and negative comments on 12 performance factors

Aspect	Number of respondents			
	Positive	Balanced	Negative	Total
Overall Design	48	8	12	68
Needs Overall	16	5	21	42
Meeting Rooms	21	0	16	36
Storage	11	3	18	32
Desk/Work Area	12	4	37	53
Comfort	24	2	4	30
Noise Sources	16	3	22	41
Lighting Conditions	26	2	8	36
Productivity	8	9	6	23
Health	18	5	11	34
Work Well	52	–	–	47
Hinder	–	–	49	54
TOTALS	252	41	204	497
PER CENT	50.7	8.3	41.0	100

Overall performance indices

For the building as a whole, the Comfort Index, based on the scores for comfort overall, noise, lighting, temperature, and air quality, works out at +2.19, while the Satisfaction Index, based on the design, needs, health, and perceived productivity scores, is +2.38, both higher than the scale mid-point (noting these indices are scaled from -3 to +3).

The Summary Index, being the average of these, works out at 2.29, while the Forgiveness Factor, calculated to be 0.99 in this instance, indicates that staff as a whole are likely to be fairly ambivalent regarding minor shortcomings in individual aspects such as winter and summer temperatures, air quality, lighting, and noise (a factor of 1 being the mid-point on a scale that normally ranges from 0.8 to 1.2).

As might be expected, there were clear differences in these indices between the AC and the PDEC buildings, the former with Comfort, Satisfaction and Summary values of 2.73, 2.93, and 2.83 respectively; the latter with values of 1.87, 2.04, and 1.95.

In terms of the Ten-Factor Rating Scale, these buildings (whether taken together or considered separately) were 'Excellent' on the 7-point scale, with a calculated percentage value of 100 per cent. When All-Factors were taken into account, the percentage value worked out at around 85 per cent – at the top end of the 'Good Practice' band.

OTHER REPORTED ASPECTS OF PERFORMANCE

A major criterion for the Torrent building was to maximise its low-energy outcomes. In this respect, the building has performed well. The total energy consumption for the six buildings in 2005 (including lights, equipment, and air conditioning for two of them) was 647,000kWh (Dutt, 2005). This equates to an energy use index of around 54 kWh/m².yr based on a floor area of 12,000m² for the surveyed buildings. The energy consumption at Torrent is thus much lower than the typical energy consumption in Indian commercial buildings which has been reported to be in the range of 280–500kWh/m^2.yr (Singh and Michealowa, 2004).

This energy performance coupled with positive user feedback seen in Torrent certainly reinforces the value of a climate-responsive approach to building design in any location. In the context of global environmental concerns, as discussed elsewhere (Thomas and Baird, 2006). it also highlights the value for strategic low-energy approaches to the energy-intensive air-conditioned glass box that is currently being adopted as the model for the rapidly developing subcontinent.

ACKNOWLEDGEMENTS

The post-occupancy study was completed with funding from the University of Technology, Sydney. This study also draws on earlier research conducted by Professor George Baird including interviews at the time with Nimish Patel (Abhikram) and Brian Ford (Short + Ford Associates). A number of individuals associated with the Torrent Research Centre have been of great assistance. We wish particularly to thank Dr C. Dutt for providing access to the building, monitored data, and permission to survey the occupants. The present study would not have been possible without the interest and participation of architects Nimish Patel and Parul Zaveri (Abhikram) who gave their time generously to participate in interviews and provided drawings as well as information relating to the design development of the building included in this chapter.

REFERENCES

Abhikram (1998) Torrent Research Centre, Entry for the Indian Architecture of the Year (Environmental Category) Award, 24pp.

ASHRAE (2001) *ASHRAE Handbook: Fundamentals, SI Edition*, Atlanta, GA: American Society of Heating Refrigerating and Air-Conditioning Engineers.

Baird, G. (2001) *The Architectural Expression of Environmental Control Systems*, London: Spon.

Chauhan, U. (1998) 'Rites of Initiation', *Indian Architect and Builder*, 11(11): 22–30.

Dutt, C. (2005) Personal communication discussing in-house metering and electricity bills.

Leaman, A. and Bordass, W. (2005) 'Productivity in Buildings: The Killer Variables', in updated edition of D. Clemence-Croome (ed.) *Creating the Productive Workplace*, London: Spon.

Majumdar, M. (2001) 'Torrent Research Centre Ahmedabad', in *Energy-efficient Buildings in India*, New Delhi: Tata Energy Research Institute, MNES, pp. 155–60.

Singh, I. and Michealowa, A. (2004) *Indian Urban Building Sector: CDM Potential through Energy Efficiency in Electricity Consumption*, Hamburg Institute of International Economics, available at: www.hwwa.de/Publikationen/ Discussion_Paper/2004/289.pdf.

Thomas, L. and Baird, G. (2006) 'Post-Occupancy Evaluation of Passive Downdraft Evaporative Cooling and Air-Conditioned Buildings at Torrent Research Centre, Ahmedabad, India', in S. Shannon, V. Soebarto, and T. Williamson (eds) *40th Annual Conference of the Architectural Science Association ANZAScA – Challenges for Architectural Science in Changing Climates*. Adelaide, Australia, the University of Adelaide and The Architectural Science Association ANZAScA, November, pp. 97–104.

Thomas, L. and Hall, M. (2004) 'Implementing ESD in Architectural Practice – An Investigation of Effective Design Strategies and Environmental Outcomes', in M. H. deWit (ed.) *PLEA 2004, 21st International Conference on Passive and Low Energy Architecture, Built Environments and Environmental Buildings, Proceedings*, vol. 1, Eindhoven, The Netherlands, pp. 415–20.

Index